13.95

W9-BVA-866

Political Traditions in Foreign Policy Series

Kenneth W. Thompson, Editor

The values, traditions, and assumptions undergirding approaches to foreign policy are often crucial in determining the course of a nation's history. Yet, the interconnections between ideas and policy for landmark periods in our foreign relations remain largely unexamined. The intent of this series is to encourage a marriage between political theory and foreign policy. A secondary objective is to identify theorists with a continuing interest in political thought and international relations, both younger scholars and the small group of established thinkers. Only occasionally have scholarly centers and university presses sought to nurture studies in this area. In the 1950s and 1960s the University of Chicago Center for the Study of American Foreign Policy gave emphasis to such inquiries. Since then the subject has not been the focus of any major intellectual center. The Louisiana State University Press and the series editor, from a base at the Miller Center of Public Affairs at the University of Virginia, have organized this series to meet a need that has remained largely unfulfilled since the mid-1960s.

The
Indochinese
Refugee
Dilemma

The
Indochinese
Refugee
Dilemma

Valerie O'Connor Sutter

LOUISIANA STATE UNIVERSITY PRESS
Baton Rouge and London

Copyright © 1990 by Louisiana State University Press
All rights reserved
Manufactured in the United States of America
First printing

99 98 97 96 95 94 93 92 91 90   5 4 3 2 1

Designer: Pat Crowder
Typeface: Linotron 202 Palatino
Typesetter: The Composing Room of Michigan, Inc.
Printer and binder: Thomson-Shore, Inc.

Library of Congress Cataloging-in-Publication Data

Sutter, Valerie O'Connor.
    The Indochinese refugee dilemma / Valerie O'Connor Sutter.
      p.   cm. — (Political traditions in foreign policy series)
    Bibliography: p.
    Includes index.
    ISBN 0-8071-1556-8
    1. Refugees, Indochinese—United States.   2. Refugees,
Indochinese.   I. Title.   II. Series.
JV6891.I64S88   1989
325'.21'089959—dc20   89-34129
                                                              CIP

The paper in this book meets the guidelines for permanence and durability of
the Committee on Production Guidelines for Book Longevity of the Council on
Library Resources. ∞

To Robert

Contents

Acknowledgments

Limitations imposed on the human condition often require that a large, complicated issue such as the Indochina refugee problem be reflected in microcosm in order for us to begin to comprehend its intricacies. Chan Sao Sovann is a young Khmer refugee who, in a different time and under other circumstances, would have been the flower of his native Cambodia. Sovann's saga, including the death of his family, years of persecution during the reign of terror of Pol Pot, and his eventual escape to Thailand, mirrors the essence of the Indochina refugee's ordeal. To Sovann I am deeply grateful for the insight he has given me into human dignity amid chaos and violence as well as the understanding of what it means to be a refugee and a remnant of God's people. Likewise, Phuong Anh and her father Vu Sinh, Vietnamese refugees now resettled in the United States, are constant reminders of the human capacity for resilience and hope. Seen through the eyes of these and other refugees, the research effort moved from an academic study to become a story that had to be told.

The entire research endeavor was made possible by a number of key individuals to whom I owe many thanks. Many people involved in the refugee issue, including representatives of governments, of voluntary agencies, and of international organizations, willingly gave their time and offered valuable explanations and insights during numerous interviews. Their professional expertise, coupled with personal dedication and caring, served as incentive to me throughout. Their names appear in the bibliography of this book. I am also indebted to the

Institute for the Study of World Politics for the liberal funding of the research, field study, and writing, but especially for the risk it took with me because of a topic we both believed was an important one.

At the University of Virginia, members of the social foundations faculty gave me the perspectives of their own disciplines, plus time and advice. Colleague Randal Lemke was always willingly available for counsel and encouragement. The university's Northern Virginia Center provided a congenial setting and staff, conducive to the research process.

My teacher and preeminent scholar of international relations Kenneth W. Thompson, director of the White Burkett Miller Center of Public Affairs, was ever open to the crossing of disciplinary lines. His intellectual contributions were instrumental in interpreting the subject at hand, while his personal interest and encouragement made the study a reality. Peter Hackett, professor of comparative and international education and dean of international studies at the University of Virginia was teacher, mentor, colleague, and close friend. His provisions for professional development, financial support, and research and writing time, as well as his academic counsel and oversight, made the project feasible. The Rev. J. Bryan Hehir of the U.S. Catholic Conference patiently and eagerly gave advice and suggestions as well as moral support from beginning to end. His own remarkable commitment to social justice was a constant source of inspiration.

Several people supported and assisted in the progression of the study to publication as a book. My thanks go to Bev Klayman, whose reliability, calmness, and editing and technical expertise were essential in bringing the initial study to completion. In addition, Paul Graney and Emily Furmage assisted in preparing the revised text for publication. I am grateful to Catherine F. Barton, managing editor, and Catherine Landry at Louisiana State University Press and to Christine Cowan for their thorough editing, availability, and suggestions as they efficiently and carefully guided the manuscript to final book form.

The twin exoduses of my grandparents from the Ukraine and Ireland at the beginning of this century have been a prologue to this academic pursuit that has made the effort a personal odyssey as well. To them I owe an interest in human migrations and a sense of history, for the story told herein could have been theirs. To my late parents, I am grateful for life's values and the opportunities bequeathed to the third generation of an immigrant family by the hardships, toil, and expectations of the second.

Finally, I am appreciative of my family. Thanks go to my children, Karen, John, Eui-Sook, and Matthew, who grew and changed and helped and shared in all kinds of ways large and small. Their patience, understanding, and spiritedness contributed more than they know. My deepest appreciation goes to Bob, my spouse, whose professional expertise, prudent advice, endurance, and especially love made the entire effort possible and worthwhile.

The
Indochinese
Refugee
Dilemma

Introduction

Victims of persecution and intolerance have sought refuge outside their homelands throughout the ages. The existence today of well over 14,000,000 refugees in need of assistance all over the world, however, demonstrates compellingly that the refugee crisis, characterized by its protractedness and unpredictability and the frequency of exoduses, is a dilemma belonging uniquely to the twentieth century. The political and ethical dimensions of the refugee issue are inherent in the very definition of a refugee put forth by United Nations international legal declarations, specifically the Convention and the Protocol, issued in 1951 and 1967 respectively, relating to the status of refugees: a refugee is a person who, "owing to a well-grounded fear of being persecuted for reasons of race, religion, nationality, membership of a particular social group or political opinion, is outside the country of his nationality and is unable or, owing to such fear, is unwilling to avail himself of the protection of that country."[1] Therefore, the rights of those who flee are inextricably bound up in the politics and principles of the nations that expel refugees and those that receive them.

The Indochina refugee problem, a major component of the global refugee issue, is rooted in the upheaval that has characterized

1. Virginia Hamilton (ed.), *World Refugee Survey: 1988 in Review,* U.S. Committee for Refugees (Washington, D.C., 1989), 31–32; U.S. House of Representatives, Committee on Foreign Affairs, *Reports on Refugee Aid,* 97th Cong., 1st Sess., No. 74-150 0, p. 1; definition cited in Rosemary E. Tripp (ed.), *World Refugee Survey: 1984 in Review,* U.S. Committee for Refugees (Washington, D.C., 1985), 1.

this region of Southeast Asia for a few decades. Since April, 1975, over 2,000,000 refugees have left Vietnam, Laos, and Cambodia in the wake of the American withdrawal from the area, the takeover of South Vietnam by the North, the establishment of a new regime in Laos, and the holocaust in Cambodia, which was followed by the invasion and occupation of Cambodia by Vietnam. This estimate includes refugees who have arrived in first asylum countries, those who left directly for resettlement countries from Vietnam, as well as more than 300,000 displaced persons near the Thai-Cambodian border and untold thousands of "boat people" from Vietnam who died at sea before ever reaching first asylum camps.[2]

Although their numbers have declined considerably since 1979, refugees continue to flee and seek asylum, arriving daily, by land and sea, in the other countries of Southeast Asia and in Hong Kong. En route, these people are frequently victims of vicious pirate attacks in the Gulf of Thailand. Passing ships often ignore their pleas for rescue at sea in order to avoid economic losses and political entanglements.

At the end of 1988, nearly 168,000 Indochinese refugees remained in temporary first asylum camps, in Thailand for the most part, but also in Malaysia, Singapore, Indonesia, the Philippines, and Hong Kong.[3] In their desire to deter the influx, some governments have resorted to "humane deterrence" measures, including the screening of arrivals to determine refugee status and the incarceration of refugees in austere "closed camps," where they are given only minimal provisions and have small chance for resettlement. Some refugees have been in the camps for years because they have been denied resettlement abroad and because voluntary repatriation and local integration efforts have failed.

In addition, an intractable, Palestinian-type situation remains near the Thai-Cambodian border, where more than 300,000 displaced persons from Cambodia are held in makeshift camps in Thailand amid a coalition of anti-Vietnamese resistance forces. These resistance fighters, 50,000 strong and growing, frequently engage in attacks on communication and supply links across the border in Cambodia in efforts to undermine the Vietnamese occupation forces there. The camps at

2. *Refugee Reports,* VIII (December 18, 1987), 8.
3. *Refugee Reports,* IX (December 16, 1988), 12.

the border, targets of occasional retaliatory attacks by the Vietnamese, received severe shelling during the November, 1984–April, 1985 dry season, prompting the emergency evacuation of the displaced Cambo- dians—civilians and resistance fighters alike—to sites a few kilometers inside Thailand, where they now remain. In early 1989, reports indi- cated that large segments of this highly vulnerable population were being used as forced labor and were secretly being moved from the border area to strategic points inside Cambodia by the Khmer Rouge resistance forces. It is feared this activity may be evidence that the refugee population will figure in a Khmer Rouge attempt to return to power once Vietnamese forces withdraw from Cambodia.[4]

The Indochina refugee issue is caught up in the social, political, economic, and strategic interests of several nations. In the Indochina states, the issue, which includes the massive expulsion of ethnic Chi- nese from Vietnam, is related to internal social, economic, and political conditions. For the countries of temporary first asylum, the refugee issue affects national interests as they are manifested in domestic and foreign policies. The unwillingness of the Association of Southeast Asian Nations (ASEAN) and Hong Kong to integrate these refugees and the seeming unfeasibility of repatriation have resulted in a massive and costly resettlement program that involves not only the United States but also Canada, Australia, France, and other nations. By 1988 the United States alone had resettled nearly 883,000 refugees since 1975. The political biases of this refugee issue, on all sides, are exacer- bated by larger strategic and balance-of-power interests involving ASEAN, China, and the United States, on the one hand, versus Indo- china and the Soviet Union on the other. The most contentious issue in this larger competition of interests has been the military occupation of Cambodia by Vietnam.

To take into account the clearly important effect of national in- terests, this study examines the Indochina refugee issue from a nor- mative-political perspective. Specifically, it deals with what the impor- tant national interests that contribute to the Indochina refugee issue are, why they exist, and how they relate to humanitarian concerns for the Indochina refugees. Assuming that national interests of the major

4. M. R. Sukhumbhand Paribatra, "Can ASEAN Break the Stalemate?," *World Policy Journal*, III (Winter, 1985–86), 85–106; Washington *Post*, January 20, 1989, p. 27.

participants, as reflected in their policies, assessments, and actions, affect and are affected by the Indochina refugee issue, this study goes further to delineate the relationship of these forces to ethical concerns for the rights and welfare of the refugees.

This book considers at least five major areas of inquiry. First, it discusses the important foreign policy interests related to the Indochina refugee issue and investigates how these interests affect and are affected by the refugees. The regional and global foreign policy interests examined are those of the Indochina states (Vietnam, Laos, and Cambodia), as sources of refugees; of the ASEAN states (especially Thailand, but also Malaysia, Singapore, Indonesia, and to a lesser extent the Philippines) and Hong Kong, as nations in close proximity to Indochina and, therefore, major countries of first asylum; and of China, the United States, and the Soviet Union, as nations whose interests in the region of Southeast Asia have ramifications in super-power politics.

Second, this study identifies the domestic interests of nations in regard to this issue and details how these internal interests affect and are affected by refugees. To explore this topic, the investigation considers social, economic, and political factors in Indochina, the ASEAN states and Hong Kong, and the United States. Brunei, the sixth member of ASEAN, is a tiny principality without any involvement in the refugee issue; it does not figure in this study.

The third area of inquiry concerns whether the national interests of the Indochina refugee issue are similar to the interests evident in other refugee problems. The book examines the Hungarian refugee exodus of 1956 for comparative and historical analysis. Specifically, it compares the American involvement in the Hungarian problem with the American response to the Indochina issue.

Fourth, the study discusses the relationship between national interests and humanitarian efforts to assist refugees. To provide a solid basis for this discussion, the study explores the role of international humanitarian and human rights organizations, which have been mandated to protect and provide assistance to refugees. In particular, it considers the effectiveness of the United Nations High Commissioner for Refugees (UNHCR) in response to the Indochina issue. It also discusses, in this context, the relevance of international law, the definition of refugees, and the rights and responsibilities of individuals and states.

Last, in a review of the investigation of national interests in the Indochina issue, this book looks at the implications for resolution, stalemate, or expansion of the crisis. It is concerned, too, with the ways in which its own conclusions might contribute to an understanding of other refugee problems around the world.

This research is important for at least three major reasons. First, the size, scope, and complexity of the global refugee problem warrant study of any component of the phenomenon. Second, the lack of attention to refugee issues has led scholars and policy makers to call for objective academic research. Specifically mentioned throughout the literature is the need to investigate normative-political aspects in refugee issues. Too often, the normative, or ethical, dimensions of these problems are addressed apart from or seen in opposition to politics. However, a comprehensive understanding demands an appreciation of the interplay between the normative and the political factors. Third, the Indochina refugee issue, though not the largest or longest standing refugee dilemma, clearly reflects the interests, concerns, and involvement of several nations in the international arena, making it one of the more complex refugee problems.

The enormity of the world's refugee problem has prompted German novelist Heinrich Böll to characterize the age as "a century of refugees and prisoners." Frances D'Souza suggests that since 1945, "there have been perhaps 60–100 million refugees in the world." Included in this estimate are those displaced in Europe after World War II, as well as all those displaced by the partition of India, the division of Germany, the exodus from Cuba, the Indo-Pakistani War, the formation of Bangladesh, the wars of nationalism in Africa and elsewhere, and the strife brought about by oppression all over the world.[5] At the present time, major conflicts and trouble spots throughout the world—in Africa, the Middle East, Central America, and South and Southeast Asia—all include refugee components.

A survey by the U.S. Committee for Refugees at the end of 1988 reported over 4,000,000 refugees in Africa, nearly 9,000,000 in the Middle East and South Asia, nearly 280,000 in Latin America and the Caribbean, over 625,000 in East Asia and the Pacific, and almost 350,000 in Europe, for a total of over 14,000,000 refugees worldwide.

5. Barry Wain, *The Refused: The Agony of the Indochina Refugees* (New York, 1982), 262; Frances D'Souza, *The Refugee Dilemma: International Recognition and Acceptance*, Minority Rights Group, XLIII (London, 1985), 6.

These figures merely scratch the surface, however, because reliable statistics are difficult to collect. The numbers do not include, for example, refugees recently resettled, those not in need of international assistance, others—possibly millions—labeled internally displaced and therefore not entitled to international legal status as refugees, and any people displaced due to natural disasters.[6]

A major theme in the global refugee debate is the relationship of the individual to the state. The existence of these vast numbers of refugees is evidence, in part, of man's inhumanity to man. Yet, ironically, this inhumanity has elicited numerous instances of man's compassion and magnanimity in the care and concern for refugees expressed by nations, international organizations, voluntary agencies, and individuals. Heightened interest in human rights since World War II, augmented by pervasive media attention, has sparked considerable interest in the rights and well-being of refugees. However, the recognition of the right to exit a country in order to escape persecution or simply because of the fear of persecution is not always complemented by the right to enter another country for asylum. The individual's right to flee conflicts with the fundamental right of states to control entry at a time when a power- and security-conscious world of nation-states has laid claim to all the earth's inhabitable spaces. The factors related to expulsion and flight are thus exacerbated by a fundamental concern about where refugees can find asylum. Commenting on the European refugee problem following World War II, Hannah Arendt, a refugee from Hitler's Germany, has remarked: "In the long memory of history, forced migrations of individuals or whole groups of people for political or economic reasons look like everyday occurrences. What is unprecedented is not the loss of a home but the impossibility of finding a new one." With the interstices between states virtually eliminated, refugees in search of asylum today are dependent on the mercies, whims, and interests of nations whose ultimate sovereignty is expressed in the control of their borders.[7] Statelessness is, as a result, an untidy anomaly in a world defined by national affiliations.

6. Virginia Hamilton (ed.), *World Refugee Survey: 1988*, 31–32.
7. Hannah Arendt, *The Origins of Totalitarianism* (Cleveland, 1969), 293; John George Stoessinger, *The Refugee and the World Community* (Minneapolis, 1956), 8–9; D'Souza, *Refugee Dilemma*, 9.

The complexity of the global refugee phenomenon is related to the establishment and maintenance of nation-states, processes often attended by internal instability and regional strife and fraught with international ramifications in a world that is increasingly interdependent. Since World War II, millions of refugees have been generated by the demise of colonialism, the increase in nationalistic independence movements, and the larger balance-of-power maneuverings as the superpowers and other nations jockey for political, military, and psychological superiority. The problem is exacerbated as these scenarios are played out predominantly in the developing world—in areas that can least afford to accommodate refugees—adding a rich-poor dimension to the issue. The superimposition of North-South relations on East-West relations has complicated a problem traditionally characterized by Manichean political biases that divide the world simplistically into good and evil people and governments, whereby states generating refugees perceive those who flee as traitors, whereas the receiving states often view refugees as "voting with their feet."[8] The unpredictability, protractedness, and frequency of exoduses in the refugee dilemma fuel an increasingly frustrated, even apocalyptic, assessment of the situation. Intensifying this perception is the anxiety about economic uncertainty, a psychological weariness of the human conscience with regard to victims of calamity known as "compassion fatigue," and concern for security and control of borders in the developed world. The global refugee problem, and the Indochina refugee issue in particular, thus raises important questions for consideration from a normative-political perspective.

This research is, in part, a response to the call by scholars and policy makers for objective, academic investigations of any aspect of the global refugee problem. Prince Sadruddin Aga Khan, former United Nations High Commissioner for Refugees, typifies the attitude prevalent among this group: "Any objective and frank analysis of the contemporary refugee situation is a welcome addition to our understanding of this tragic testimony of man's inhumanity to man. More importantly let us hope that it will contribute to bringing the problem closer to a just and lasting solution."[9]

8. Astri Suhrke, "Global Refugee Movements and Strategies: An Overview" (Typescript, American University, 1981), 15.
9. D'Souza, *Refugee Dilemma*, 3.

Scholars of refugee studies, Barry Stein and Sylvano Tomasi comment that too often journalistic accounts substitute for academic research. They indicate that traditionally refugee movements have been viewed as isolated, localized, nonrecurring events. In addition, these exoduses have been undefined and undocumented. Stein and Tomasi call for research reflecting both fresh thinking and comprehensive interdisciplinary, comparative, and historical perspectives that consider patterns and consistencies across different refugee issues. Noting the lack of standard texts, of systematic collection of data, and of clear definitions of subject matter and field, they suggest that research should aim toward forming a body of knowledge and an institutional memory. In this way, those who grapple with new and emerging refugee events might draw on the documentation of past refugee problems.[10]

Within the context of the study of refugee exoduses, Aristide Zolberg notes the lack of attention given "the political dimension that is a constitutive element in all international migrations." In a paper that interprets global refugee movements and strategies, Astri Suhrke writes that research has focused on refugee resettlement and on national and international law and has failed to acknowledge and examine foreign policy determinants in refugee issues. Too often, foreign policy aspects are shoved "under a cover of humanitarian concern." Suhrke writes further: "A central theme in the public policy debate in some major receiving countries is to what extent refugee policy should reflect domestic and foreign political considerations, as opposed to humanitarian concerns. . . . The determinants of refugee policy, and the conditions that encourage politicization, have not been studied systematically." She suggests moving beyond single-factor analysis toward consideration of the complexities of various issues, among them the individual's rights versus the state, the newer North-South dimension now imposed on East-West relations, and the existence of "pull" as well as "push" factors in exoduses.[11]

10. Barry N. Stein and Sylvano M. Tomasi (eds.), "Refugees Today," *International Migration Review,* XV (Spring-Summer, 1981), 5–6.

11. Aristide R. Zolberg, "International Migrations in World Perspective," in Mary M. Kritz, Charles B. Keely, and Sylvano M. Tomasi (eds.), *Global Trends in Migration: Theory and Research on International Population Movements* (New York, 1981), 3; Suhrke, "Global Refugee Movements," 3; Astri Suhrke, "Global Refugee Movements and Strategies of Response," in Mary M. Kritz (ed.), *U.S. Immigration and Refugee Policy, Global and Domestic Issues* (Lexington, 1983), 158, 170.

Objectivity in refugee research can be problematic. The crisis nature of refugee problems and their emotion-laden, sensational aspects, enhanced by on-the-spot media coverage, can justifiably solicit the attention and response of the international community. However, these situations can inhibit the comprehensive, rational description and analysis that consider the larger context and all sides in the event. The refugee dilemma lends itself to moralizing, political bias, and even hypocrisy in lieu of the more difficult process of moral reasoning. A case in point: when an exasperated Malaysia pushed Vietnamese boat people seeking asylum away from its shores in 1979, the world community, including the United States, moralized about Malaysia's inhumanity. The complexity of this moral dilemma was perhaps not fully realized until a similar incident occurred in 1980, this time involving the interdiction of boats of Haitians headed toward American shores by the U.S. Coast Guard.

A recognition of the problems associated with the pursuit of objectivity would be more honest than a claim to have attained that objectivity. A colleague has noted that "not only the political inference we may draw from facts, but also the selective process of observing and interpreting the world is conditioned by value." Western perceptions of refugee issues are colored by religious tradition that includes such sagas as the Exodus and by philosophical thought that includes the belief in human rights rooted in natural law. Past experiences in Europe, including the repatriation of thousands of Russians against their will after World War II, the Jewish Holocaust, and the Cold War, and ideas of freedom embodied in democratic ideology influence the questions we ask. In his profound analysis of knowledge, Michael Polanyi reminded us that the tacit union of data and values results in knowledge and meaning. Adda Bozeman, noting that not all nations subscribe to the same idea of what constitutes the correct relationship between the individual and the state, suggested that seemingly universal human rights, of which refugee rights are a part, may actually be influenced by culture and also by national interests. Anyone who has witnessed the vacant stares of refugees confined to camps in Southeast Asia can probably never again claim detachment. After viewing such a scene, one can appreciate the opinion of a U.S. State Department official who wondered if the overwhelming emotional and political aspects of refugee problems, including the Indochina issue, could, or even should, be intellectualized. Perhaps the best that can be done is at least to recognize the problems associated with the pursuit of objectivity.[12]

Research focused on the national interests that contribute to the Indochina refugee issue is warranted because this particular case reflects the important involvement and concern of several states in the international arena. The Indochina refugee problem, over the years and especially at its height in 1979 and 1980, has prompted moralizing by nations, often noble but at times contradictory. It has also prompted much soul searching and has been linked to memories of the Jewish Holocaust; recriminations concerning national responsibility and liability have been voiced on all sides. Although practical recommendations and programs to relieve suffering can be judged to have been moderately successful, little effort has been given to a careful, comprehensive examination of the complex, multiple factors—an examination that could lead to an understanding of and possible long-term solutions to the problem.[13] Consequently, the Indochina refugee issue remains a significant quandary in international relations. It is an illustration of the conflict between national interests and humanitarian concerns for refugees, a dilemma of power and conscience.

The Indochina refugee issue readily lends itself to a study of national interests because of its relationship to internal tensions, regional instability, and global politics, as already indicated. Clearly, a study of this event is needed: though some observers point to the problem's diminution on the whole, its protractedness is disturbing, and some important aspects of the issue are actually worsening. A study is perhaps overdue, as refugee crises elsewhere are eclipsing interest in the Indochina refugees before their dilemma has been understood and remedied.

Now, after more than a decade since the beginning of the exodus, references to the winding down of the Indochina refugee problem are being made. Some observers believe the issue to be in its concluding stages. However, Roger Winter, the director of the refugee advocacy

12. Donald L. Layman, "Education and the Egalitarian Quest: The Chinese Experience" (Ph.D. dissertation, University of Virginia, 1979), 11–12; Michael Polanyi, *Personal Knowledge* (Chicago, 1974); Adda B. Bozeman, "Human Rights in Western Thought," in Kenneth W. Thompson (ed.), *The Moral Imperatives of Human Rights: A World Survey* (Washington, D.C., 1980), 25–38; interview with Frank Sieverts, Bureau for Refugee Programs, Washington, D.C., February 3, 1984.

13. D'Souza, *Refugee Dilemma*, 5.

group the U.S. Committee for Refugees, sees a decided "managing down" overall of efforts to assist refugees, which he finds unfortunate. Resettlement, a critical and costly component in the response to the exodus, may see significant change, according to Winter and others. For the United States, the major resettlement country, "refugee resettlement will be defined by a dwindling pool of refugees eligible for admission . . . and dwindling federal funds," a result, in part, of the Gramm-Rudman-Hollings federal deficit reduction effort. George Shultz, as U.S. secretary of state under Ronald Reagan, indicated the American program to be at a "transition point." In the Congress, Senator Alan K. Simpson, chairman of the Subcommittee on Immigration and Refugee Policy, commented, "We are now coming to the conclusion of that worthy humanitarian project."[14]

In Southeast Asian countries of temporary asylum, there are noticeable changes. Far fewer refugees are now in the camps than were there in the period 1979–1982, when these nations were inundated with refugee arrivals. On the last day of 1986, Thailand officially announced the closing and phasing out of its large asylum camp for Cambodians, Khao-I-Dang Holding Center, which had been a "symbol of compassion" and hope since it had opened in November, 1979. This and other camp closings and consolidations are indications of Thailand's serious effort to limit its role as the major country of first asylum for Indochinese refugees.[15]

Amid the signs of change in the Indochina refugee issue, however, there are also indications that predictions about the end of the problem are premature. Instability in the region at the present time, specifically related to the Cambodian stalemate, could generate more refugees. The situation for the 300,000 displaced and unprotected Cambodians near the Thai-Cambodian border remains precarious. Cautious optimism in 1988 regarding the gradual Vietnamese military withdrawal from Cambodia and initiatives for a negotiated settlement for Cambodia was further tempered by wariness at the military resistance

14. Interview with Roger Winter, Director, U.S. Committee for Refugees, Washington, D.C., February 8, 1984; "Regional Consultation Reviews Future of Refugee Resettlement," *Refugee Reports*, VII (March 21, 1986), 1–2; U.S. Department of State, *Proposed Refugee Admissions for FY 1986*, No. 738 (September 17, 1985), 2; Washington *Post*, June 5, 1986, Sec. A, p. 23.
15. New York *Times*, December 30, 1986, pp. 1, 6.

holding the border population hostage. In addition, dramatic increases in the exodus from Vietnam in late 1987 and during 1988 immediately triggered alarm throughout the region. The latest influx promptly caused policy changes in the first asylum countries, particularly Thailand and Hong Kong, the recipients of the majority of the newly arriving boat people.[16]

Although the numbers of refugees in first asylum camps and processing centers had been declining before 1988, the rate of decline was slow because refugees leaving for permanent resettlement were always quickly replaced by new arrivals. In Vietnam, an estimated 12,000 Amerasians and their 18,000 close relatives are beneficiaries of recent U.S.–Vietnamese efforts to assist in their transfer to the United States. However, they face serious obstacles in the migration process. The Orderly Departure Program (ODP), which facilitates the safe and regular flow of Vietnamese to direct resettlement abroad, was in limbo from January, 1986, to August, 1987, and is still bureaucratically sluggish. No such programs actively facilitate the exiting of asylum-seekers from Laos and Cambodia. Reportedly, 1,000,000 Vietnamese are planning to leave their country, either by escaping or via the ODP.[17]

The Indochina refugee problem may appear to be manageable, to be winding down, but it is far from over or solved. The ASEAN countries and Hong Kong, where temporary first asylum camps are located, repeatedly voice their dismay over perceptions of dwindling international concern as resettlement offers decrease and thousands remain in the camps, many for years. Some refugees are forcefully pushed back, involuntarily repatriated, or denied refugee status, and several of the refugee camps remain "crowded, unsanitary and dangerous."[18] Taking the present situation into account, this study looks at national interests and humanitarian concerns as the Indochina refugee issue has evolved and changed and includes descriptions of the current

16. "Cambodia: Peace at Last or the Return of Pol Pot?," *Refugee Reports,* IX (July 15, 1988), 1–9; "Vietnamese Refugee Crisis in Thailand Continues to Elude Solutions," *Refugee Reports,* IX (March 18, 1988), 1–5; "Asylum Crisis Widens for Refugees in Southeast Asia," *Refugee Reports,* IX (May 20, 1988), 11–14.

17. "Amerasians in Vietnam: New Climate of Hope, but Problems Remain," *Refugee Reports,* IX (August 12, 1988), 1–7; Barry Wain, "Orderly Departure? Escape Is Still the Hope of a Million Vietnamese," *Asian Wall Street Journal,* May 6, 1985, pp. 6, 22.

18. Joseph Cerquone, *Refugees from Laos: In Harm's Way,* U.S. Committee for Refugees (Washington, D.C., July, 1986), 19–22.

uncertain state of affairs. It comes at a time when many observers are calling for a renewed international commitment to this problem.

With its obvious ethical themes and connotations all bound up in the interests of nations, the Indochina refugee issue forces a profound quandary on the international community as well as on this research effort. Eminent legal scholar Paul Freund has noted that "Western civilization suffers from the decline of the ancient art of moral reasoning."[19] For example, the media are sensitive to the poignant images of refugees in flight, but their chronicles are determined by the immediacy of such events. Dramatic photographic accounts of Vietnamese boat people in leaky sailing craft in the South China Sea during 1979 will probably be etched on the collective mind of the world for some time to come. These images of grief and fear mirror our own naked vulnerability and strike at the core of human dignity. The impetus behind these images, however, is pathos for the human condition, not a need for a moral, rational, and balanced perspective.

This study, though not committed to rigid, clearly defined theories of political science or models of refugee movements, is definitely guided by certain normative-political perspectives and assumptions. In seeking to avoid an idealism that easily succumbs to cynicism in the face of the grim realities of the Indochina issue, this investigation finds its guidance in the perspective known as political realism, found in the writings of masters of international thought. These major thinkers, "men of large and capacious thought," address the dilemma of politics and principles, of power and conscience, of international relations and morality.[20] Although they do not comment directly on the refugee issue at hand, their ideas are implicitly appropriate to understanding national interests and humanitarian concerns.

The selected ideas of Herbert Butterfield, Reinhold Niebuhr, Hans Morganthau, George Kennan, and Kenneth W. Thompson provide a framework for this investigation. The views of these men are rooted in their ideas about human nature, history, progress, and the politics of nation-states.[21] The normative approaches to political theory of Butter-

19. Kenneth W. Thompson, *Morality and Foreign Policy* (Baton Rouge, 1980), 75.
20. Kenneth W. Thompson, *Masters of International Thought* (Baton Rouge, 1980), xi.
21. The ideas of Butterfield, Niebuhr, Morganthau, Kennan, and Thompson discussed here are derived from the following studies by Kenneth W. Thompson: *Christian Ethics and Dilemmas in Foreign Policy* (London, 1959), *Cold War Theories: World Polarization,*

field, Niebuhr, Morganthau, and Kennan, all important twentieth-century thinkers, grew out of their realization that orthodox thinking had failed to address adequately the relationship of morality to politics, especially international politics, in the serious dilemmas that confronted nations during their lifetimes. It is Thompson who has interpreted, synthesized, and expanded on the ideas of these four individuals and who has authored numerous volumes on the normative-political aspects of political realism in his own right.

All of these thinkers share a similar view of human nature as capable of both good and evil. Butterfield recognized the limited, fragmentary nature of human existence, and he believed evil could be tempered by religion, that moral order derived from higher law. He cautioned, however, that morality is not a simple choice between good and evil but a complex process of partial goods and lesser evils. Niebuhr, a theologian, who pondered the nature of man throughout his life, remarked on the complexity of human nature: "Man has been his [own] most vexing problem. How shall he think of himself?"[22] He avoided cynicism by accepting the existential notions of choice in human destiny and of man's dual nature, human and divine, suspended between finiteness and freedom. In liberalism Niebuhr found the ideas of freedom, tolerance, and fairness, whereas from Marxist thought he apparently was influenced by the concepts of the social aspect of human life, the collective fate of existence, and the conflict within and among individuals and groups. Morganthau, a political theorist and a refugee from German anti-Semitism, tempered a pessimism regarding human nature with an appreciation for man's intellectual and moral dimensions. Although he thought people moral by virtue of their being human, he pointed out that absolute principles, if they exist, are filtered through time, place, and cultural circumstances, leading to a variety of applications. Kennan, a scholar, foreign service officer, and policy planner, brought to normative-political thinking his experiences as both participant in and observer of world politics. He, like Niebuhr, saw man as human and divine.

As a historian, Butterfield challenged the conventional historiogra-

---

1943–1953 (Baton Rouge, 1981); *Ethics, Functionalism, and Power in International Politics* (Baton Rouge, 1979), *Masters of International Thought, Morality and Foreign Policy,* and *Political Realism and the Crisis of World Politics* (Washington, D.C., 1982).

22. Thompson, *Political Realism,* 12.

phy of his day, which depicted past events as the inevitable, uninterrupted progress of civilization. Rather, he emphasized that history "at its core is a drama, often tragic in dimension, of human personalities," and he stressed the importance of putting oneself in the actors' shoes in order to appreciate the textural complexity and unpredictability of events and to understand rather than to judge them. The historian, he believed, is required to grasp the multiplicity of forces and factors that bear on events. In his own study of history, Butterfield appreciated the role of accident and the existence of irreducible dilemmas "beyond the ingenuity of man to untie." He applied his views of human nature and history to the normative aspects of international politics, advising statesmen to put themselves in others' shoes. But he also understood the role of conflict and saw politics as a natural human form, not to be avoided or scorned. Out of conflict, he thought, could come good as well as evil: "man's most creative achievements are usually born out of human distress." Warning against the excesses of moralizing, he saw religion not as prescribing or setting policy but as contributing a civilized spirit in which one could work. He advised tolerance of an imperfect world, recognition of the need to coexist, and restraint on grandiose objectives in foreign affairs. He called for prudent leadership combined with the capacity to take an extra step at times, to express a magnanimous gesture to break political impasses, and to instigate marginal experiments. Acknowledging the reality of interests, Butterfield said, "A state may fairly acquire virtue from the very fact that it construes to make its self-interest contrive with something that is good for the world in general."[23]

For Niebuhr, history itself and the events of his day invalidated the liberal view of progress. Human anxiety produces a will to power as a means of security, to safeguard against the domination of others. The natural rivalry that springs up between the self and others finds expression at every level of human life, and these forces are harmonized only when a balance of power neutralizes conflict. Society is the culmination of individual egoism; that is, no group acts for unselfish reasons. As the form that exerts control over society, politics is thus a contest for power. Transferred to the arena of nations, this concept

23. Cited, respectively, in the following studies by Thompson: *Masters of International Thought*, 9, *Political Realism*, 3, *Masters of International Thought*, 12, and *Christian Ethics*, 102.

finds states seeking security and naturally following their own interests. Niebuhr thought nations to be not particularly generous; a wise self-interest, enlightened at best, he believed to be the limit of their moral attainment.

Niebuhr rejected both optimistic reformers and cynical radicals, pointing out that a realist views the world pragmatically, understanding power politics, but this view is possibly tempered by hope, love, and forgiveness. A realist learns to live with uncertainty, is cautious, and seeks coexistence in a pluralistic world. Like Butterfield, Niebuhr warned against utopian, pretentious moralizing and overly ambitious aims in international politics. Self-righteous crusading and the search for formalized solutions must be exchanged for flexibility and the consideration of the interests of others, he argued. Foreign policy for Niebuhr thus became "a practical art linking justice and power, not an exercise in moral philosophy." He distinguished between individual and collective morality, each with different obligations. For nation-states, national interests are primary, and the defense of values cannot endanger national security and existence. Normative theory, then, must provide "guideposts" to the process of moral reasoning, which accounts for multiple factors and principles relevant to practice. "Politics will, to the end of history, be an area where conscience and power meet."[24]

History led Hans Morganthau to see both decline and improvement in civilization. Classic problems of history and his own European experiences influenced his concepts of power and national interests. According to Morganthau, power and interests form the only legitimate basis for foreign policy and are the means to international stability and harmony. Like Niebuhr, he warned of the dangers of an American inclination to cover over interest and power with law and morality, insisting that the duty of the state is to defend its interests. States that profess humanitarian, selfless aims usually fall short of these goals in practice, he pointed out. Morganthau emphasized the need for statesmanship and diplomacy to seek compromise and accommodation rather than a "crusading foreign policy based on moral abstractions," which forces idealistic aspirations of what the world ought to be.[25] He questioned whether nations should, or even could,

24. Thompson, *Morality and Foreign Policy*, 43, 95.
25. Thompson, *Masters of International Thought*, 86.

impose their principles on others. With Butterfield and Niebuhr, he looked to realism as the way to avoid reductionist theory, dangerous because it failed to account for complexities, multiple factors, and changes in political events and decisions. Morganthau warned that in foreign policy moral justification without defined interests was actually immoral, often causing conflicts to become limitless and intensifying violence and destruction. A serious critic of American involvement in the Vietnam War, he saw this event as a case in point.

George Kennan's sense of history derived from long study not only of Russia but also of the United States. In scrutinizing the latter, he found an inclination to use a moralistic-legalistic approach to foreign affairs that tends to judge other nations from a stance of moral superiority, indignation, and impatience, all of which impede moral reasoning. With the other thinkers, Kennan appreciated the primacy of power, the importance of national interests, and the necessity for the balance of power. Like Niebuhr, he distinguished between individual and collective morality. The power of nations is thus a practical function, not a moral exercise. Government is a necessary agent of citizens but not a substitute for the morality of the people it serves. If benevolent, at best government safeguards the individual rights of its citizens. This purpose, when carried out in foreign policy, provides "scant basis for international benevolence, lofty pretensions, or moral superiority."[26] Warning that when every practical measure is covered with moral virtue, then self-righteous moralism is an impediment to statesmanship, Kennan held that nations look to what is done, not what is said. Ethical progress, then, is the task of individuals, not states. The role of Christian morality in international relations is not in defining purpose but in expressing the virtues of patience, respect, honesty, decency, and forgiveness. Kennan placed high priority on statesmen as "gardeners," those who are able to make prudent choices within the narrow margins of maneuverability, and not as "mechanics," those who artlessly force solutions without regard for the organic nature of international relations.

Kenneth Thompson, a scholar of international relations, saw the common normative-political themes in the ideas and writings of Butterfield, Niebuhr, Morganthau, and Kennan and synthesized, interpreted, and expanded on these ideas, thus defining and clarifying

26. *Ibid.*, 154.

the theory of political realism. His own studies, especially of the Cold War era and of the Third World, indicate an appreciation of and dedication to understanding the complexities of international problems. For Thompson, political realism bridges the gap between theory and practice. He noted that politicians and policy makers adhere to political realism more than they realize. Commenting on the tendency to denigrate politics, Thompson remarked, "If politics is anything, it is compromise, the adjustment of divergent interests and the reconciliation of rival moral claims." In the political arena, the complex process of moral reasoning reflects morality as distinguished from moralism. For Thompson, "moralism is the tendency to make one moral value supreme and to apply it indiscriminately without regard to time and place; morality, by comparison, is the endless quest for what is right amidst the complexity of competing and sometimes conflicting, sometimes compatible, moral ends."[27]

Political realism avoids the pitfalls of an idealism becoming prey to disillusionment and the despair of cynicism. Politics is natural and necessary, not an evil to be avoided; it ought to be characterized by power and interests honestly acknowledged. Religion or morality is a guide or perspective, not a purpose or end in itself. Like his mentors, Thompson appreciated the role of human personalities in politics, noting the difference between the observer-critic, who stands in judgment after the fact, and the participant policy maker or statesman, who must often make on-the-spot choices and decisions and who is charged with protecting national interests.

The complex dilemmas of the modern age demand the art of moral reasoning, as these masters of normative-political theory in international relations have pointed out. It seems especially appropriate that the Indochina refugee issue be discussed from a normative-political perspective and that the study be guided by political realism. Some may find a limitation of the study to be its reluctance to judge the policies and views of the participants critically. The study may appear to others to be an apology for the actions of nations. I take this risk with an appreciation of the need to understand, rather than judge, to take into account the multiple factors affecting the issue, to recognize the realities of power and interests, and to be aware of the difficulty of moral reasoning.

27. Thompson, *Political Realism*, 14, and *Morality and Foreign Policy*, 75.

The research underlying this investigation has included a review and application of written materials, extensive interviews with people knowledgeable about the issue, and a field study in Southeast Asia, where the impact of the Indochina refugee exodus is dramatically evident. According to refugee studies' scholar Barry Stein, research of refugee issues can be problematic, because "refugee research extends across many disciplinary lines." Additionally, the general neglect of refugee research means that there are few materials available. Much of the material is "buried in the files of refugee agencies . . . countless valuable articles . . . in journals, obscure or major, in which one might never think to look."[28]

Interviews with a cross section of people interested and involved in the Indochina refugee issue constituted an important resource in this investigation. Although open ended and geared to each interviewee's expertise, the interviews contained key questions that were repeated throughout the series of conversations. In some cases, my willingness to honor requests for anonymity resulted in the person's sharing of valuable interpretations and assessments. The interviews covered a broad range, representing governments, organizations, and agencies in the United States and abroad. They included talks with individuals at the U.S. Bureau for Refugee Programs, the Office of the U.S. Coordinator for Refugees, and American embassies and consulates abroad; congressional offices and the Library of Congress' Congressional Research Service; UNHCR offices in Washington, D.C., and abroad; the U.S. Committee for Refugees; various voluntary agencies, including the U.S. Catholic Conference, Church World Service, the International Rescue Committee, the International Catholic Migration Committee, Catholic Relief Services, and American Friends Service Committee, among others; and offices representing the governments of Thailand, Malaysia, Singapore, the Philippines, Hong Kong, Canada, and Australia. Interviews with individuals without organizational affiliation, including refugees themselves, were also conducted.

In March and April, 1984, I conducted a field study, with visits to the ASEAN countries of Thailand, Malaysia, Singapore, and the Philippines and to Hong Kong. Its purpose was to provide me a first-hand orientation to the problem. By visiting refugee camps and holding

28. Barry N. Stein, "Documentary Note, Refugee Research Bibliography," *International Migration Review*, XV (Spring-Summer, 1981), 331.

centers and by listening to people who were directly concerned, including individuals representing governments, international organizations, voluntary agencies, and refugees, I intended to heed Butterfield's advice to put oneself in the places of others in order to appreciate the textural complexity of events.

In Thailand, where the Indochina refugee problem is still most acute, interviews were conducted at the Ministry of Interior, Supreme Command Headquarters, the U.S. Embassy, the office of the UNHCR, and relief agencies. Four sites were visited: Nong Samet, a camp along the Thai-Cambodian border; Khao-I-Dang, a large holding center for Cambodian refugees; Ubon Repatriation Center, a camp for lowland Lao and hill tribe Lao expecting to return to Laos; and Phanat Nikhom Holding and Transit Center, for refugees anticipating resettlement abroad.

There were approximately 108,000 refugees inside Thailand and 300,000 displaced Cambodians near the border in late 1988.[29] The refugees pose concerns for national security, as Thailand has common borders with Laos and Cambodia. The refugee situation in Thailand is characterized by an emphasis on "humane deterrence" to curb the influx and includes the considerable outside involvement of international organizations, relief agencies, and governments.

In Malaysia, interviews were held at the UNHCR, Malaysian Task Force Seven (VII), which is the government unit charged with responsibility for the refugee issue, the Malaysian Red Crescent Society (MRCS), the U.S. Embassy, the Joint Voluntary Agency, and the High Commission of Australia. Sungei Besi Transit Center, near Kuala Lumpur, where refugees wait for resettlement offers, was also visited. Malaysian concerns vis-à-vis the refugee issue are mainly internal. Malaysia is a developing country where race and ethnicity have important political ramifications. It perceived the many refugees, especially those of Chinese extraction, as posing a political threat. This attitude is especially true in the conservative, indigenous Malay-Muslim area of Trenganuu, located on the east coast of Malaysia where the refugees disembark. As of late 1988, there were nearly 12,500 refugees in Malaysia, divided between the Pulau Bidong island camp and Sungei Besi. The refugee situation in Malaysia is marked by an absence of major involvement of outside relief agencies, except for the UNHCR.

29. Camp populations as of September, 1988, as reported in *Refugee Reports*, IX (December 16, 1988), 6; X (May 19, 1989), 10.

In Singapore, interviews were held with representatives from the Foreign Ministry of Singapore, the office of the UNHCR, the International Committee for Migration (ICM), the U.S. Embassy, and the high commissions of Canada and Australia. Refugees in Singapore are few because of a consistent hard-line government policy that includes a refusal to allow refugee boats to stop in Singapore. Only those refugees rescued at sea by passing ships are allowed to disembark. A visit was made to the Hawkins Road Camp, where refugees are held temporarily until they can be moved quickly to resettlement countries. In late 1988, less than 350 refugees were at the camp, in stark contrast to the thousands of refugees in other facilities throughout Southeast Asia and Hong Kong.

Although not a major country of first asylum because of its distance from Indochina, the Philippines, along with Indonesia, is a site for a large refugee processing center. Personnel from the U.S. Embassy, the Joint Voluntary Agency, the ICM, and the Philippines' government were interviewed. The Bataan Refugee Processing Center, where 15,000 refugees were participating in a six-month English language and orientation program before embarking for resettlement in the United States, was visited as well. A second major processing center, located at Galang, Indonesia, but now closed, was not visited because of time constraints. In late 1988 there were nearly 18,500 refugees in the Philippines and over 2,000 in Indonesia.

In Hong Kong, where there were more than 38,000 refugees by mid-1989, interviews were conducted with personnel from the Hong Kong government, the political and refugee sections of the American consulate, the office of the UNHCR, the Joint Voluntary Agency, and the U.S. Immigration and Naturalization Service (INS). Both Kai Tak Camp and Argyle Street Center were visited. The refugee issue in Hong Kong includes concern about long-term camp residents, dramatic increases in arrivals, and a recently installed screening process to discourage refugees from entering Hong Kong. The larger implications of the issue have to do with the high rate of illegal aliens from China, a sense of political powerlessness vis-à-vis the international community, and a preoccupation about the future of Hong Kong. Of the first asylum countries, Hong Kong has the largest number of boat people from Vietnam, with large increases in arrivals beginning in 1987 and continuing in 1988 and 1989.

This study actually begins with a look at another refugee event, the exodus from Hungary in 1956 and 1957. An examination of the national interests evident in that incident provides a valuable historical comparison for the Indochina case. Chapter II traces the forces and factors at the roots of the exodus from Vietnam, Laos, and Cambodia, with attention to the larger scope of relations between and among the nations of Southeast Asia, as well as the superpowers. The next two chapters look at the refugee issue from the perspectives of the countries that provide temporary first asylum. Thailand, Malaysia, Indonesia, the Philippines, and Hong Kong all play a vital part in providing for the protection and well-being of the refugees, yet their reactions to the influx clearly reflect their respective national interests. The role of the United States, a major donor and resettlement country, is reviewed in Chapter V, which also highlights refugee policy issues involving the balancing of foreign policy and domestic interests. Humanitarian concerns related to Indochina refugees are examined in Chapter VI, with special attention given to the performance of the UNHCR and to some of the disconcerting and thorny human rights dilemmas raised by this refugee event.

In essence, the purpose of this book is to discern, describe, and synthesize the multitude of elements and influences that comprise the Indochina refugee issue. Achieving that purpose involves looking at this complex problem from a variety of perspectives by putting ourselves in the shoes of others, as Butterfield suggests. It is my hope that in acknowledging the reality and legitimacy of national interests along with the compelling need to restore human dignity to thousands of Indochinese refugees, the book may, in some small way, foster a recommitment to seek fresh solutions to a dilemma that has gone on too long.

I

Hungarian Refugees
1956

To the world's surprise and in the midst of the Cold War, Hungary defiantly and dramatically challenged Soviet hegemony in eastern Europe on October 23, 1956. The brief Hungarian revolution, swift and brutal Soviet military intervention and suppression on November 4, and the ensuing confusion generated the sudden migration of Hungarians across the border into Austria and Yugoslavia. Approximately 200,000 refugees left Hungary before the borders were resealed a few months later. To the free world, the refugees were highly visible symbols of the oppression going on behind the iron curtain. While the refugee problem quickly became a significant part of the larger political crisis, humanitarian concerns for the well-being of the refugees resulted in considerable assistance programs involving several nations, international organizations, and voluntary relief and resettlement agencies. Eventually, most of the Hungarian refugees were integrated into Austrian society or resettled in other European countries, the United States, Canada, and Australia.

A former U.S. refugee coordinator, Victor A. Palmieri, noted the following about the history of American immigration policies: "The warmth of our welcome to the huddled masses relates closely to our own interests. . . . Our romance with the Statue of Liberty has been a hot and cold affair."[1] With this idea as a guiding principle, this chapter examines the national interests that underlay the response of the

1. Kritz (ed.), *U.S. Immigration and Refugee Policy*, xi.

United States to the Hungarian refugees, as well as humanitarian concerns in relation to these interests. What emerges is a historical, comparative, and descriptive analysis of a refugee problem that, in turn, provides a context for the study of the Indochina refugee issue.

This investigation utilizes reviews of the press, especially the New York *Times*, and the debate over Hungary in Congress as found in the *Congressional Record*. A few works by journalists are on-the-spot, moving accounts of the uprising that include commentary on the refugees' experiences and provide important contextual information. Marten A. Bursten's *Escape from Fear*, James A. Michener's *The Bridge at Andau*, Leslie B. Bain's *The Reluctant Satellites*, and *The Hungarian Revolution* edited by Melvin J. Lasky are especially noteworthy. Sympathetic to the Hungarian cause, frustrated by the unwillingness and seeming inability of the free world, especially the United States, to intervene, these authors are critical of the American response to the uprising and to the refugees' plight. The story of one refugee, Vilmos Solyom-Fekete, as dramatized by John Hersey in *Here to Stay*, is all the more valuable here because it is complemented by an interview with Solyom-Fekete specifically for this study.[2]

The memoirs of political leaders of the time, including former president Dwight D. Eisenhower, U.S. State Department officer Robert Murphy, and former American ambassador to the Soviet Union Charles Bohlen, provide perspectives of those in positions of power who made and executed policy decisions. Louise Holborn's study of the UNHCR, *Refugees: A Problem of Our Times*, and Aaron Levenstein's *Escape to Freedom* discuss the issue from the standpoint of international organizations and relief agencies charged with protecting and providing assistance to the refugees. Holborn's work, though mainly descriptive and testimonial to the UNHCR, objectively considers the views of the new Hungarian regime regarding the refugee problem. Levenstein's account, a history of the work of the International Rescue Committee, offers a good example of how humanitarian concern for refugees is inextricably bound up with larger political interests. The single most important study relevant to this investigation is Arthur A. Mark-

---

2. Marten A. Bursten, *Escape from Fear* (Syracuse, 1958); James A. Michener, *The Bridge at Andau* (New York, 1957); Leslie B. Bain, *The Reluctant Satellites: An Eyewitness Report on East Europe and the Hungarian Revolution* (New York, 1960); Melvin J. Lasky (ed.), *The Hungarian Revolution* (New York, 1957); John Hersey, *Here to Stay* (New York, 1963).

owitz's "Humanitarianism Versus Restrictionism," which describes congressional reaction to the Eisenhower administration's proposed response to the Hungarian refugees. An initially generous American offer to resettle large numbers of refugees was opposed ultimately by those in Congress who favored a conservative immigration policy as manifested in the Immigration and Nationality Act of 1952. These critics of a liberal refugee policy questioned the legitimacy of the refugee status accorded some of the Hungarians and expressed concern for national security, seemingly jeopardized by careless screening of those admitted into the United States.[3]

The response to the Hungarian refugee crisis was influenced by at least four factors that affected the interests of the United States and various other nations. First, Hungarian refugees added to an already aggravated and growing problem in Europe. Thousands of refugees from World War II still remained unsettled and new refugees were leaving daily from the Soviet-bloc countries. Second, the issue of the refugees was encompassed by the rhetoric and reality of the Cold War. The exodus from Hungary was viewed in the West as proof of Soviet malevolence. Third, the refugees were part of both the revolution itself and the American government's reaction to that event. U.S. response to the exodus reflected American humanitarianism but also foreign policy interests. Finally, heightened interest in human rights included an appreciation of the rights of refugees based on recent wartime experiences in Europe. This interest is reflected in the international legal instruments related to refugees devised by the UN in 1951.

Holborn indicated that one result of the Hungarian refugee crisis was the realization that "the refugee problem was not a matter of past events, but a phenomenon of the twentieth century." Displaced persons in the postwar era seemed to be rather permanent fixtures, lingering by-products, and costly nuisances obstructing the physical and psychological recovery and rehabilitation of nations devastated by

3. Charles Bohlen, *Witness to History, 1929–1969* (New York, 1973); Dwight D. Eisenhower, *Waging Peace, 1956–1961* (Garden City, N.Y., 1965); Robert Murphy, *Diplomat Among Warriors* (Garden City, N.Y., 1964); Louise Holborn, *Refugees: A Problem of Our Time: The Work of the United Nations High Commissioner for Refugees* (Metuchen, N.J., 1975); Aaron Levenstein, *Escape to Freedom: The Story of the International Rescue Committee* (Westport, Conn., 1983); Arthur A. Markowitz, "Humanitarianism Versus Restrictionism: The United States and the Hungarian Refugees," *International Migration Review,* VII (Spring, 1973), 46–59.

war. John George Stoessinger's *The Refugee and the World Community* describes how organizations such as the International Refugee Organization had tugged wearily for years at the hearts and pockets of the countries of Europe and beyond, seeking solutions to the refugee problem.[4]

On the eve of the Hungarian revolution, thousands of hard-core, residual refugees remained languishing in camps, victims of a war that had been over for nearly a decade. For the most part, the "old refugees" were in Austria, Italy, Greece, Germany, and what had been the Free Territory of Trieste, clustered in camps near the borders of their homelands. Holborn wrote: "These countries had experienced the destruction and damage caused by war, and serious dislocations had undermined the fabric of their societies. In addition, they were caught between two opposed and ideologically irreconcilable power centers."[5]

Well after the war, a steady stream of refugees was still leaving the iron curtain countries, exacerbating the problem posed by the residual refugees. Stoessinger estimated that there were, for example, 700,000 old and new refugees in Europe in 1953. In mid-1952 there were nearly 200,000 refugees in reception centers in West Germany and West Berlin. At times, the flow to these two havens reached 15,000 per month. Prior to the Hungarian exodus in 1956 and 1957, the UNHCR and others launched a concerted effort to address this problem.[6]

Out of some 200,000 Hungarian refugees from the failed revolution, 180,000 sought temporary first asylum in Austria. When the refugees started entering in late 1956, Austria already had 30,000 refugees and 150,000 "Volksdeutsche," or people displaced from their German homelands from the war era. Many had not been fully integrated, and some still lived in camps. Austria had regained its independence only sixteen months earlier, in July, 1955, had pledged permanent neutrality, and was geographically wedged between two ideologically opposed camps of nation states.[7] The sudden influx of refugees presented it with a complicated political and humanitarian problem, which had implications for the national interests of several countries on both sides of the iron curtain.

4. Holborn, *Refugees*, 407; Stoessinger, *Refugee and the World Community*.
5. Holborn, *Refugees*, 162.
6. Stoessinger, *Refugee and the World Community*, 223, 162; Holborn, *Refugees*, 391.
7. Holborn, *Refugees*, 391.

If refugees are practical and political liabilities, they also serve some political advantage in the context of national interests. Political scientist Suhrke wrote that "one obvious connection is the negative judgment on the country of origin implied by conferring refugee/*asylee* [*sic*] status on the people who are leaving."[8] The philosophical underpinnings of the rights of refugees, when reduced to the protest ideology of the individual versus the state, translate neatly into Cold War rhetoric that includes self-righteous moralizing and the division of the world into good and evil, free and communist camps.

The Hungarian revolution and subsequent exodus of refugees occurred in the midst of the Cold War. Eisenhower was in the final stretch of his second presidential election campaign, John Foster Dulles was secretary of state, and terms such as "liberation" and "roll back the Iron Curtain" were popular. Affectionately called "freedom fighters" who were "voting with their feet," the refugees were living proof to many of the diabolical nature of the Soviet Union. If the Cold War saw the demise of the art of diplomacy and the rise of an ideological war of words that was based on realities but also on misunderstandings on both sides, the Hungarian revolution, by permitting a glimpse through a crack in the iron curtain, gave cold warriors and suspicious others proof for their arguments. The refugees, caught up in an international political entanglement, were one side's heroes but the other side's traitors. Journalist François Bondy captured the feeling in the West: "Their escape from Hungary represents a ballot cast against the land of Soviet Kommandaturas and of the Kadar government, the most tragic but also the clearest of all possible plebiscites."[9]

According to historians, the foundations of the Cold War were formed as the Soviet Union reaped the rewards of victory in World War II by establishing a sphere of influence along the periphery of its western borders. Hungary, along with other eastern European states, became a satellite in the strategic interests of the Soviet Union. Joseph Stalin's iron grip on the peripheral countries fed the fear of an escalating Cold War. This control of eastern Europe reflected Soviet ideological pronouncements about the spread of communism, a goal that the free world found offensive. The American view of an aggressive Soviet Union bent on controlling the world overshadowed consideration both

8. Suhrke, "Global Refugee Movements," 28.
9. Lasky (ed.), *Hungarian Revolution*, 318.

of the historical roots of Soviet interests in a sphere of influence in eastern Europe, which predated communism, and of the devastation of Russia during the war, wrought by German control of this region. Hungary was the last East European nation to abandon its alliance with Nazi Germany, a fact probably not lost to Soviet memory.[10]

In 1953, the new regime, for which Nikita Khrushchev set the tone, brought an easing of Soviet control on eastern European satellites, and in 1956 it denounced Stalin. During this time period, these satellites were becoming restless, with riots in East Berlin in 1953 and in Poznan, Poland, in 1956. The liberalizations of Josip Broz Tito in Yugoslavia and Wladyslaw Gomulka in Poland were tolerated as long as these governments remained firmly loyal to the Soviet Union. Historian Louis Halle indicated that this easing of Soviet control, however, was a gamble and that Hungary was different. During the uprising in Hungary, Imre Nagy could not establish the firm authority he needed as head of a new communist regime to assure the stability of an alliance with the Soviet Union. When the revolution spread and Hungary broke with the Warsaw Pact, proclaimed neutrality, and sought United Nations' protection on November 1, 1956, the Soviets decisively and brutally quelled the revolution within a few days. With the Soviets unable to hold the liberalization movement in check, "destalinization, going too fast, too far led to restalinization," in the fear that the overthrow of communism in Hungary would influence all of eastern Europe in a "domino" effect. Khrushchev later commented, "Believe me, my friends, we spent painful days and nights before coming to a decision."[11]

Although statesman George Kennan warned the United States not to ridicule and therefore jeopardize the destalinization efforts, "Secretary Dulles from the beginning identified American purpose with the aspirations of the revolting Hungarians," according to historian Norman Graebner. Radio Free Europe denied, but still stood accused of, calling for the overthrow of Nagy and for free elections, that is, nothing short of complete liberation. When it sounded the cry for courage and

10. Norman A. Graebner, *Cold War Diplomacy: American Foreign Policy, 1946–1975* (New York, 1977), 12, 62–65; Louis J. Halle, *The Cold War as History* (New York, 1967), 67–68, 328–30; Paul Tabori, *The Anatomy of Exile: A Semantic and Historical Study* (London, 1972), 252.

11. Graebner, *Cold War Diplomacy*, 61; Halle, *Cold War as History*, 329; David Pryce-Jones, *The Hungarian Revolution* (London, 1969), 119.

boldness, Radio Free Europe had implied support and promised success. One analysis found that though Radio Free Europe may not have
incited the uprising in Hungary, it did broadcast its support once the
revolution was underway. James R. Price commented that "the question remains unanswered as to exactly what RFE did hope to accomplish in the face of massive Soviet power and the virtually certain
knowledge that Western intervention would not occur." Another critic
remarked, "American Cold War propaganda had been harmful, inspir-
ing hopes which could only be disappointed, and at a most anguishing
moment." The Soviet Union and others complained and implicated the
United States in the Hungarian revolt. The situation was exacerbated
by Eisenhower's open appeal to the Soviet Union to remove its forces
from Hungary and to allow freedom for the Hungarians.[12]

For all the Cold War rhetoric in support of liberating eastern Europe
from communism, the American response to the Hungarian revolution was "conspicuous by its absence." In his memoirs, Eisenhower
described the time that included the uprising as the "most crowded
and demanding three weeks of my entire Presidency." The 1956 presidential election was imminent, fostering a reluctance for risky political
decisions; Congress was in recess; severe drought was plaguing the
southwestern United States; the Suez crisis had triggered immediate
concern for the western alliance itself, as well as curtailing the ship-
ment of supplies to western Europe; Secretary Dulles was in the hospital for emergency cancer surgery; Democratic political opponent Adlai
Stevenson was calling for a new foreign policy; and the Hungarians
had revolted. Whether these other events and circumstances were
used intentionally to deflect attention away from the Hungarian crisis,
or whether the Hungarian cause was simply affected by the natural
flow of time and circumstances, the United States did not seek any
action in Hungary beyond a UN reprimand of the Soviet Union. British
statesman, Anthony Eden, recalled his frustration with American pro-
crastination at the UN: "Five days passed without any Council meeting
on Hungary despite repeated attempts by ourselves and others to
bring one about. The U.S. representative was reluctant, and voiced his
suspicion that we were urging the Hungarian situation to divert atten-

12. Graebner, *Cold War Diplomacy*, 62; Library of Congress, *Radio Free Europe: A
Survey and Analysis*, No. JX 1710 US B (March 22, 1972), pp. 25–30, esp. 29; Pryce-Jones,
The Hungarian Revolution, 117–18; Murphy, *Diplomat Among Warriors*, 429.

tion from Suez. The U.S. government appeared in no hurry to move. Their attitude provided a damaging contrast to the alacrity they were showing in arraigning the French and ourselves."[13]

Robert Murphy, an official at the State Department at the time, also noted the rush of events and recalled that "the ruthless suppression of the Hungarian rebellion was somewhat dimmed by the Suez crisis, which could not have been timed more advantageously for the Russians." Hungarian refugee Solyom-Fekete, a former member of the noncommunist Smallholders' party who served briefly in the Hungarian Parliament of 1947 during the short time between German rule and a communist regime in Hungary, agreed that the United States could have done nothing to intervene directly. However, he did question the reluctance of the United States, calculated or not, to send in UN observers as a minimal guarantee of Hungary's neutrality. He said he and others inside Hungary were horrified to hear Radio Free Europe announce on November 3 that UN Ambassador Henry Cabot Lodge had suggested postponing any UN discussion or vote on Hungary. However, measures adopted eventually by the UN, including resolutions calling for an end to the Soviet intervention and the sending of outside observers to Hungary, were ineffective. The Soviet Union remained adamant on its position to suppress the uprising, and American policy, according to Murphy, was to render assistance as long as it was "action short of war."[14]

Idealistically, the United States, in a position of power, had the utopian goal of eliminating the Soviet threat in eastern Europe. Realistically, the Hungarian revolution presented the United States with a test case in Soviet hegemony. The uprising caught the United States by surprise, "without advance information" and a "plan of action." U.S. foreign policy leaders faced the stark realization that the liberation of Hungary was not within U.S. capability without the risk of atomic war, nor was it, they discovered, within the scope of U.S. vital interests. In his memoirs, Eisenhower recounted the dilemma: "Unless the major

13. Bursten, *Escape from Fear,* 49; Eisenhower, *Waging Peace,* 58; Markowitz, "Humanitarianism Versus Restrictionism," 46; Endre Marton, *The Forbidden Sky: Inside the Hungarian Revolution* (Boston, 1971), 286.

14. Murphy, *Diplomat Among Warriors,* 430; interview with Vilmos Solyom-Fekete, European Law Division, Library of Congress, Washington, D.C., April, 1983; Murphy, *Diplomat Among Warriors,* 430–31.

countries of Europe would, without delay, ally themselves with us (an unimaginable prospect), we could do nothing. Sending United States troops alone into Hungary through hostile or neutral territory would have involved us in a general war." Murphy deemed the situation the most critical for the United States since the Korean War. In particular, he saw the danger of direct contact between American and Soviet troops.[15]

Usually verbose in the crusade to "roll back the Iron Curtain," John Foster Dulles gave this terse reply to a reporter's inquiry about intervention: "Well, there was no basis for our giving military aid to Hungary. We had no commitment to do so, and we did not think that to do so would either assist the people of Hungary or the rest of Europe or the rest of the world." Late 1956 was reported to be the bleakest period in Dulles' career. A biographer of his wrote: "All he had ever said about liberation and the rolling back of Soviet rule in Eastern Europe was thrown in his face by the agonizing, yet inevitable decision that the U.S. could not and would not interfere to help the Hungarians."[16]

Charles Bohlen, the American ambassador to the Soviet Union, recalled the following, which occurred on October 29, 1956, a few days prior to Soviet intervention in Hungary: "I had just received a cable from Dulles who urgently wanted to get a message to the Soviet leaders that the United States did not look at Hungary or any of the Soviet satellites as potential military allies. . . . But the American assurance carried no weight with the Kremlin's leaders." Two weeks later, Eisenhower publicly explained that he had never intended to encourage any revolution "by an undefended population against forces over which they could not possibly prevail."[17]

Subsequent analyses of the Hungarian revolution have absolved the United States of any major responsibility by concluding that the uprising was an internal, spontaneous event.[18] If the United States, for whatever reasons, chose not to become embroiled militarily in the Hungarian Revolution of 1956, it did become involved in the assistance

15. Murphy, *Diplomat Among Warriors*, 428; Eisenhower, *Waging Peace*, 89; Murphy, *Diplomat Among Warriors*, 429.
16. U.S. Department of State, *Bulletin*, XXXVI, No. 927 (April 1, 1957), 533; Richard Goold-Adams, *John Foster Dulles: A Reappraisal* (New York, 1962), 234.
17. Bohlen, *Witness to History*, 433; Murphy, *Diplomat Among Warriors*, 429.
18. For example, see Marton, *Forbidden Sky*, 288.

to and resettlement of the refugees who fled to Austria and Yugoslavia in the few months before the borders were sealed once again. If the American response to the needs of refugees was based on genuine humanitarian concern, it was also based on political motivations that seized an opportunity to battle the Soviet Union with a perpetuation of Cold War rhetoric. In fact, assistance to the refugees was about the only action permitted even the powerful United States in this event. Robert Murphy summed up the situation in this way: "Perhaps history will demonstrate that the free world could have intervened to give the Hungarians the liberty they sought, but none of us in the State Department had the skill or imagination to devise a way. . . . But in the end, our government was reduced to the minimal policy of providing assistance to Hungarian refugees, and to impact on world opinion—whatever that may mean."[19]

The tenor of the times also included heightened interest in the rights and welfare of refugees as part of both a concern on the part of many individuals for human rights in general and a revival of natural law theory. This renewed interest in human rights appears to have been rooted in the devastating experiences of two world wars and of the Jewish Holocaust. The rights basic to all human beings were codified in the UN Declaration of Human Rights in 1948, which was followed by the UN Convention on Refugees and the creation of the UNHCR, mandated to protect those who flee because of persecution, in 1951. The Cold War mentality seems to have been influenced by the vivid memory of the exile and execution of over a million post–World War II refugees who had been forcibly repatriated in the Soviet Union as a result of an agreement reached at Yalta in 1945. Thus, practical, political, and philosophical factors together form the proper context for understanding the Hungarian refugee problem.

The resettlement of 38,000 refugees in the United States during late 1956 and early 1957 was deemed a success, an expression, for the most part, of the humanitarian spirit that is part of American democratic ideology. Swift, organized government assistance and the help of several voluntary agencies and generous individuals prompted Tracy S. Voorhees, chairman of the President's Committee for Hungarian Refugee Relief, to remark, "No comparable mass movement into America

19. Murphy, *Diplomat Among Warriors*, 432.

had ever occurred in so short a time."[20] Vilmos Solyom-Fekete attested to and was grateful for the warm welcome and support he and other refugees received from the U.S. government, relief agencies, and the American people.

Genuine, strong cultural and sentimental ties with the people of Hungary, fostered in part by the presence of a sizable, ethnically Hungarian population in the United States, probably prompted a generous response by many Americans, according to Joseph Whelan, a specialist in East European affairs. Whelan recalled the 1952 presidential campaign in Buffalo, New York, where the eastern European ethnic populations heard Republican candidates denounce Soviet hegemony and promise the "roll back" of the iron curtain in eastern Europe. Religious ties were evident, too. Catholic leader Francis Cardinal Spellman of New York was a close friend of Josef Cardinal Mindszenty, leader of the Catholic Church in Hungary, who sought refuge at the American embassy in Budapest when the Soviets invaded and quelled the uprising. In the late 1940s, the communists had accused Spellman of "directing espionage, sabotage, and various other disturbances in countries that refused to submit to capitalism." They also charged that Spellman, with the assistance of Cardinal Mindszenty, was plotting to restore the monarchy in Hungary.[21]

The media were influential in portraying the dramatic events of the revolution and the plight of the refugees. *Life* magazine, in a special edition entitled "Hungary's Fight for Freedom," along with other periodicals and newspapers, published a series of moving photographs taken at the scene. American society was experiencing, as never before, a media revolution as the widespread availability of television brought world news into the living room. Media coverage of the daring exploits of escapees from eastern Europe reaching freedom in the West served as prologue to full-scale reporting on the Hungarian refugees.[22]

Humanitarian concerns for the refugees were soon joined by compelling foreign policy interests. Like Robert Murphy, Eisenhower later

20. Markowitz, "Humanitarianism Versus Restrictionism," 57.

21. Interview with Joseph Whelan, Senior Specialist on International Affairs, Congressional Research Service, Library of Congress, Washington, D.C., April, 1983; Robert I. Gannon, *The Cardinal Spellman Story* (Garden City, N.Y., 1962), 340.

22. *Hungary's Fight for Freedom: A Special Report in Pictures, Life* special issue (Chicago, 1956); interview with Joseph Whelan, April, 1983.

recalled in his memoirs the frustration he felt over the nation's inability to intervene in Hungary: "So, as a single nation the United States did the only thing it could: We readied ourselves in every way possible to help the refugees fleeing from the criminal action of the Soviets, and did everything possible to condemn the aggression." The Eisenhower administration was on record as condemning the sellout of refugees at Yalta and the loss of China and as promising the liberation of eastern Europe. Therefore, the administration's decision not to intervene in Hungary must have seemed hypocritical. Members of Congress reprimanded the State Department and the government's intelligence agencies for having been caught by surprise. There was criticism of possible complicity between the State Department and Radio Free Europe. Many people were clamoring for at least some action by the United States.[23]

Perhaps out of a sense of guilt and with the opportunity to recoup the loss of face from appearing powerless, even "soft on communism," the Eisenhower administration quickly organized a refugee assistance effort to its political advantage. The option of military intervention in Hungary was exchanged for a moral crusade against the Soviet Union that utilized the refugees. One observer noted that the refugee relief operation appeared out to win a consensus from the American people for the administration's Cold War policies. Journalist Marten A. Bursten sardonically noted this fact in his volume on the revolution: "It was hard to show some people that the warm hospitality shown to the victims of communism had more purpose than the humanitarian aspects—that the treatment of these self-banished people was part of America's foreign policy to win friends, and help care for those who broke with communism. It was part of the 62 billion dollar foreign aid investment made by the United States' taxpayers since 1945 to keep communist bedeviled countries . . . from slipping into the eager grasp of the Kremlin."[24]

The exploitation of the Hungarian revolution and its refugees took on international ramifications. Films, photographs, and Voice of America broadcasts were disseminated around the world. Arthur Lawson, director of the United States Information Agency (USIA), made specific mention of the broad distribution of such materials in Vietnam. Ac-

23. Eisenhower, *Waging Peace*, 89; Murphy, *Diplomat Among Warriors*, 429.
24. Bursten, *Escape from Fear*, 164.

cording to Lawson, "a wall poster, for example, appeared in every Vietnamese village." A dramatic account of events written by a young Hungarian refugee and accompanied by photographs was "sent to all the Agency's posts eleven days after his arrival in this country." In a report to Congressman Michael A. Feighan, Lawson indicated what the revolution meant: "This historic event presents an unparalleled opportunity to expose communism for what it is. . . . As to the future, one of our major themes will be the Hungarian freedom revolution." Even the U.S. Postal Service was not spared involvement in propaganda efforts. Soon after most refugees were resettled, Hungary complained of personal letters arriving from the United States with stamps bearing the inscription "Support Your Crusade for Freedom."[25] Presumably, some of these letters were coming from recently resettled refugees.

The first offer of assistance to refugees by the United States was for $20 million in relief aid for food and other emergency services for those streaming into Austria, and it came on November 2, 1956. Five days later, on November 7, the day following the presidential election, Eisenhower announced that 5,000 refugees would be admitted to the United States "as expeditiously as possible," with immigrant visas available under the Refugee Relief Act of 1953, due to expire less than two months later, at the end of December, 1956. This relief act had actually been a result of Eisenhower's interest and initiative. It began as an administration-authored bill based on the problems of overpopulation and war refugees in Europe. Eisenhower sought such legislation to "guard our legitimate national interests and be faithful to our basic ideas of freedom and fairness to all."[26] On December 1, 1956, Eisenhower increased to 6,500 the number of visas for Hungarian refugees. In addition, another 15,000 were to be admitted as parolees under a provision of the Immigration and Nationality Act that allowed such measures to be taken by the attorney general in emergency situations. In his eagerness to do all he could under existing law, Eisenhower said that tough restrictions on the admittance of refugees into the United

25. U.S. Congress, *Congressional Record*, 85th Cong., 1st Sess., CIII, Pt. III, 3869; Janos Radvanyi, *Hungary and the Superpowers: The 1956 Revolution and Realpolitik* (Stanford, 1972), 31.

26. Library of Congress, "Chronology of the Hungarian Refugee Program" (Typescript, May 19, 1975), 1; U.S. Senate, Committee on the Judiciary, *U.S. Immigration Law and Policy: 1952–1979*, 96th Cong., 1st Sess., No. 44-151, pp. 15–16.

States might have to be bent to meet the crisis, a statement that would soon haunt the administration's efforts. Meanwhile, other European countries were moving refugees to resettlement at a much quicker pace, as noted by the UNHCR. During the first month of the exodus, until November 28, 1956, the United States took in considerably fewer refugees than other nations:

3,917 to Switzerland	1,976 to the Netherlands
3,369 to Germany	1,172 to Italy
3,345 to the United Kingdom	1,122 to Sweden
3,002 to Belgium	630 to the United States
2,976 to France	151 to Ireland[27]

The transfer of refugees from Austria to the United States took on the elements of a military campaign. Labeling the transfer "Operation Mercy" and "Operation Safe Haven," the Intergovernmental Committee for European Migration (ICEM) took refugees to a former army installation, Camp Kilmer in New Jersey, in red, silver, and blue DC-4 planes. Flight schedules were adjusted to allow for maximum media coverage. One group went directly to Milwaukee for an observance of "Free Hungary Day." Another group of weary travelers had its schedule adjusted to allow for daytime arrival on Thanksgiving Day; dubbed "Delayed Pilgrims," these refugees met reporters against a backdrop that read, "Providence Brought You Here." Refugees were in demand for television quiz shows, ribbon cuttings, and parades. Voorhees, who had been appointed by President Eisenhower to head the relief effort, was criticized by some for his lack of experience with refugees. Despite his inexperience, however, he knew what had to be done to make the refugee resettlement a success; upon appointment, he immediately hired a large advertising firm to sell the refugees to the American public. Commenting on the powerful influence of the United States as it responded to the Hungarian uprising, Vice-President Richard Nixon said, "I am convinced that the events of Hungary will prove to be a major turning point in the struggle to defeat communism without war." Similarly, the President's Committee for Hungarian Refugee Relief saw the importance of the American response to the refugees: "While Russian tanks were firing on Hungarians, U.S. military planes

27. Library of Congress, "Chronology of the Hungarian Refugee Program," 1–2; Elmo Roper, "The Americans and the Hungarian Story," *Saturday Review*, XL (May 11, 1957), 24; Holborn, *Refugees*, 401.

were carrying many thousands of them to the safe haven of our free land. Like the Berlin Airlift, the meaning of this operation was not lost on the peoples of the world."[28]

All in all, the 38,000 refugees who came to the United States were quickly resettled, with generous employment and educational opportunities from individuals, businesses, and universities throughout the country. Nevertheless, some aspects of the resettlement program would read like a comedy of errors. For example, a farmer in Vermont, in need of laborers, agreed to take a group of refugees who wanted to be resettled together. Upon their arrival by bus from Camp Kilmer, the farmer discovered he had a band of gypsies on his hands.[29]

According to a study of the acculturation of the refugees conducted by Alexander S. Weinstock, the Hungarians who had migrated to the United States over the years were primarily of peasant origin, having little in common with this new group of mostly young, male, middle-class, and educated refugees. The latter tended to look down on and remain aloof from their predecessors. Some immigrant and minority groups seemed to resent the special treatment accorded the new refugees. For example, pressing hard for civil rights and having made it a campaign issue, American blacks questioned why charity did not begin at home: "[They] found themselves wondering why comparable zeal had never been harnessed to find proper homes and jobs for as many American-born Negroes. Why . . . did the Vice President, rather than going such a long way to Austria, not simply catch a plane for Mississippi?" In fact, civil rights legislation competed with the plight of the Hungarian refugees for attention in Congress in early 1957. Once the fanfare and attention subsided, however, some of the Hungarian refugees felt isolated and neglected.[30]

The American effort at resettlement was not without criticism both at home and abroad. At home, restrictionism, long a theme in American immigration debates and policies, became a formidable challenge to American foreign policy. The consequent delays and final curtail-

28. Bursten, *Escape from Fear*, 155–63; U.S. Department of State, *Bulletin*, XXXV, No. 912 (December 17, 1956), 943.
29. Bursten, *Escape from Fear*, 185.
30. Alexander S. Weinstock, *Acculturation and Occupation: A Study of the 1956 Hungarian Refugees in the United States* (The Hague, 1969), 42–43; Peter Lyon, *Eisenhower: Portrait of the Hero* (Boston, 1974), 733; U.S. Congress, *Congressional Record*, 85th Cong., 1st Sess., CIII, Pt. V, 6115–17.

ment of the resettlement of refugees by the United States brought criticism from the international community, especially Austria, as the promise of sustained and generous assistance proved empty.

Eisenhower's objective to admit large numbers of refugees was constrained by existing conservative immigration laws and parole authority. A more liberal refugee admissions policy for the Hungarians required congressional approval. In December, 1956, the president sent a reluctant Vice-President Nixon on a fact-finding trip to Austrian refugee camps, which resulted in a much-publicized report to Congress attesting to the fact that those seeking asylum were bona fide refugees who indeed needed emergency assistance. Nixon "brushed aside fears that large numbers of the refugees were communist spies or undesirables." He further insisted that "the quality of nearly all of them . . . was of the highest order." Nixon recommended that no ceiling be set on the number of refugees the United States would take in and that the refugees be admitted with regular, not parole, status. In January, 1957, Eisenhower essentially repeated Nixon's recommendations, asking for the liberalization of measures restricting further entry of the refugees. Congress, however, did not oblige.[31]

By April, 1957, without congressional permission to do otherwise, Eisenhower announced that "the number of refugees admitted . . . will be on a diminishing basis."[32] Although it was true that fewer refugees were entering Austria and Yugoslavia as Hungary tightened its border security, thousands still remained in camps. Many of those remaining had hoped to enter the United States. In addition, thousands of others had reluctantly resettled in other countries on a temporary basis, believing the assurances from Eisenhower that eventually they would be allowed to come to the United States.

In a special report in 1979, Senator Edward M. Kennedy noted that immigration and refugee policy has been a major theme but also a most contentious issue in American history. Referring to the Immigration and Nationality Act of 1952, which was in effect at the time of the Hungarian revolution, Kennedy commented that it was passed over the veto of President Harry S. Truman, "at the depth of the Cold War and restrictionist atmosphere of that era." The law had borrowed heav-

31. Markowitz, "Humanitarianism Versus Restrictionism," 51; New York *Times,* January 19, 1957, p. 6.
32. Library of Congress, "Chronology of Hungarian Refugee Program," 3.

ily from similar legislation passed in 1924, which had established the national origins quota formula. In addition to restricting immigration, the Immigration and Nationality Act of 1952, popularly known as the McCarran-Walter Act in honor of its congressional sponsors, provided for careful screening and the deportation of subversive immigrants thought to be communists or communist sympathizers. This legislation "reflected the view that communist subversion represented a serious danger to the country, against which our immigration law formed a vital line of defense."[33] It was the coauthor of this law, Congressman Francis E. Walter, chairman of the House Subcommittee on Immigration and Naturalization, who led the opposition to the Eisenhower administration's proposal to liberalize admissions for Hungarian refugees.

The administration was politically astute to include Walter in the special delegation headed by Nixon that visited refugee camps in Austria in late 1956. At the time, Walter expressed his support for U.S. intentions and promised to do all he could to bring the refugees to the United States. He predicted that most of the refugees would return to Hungary to fight the Soviet invaders. But Walter's sympathies soon changed as the image of the idealized freedom fighters became tarnished. In February, 1957, both the *Times Herald* and the Washington *Post* reported the arrest of two Hungarians, thought to be secret communist agents, who were apprehended by Austrian police just as they were about to board a plane for the United States. Walter began to accuse immigration authorities of faulty and hasty screening, which thus allowed communist subversives into the country. He claimed that the 6,130 visas available under the Refugee Relief Act had been given indiscriminately to the wrong people, as the first wave of refugees were actually communists fleeing the wrath of the true revolutionary freedom fighters, who had stayed behind to fight. Others who fled he accused of opting out of the revolution to seek economic opportunity abroad. Congressman George S. Long of Louisiana agreed with Walter's assessment in his own comments on President Eisenhower's request for generous quotas for the refugees from Hungary: "I find it hard to generate much enthusiasm over the Hungarian refugees who have deserted their homeland in time of crisis and who under the guise

33. Senate Judiciary Committee, *U.S. Immigration Law and Policy*, 1, 5–6.

of Freedom Fighters have migrated in wholesale lots to the promised land—America." Journalist Leslie Bain reported that a greater number of genuine freedom fighters could be found among those who escaped later but that resettlement offers for later refugees had diminished. Many of these people went to Yugoslavia, as access to Austria was blocked by the Hungarian government.[34]

Asked if some of the refugees were communists, Vilmos Solyom-Fekete said they were, but in name only. Realistically, one way to cope under communist rule in Hungary, to avoid suspicion and harassment, was nominally to join the Communist party. In addition, for middle-class professionals in urban areas, the ticket to employment was a party card. However, neither Congressman Walter nor the tenor of the times permitted any explanation of this type of accommodation to the system. A Cold War perspective did not allow for an appreciation of the complexity of the factors that motivate refugees to flee. Instead, it employed simple reductionism to characterize events and issues in terms of good or evil, communist or free.[35]

In his analysis of the reception of the Hungarian refugees, Weinstock found that "the fact that relatively few had actually fought was of little consequence" to the granting of heroic refugee status. The idealizing of the Hungarian refugees for Cold War propaganda purposes precluded a comprehensive understanding of the myriad factors that influenced their decisions to leave. In addition to the immediate fear of persecution, a number of other factors probably combined to influence their decisions to seek asylum, including the general political situation in Hungary, uncertainty about the future, the attraction of a better way of life elsewhere, relatives and friends abroad, the sudden opening of the border during the chaos of the uprising, and personal reasons unique to each refugee. Paul Tabori, chairman of the Hungarian Relief Fund in London later described what he found to be the general reason for leaving Hungary: "It became evident . . . that the vast majority were not political refugees, had not taken an immediate,

34. New York *Times*, December 3, 1956, p. 6; U.S. Congress, *Congressional Record*, 85th Cong., 1st Sess., CIII, Pt. III, 2938; New York *Times*, January 5, 1957, p. 2; U.S. Congress, *Congressional Record*, 85th Cong., 1st Sess., CII, Pt. II, 2365; Bain, *Reluctant Satellites*, 187.
35. Interview with Vilmos Solyom-Fekete.

active part in the revolution, but had simply left a life that was drab and hopeless."[36]

Solyom-Fekete indicated that many of the younger Hungarian refugees had genuine fears of imprisonment and death if they remained in Hungary. He thought that the accusations by the West of large-scale forced exiles of revolutionaries to the Soviet Union were probably exaggerated, though the possibility of wholesale exile loomed large when one considered Soviet behavior since the end of the war. In his own case, he had experienced imprisonment and harassment by the communists over many years. Although he did not necessarily fear for his life, he had had enough of life under communist rule. Solyom-Fekete did not fight in the Hungarian Revolution of 1956, yet his story is representative of many who fled, and his account is an example of the difficulties one encounters in ascribing refugee status. In her work, Astri Suhrke discusses how the interactions of various pull and push factors can precipitate the choice to leave one's country, of how fears of persecution combine with the opportunity to leave—for example, a suddenly opened border—and with the anticipation of a warm reception and resettlement elsewhere. These factors need not diminish the validity of refugee status, unless they conflict with some idealized notion of what a refugee ought to be.[37]

Additionally, the refugee program had to contend with outbreaks of anti-Semitism. The American refugee program was marred by charges of anti-Semitism that surfaced when a few issues of *Szabad Magyarsag* (*Free Magyardom*), a pro-Nazi paper, were found at Camp Kilmer. In Salzburg, Austria, anti-Semitic rioters accused refugee agencies of favoring Jews for resettlement. Solyom-Fekete acknowledged that anti-Semitism existed among the refugees, but its extent, in his view, was exaggerated by the press. Bain found anti-Semitic outbreaks to be more prevalent in camps with refugees destined to go to the United States, because American screening authorities favored asylum seekers who were rightists politically and oftentimes anti–Jewish as well. Edward H. Meyerding, supervisor of the Quaker refugee relief program in Austria, confirmed reports of anti-Semitism,

36. Weinstock, *Acculturation and Occupation*, 31; Tabori, *Anatomy of Exile*, 254–55; Bain, *Reluctant Satellites*, 189.
37. Suhrke, "Global Refugee Movements," 3.

caused in part by the fact that some of the Hungarian communist leaders were Jewish.[38]

Meyerding also complained that the picking and choosing of refugees for resettlement, especially by the United States, enflamed tensions. As time passed and Western nations were less generous in their refugee quotas, frayed nerves erupted in anger and violence as the refugees competed for fewer resettlement offers. Suicide attempts were reported. Many who wanted to go to the United States refused resettlement elsewhere, as word spread that those who had gone to other resettlement countries earlier, particularly Great Britain, secure in the promise that they would move on to the United States, were unable to do so. Austria pleaded with the resettlement countries, especially the United States, and with their sponsoring agencies to discontinue the screening of refugees along religious, racial, and state-of-health lines. The voluntary agencies, affiliated with religious institutions for the most part, used religious criteria in a selection process that was problematic to the American refugee resettlement effort.[39]

If Congressman Walter spearheaded the opposition to Eisenhower's planned refugee policy, he did not act alone. John Eastland and others from the Senate joined him. Other legislators, perhaps influenced by public opinion polls, were apprehensive about liberal quotas. A sample survey found that 32 percent of the American people thought the refugees would have a bad influence on American society, 21 percent believed they would have no effect, and only 26 percent thought the country would benefit. Some expressed the fear that conditions behind the iron curtain were so bad that a liberal immigration policy would attract a flood of refugees from all over eastern Europe. Senator Jacob Javits urged that refugees generated by the Suez crisis in the Middle East be included in the new refugee quotas. Such requests, including demands for resettlement for 160,000 other refugees in Europe, may have fueled a growing apocalyptic view of the refugee problem. Even those politicians who were sympathetic to the Hungarian refugee cause were faced with some public opposition to their position. For example, Senator Richard L. Neuberger from Oregon needed to

38. New York *Times*, January 29, 1957, p. 36, January 13, 1957, p. 13; Bain, *Reluctant Satellites*, 193; U.S. Congress, *Congressional Record*, 85th Cong., 1st Sess., CII, Pt. II, 2408.

39. U.S. Congress, *Congressional Record*, 85th Cong., 1st Sess., CII, Pt. II, 2408; New York *Times*, January 15, 1957, p. 3.

address the fears of his constituency that the refugees would have an adverse economic effect on the country as they competed with American citizens for jobs. The senator countered opposition by claiming that instead of competing the refugees would actually benefit the economy since they would bring high-level skills and expertise needed in industry. Senator John Stennis perhaps summarized the opposition's major arguments by emphasizing the threat the refugees posed to internal security and to the economy: "Again, let me emphasize that while we all admire the gallant people of the satellite countries in their heroic struggle for freedom and liberty, I do not believe that America can be made more strong or resolute in its determination to stop Communist imperialism by weakening our security structure, nor by disrupting the domestic economy by preempting jobs otherwise available to unemployed American citizens." Stennis saw a possible solution in the creation of a freedom corps of refugees from the iron curtain countries to be made into combat units within the North Atlantic Treaty Organization (NATO).[40]

As American foreign policy interests collided with domestic restrictionism, the pace of resettlement slackened. Other countries also reduced their efforts, causing complaints from Austria. Vienna's approval for the visit of a Hungarian delegation to the camps came as an embarrassment to the West, which feared that the delegation would report "the worst aspects of refugee life" for propaganda purposes. Austria hoped that the visit would prompt an improvement in the resettlement process. Soon after the delegation's visit on January 17, 1957, Hungary charged that refugees were being abused, that they were being discriminated against in asylum screenings, and that many were runaway minors and children who had been kidnapped. Refugees sent to Great Britain, it said, were being exploited in the coal mines. Ironically, Hungarian refugees were actually excluded from work in the mines by irate British unionists, even though a labor shortage existed. On January 20, 1957, Hungary announced amnesty for refugees who returned and asked the West to stop using refugees for propaganda purposes. Western propaganda was undermined even before the Hungarian delegation's visit to Austria. A New York *Times*

40. Markowitz, "Humanitarianism Versus Restrictionism," 54; U.S. Congress, *Congressional Record*, 85th Cong., 1st Sess., CIII, Pt. IV, 5223–24, Pt. VII, 9764, and Pt. III, 2938.

headline of January 9 ("Austrian Officials Bar Asylum for 11 Boys, Aged 13, Who Fled Out of Dislike for Teacher") suggested that not all the asylum seekers were bona fide freedom fighters.[41]

Why did the Soviets allow thousands of Hungarians to flee, especially if the issue served to give the advantage to American Cold War propaganda? One reason is that the authorities were glad to be rid of disgruntled, rebellious elements, described as deserters and traitors by the Hungarian press.[42] This is not to say flight was easy; it still had to be carried out clandestinely, but the rigid security measures usually expected of totalitarian governments were lacking, and the Voice of America provided encouragement. In an immediate sense, the confusion in Hungary kept authorities preoccupied with quelling the uprising and reestablishing control rather than with worrying about those who were fleeing the country. It is also possible that ethnic solidarity overtook ideology, so that Hungarian border guards were willing to turn their eyes and guns away from those fleeing. As with many refugee exoduses, it all happened quickly in just a few weeks. When the border between Austria and Hungary was sealed again, after 180,000 had arrived in Austria, still 20,000 more refugees escaped by way of the more arduous journey to Yugoslavia.

The Hungarian authorities were not completely without misgivings about the exodus. As early as December, 1956, the new Kadar regime in Hungary became concerned about the loss of thousands of educated, middle-class professionals. In addition, the new government may have feared that a resistance force that could eventually mean trouble was forming among the refugees outside the country. Tabori indicated the existence of a Hungarian historical penchant to form political parties in exile: after World War II, groups of Hungarian socialists, liberals, Nazis, peasants, and workers were active in Europe, the United States, and South America. In his book *Hungary 1956*, Bill Lomax discussed the possibility that Hungarian exiles were recruited by the West at about the time of the uprising to go into Hungary to bring out information.[43]

41. New York *Times,* January 17, 1957, p. 8, January 20, 1957, p. 1, January 9, 1957, p. 10.
42. Tabori, *Anatomy of Exile,* 328.
43. Lasky (ed.), *Hungarian Revolution,* 314; Tabori, *Anatomy of Exile,* 253; Bill Lomax, *Hungary 1956* (London, 1976), 128.

Repatriation efforts moved ahead slowly, discouraged by the United States for political reasons and affected by memories of other forced repatriations. Anxious for durable solutions to the refugee problem but wanting to remain nonpolitical, the UNHCR cooperated with Austria, Yugoslavia, and Hungary by seeing to it that refugees returned only by choice. The UNHCR remained committed to the principle of family reunification and expressed special concern for the many unaccompanied minors. Nearly 10 percent of the refugees, or approximately 18,200 people, returned to Hungary.[44] It remains to be determined if some returned only because permanent resettlement offers had dwindled.

The refugee par excellence to many Americans was Josef Cardinal Mindszenty, archbishop of Budapest, primate of Hungary, and an intriguing, highly symbolic figure. Mindszenty had suffered at the hands of both the Nazis and the communists for many years and had become "the leader of the opposition to Communism of all denominations."[45] Reaching safety in the American embassy compound in Budapest during the revolution, he remained there, steadfastly denouncing any rapprochement with the communists. Upon his release years later, he traveled to the United States as a leader of the Hungarians in exile.

During his exile inside the embassy, Mindszenty proved to be an obstacle, if not an embarrassment, to Vatican efforts to reach an accord with communist authorities over the delicate problem of the role of the church behind the iron curtain. Solyom-Fekete, along with others, questioned Mindszenty's effectiveness in stubbornly refusing to budge from the American embassy, noting that the cardinal may have done more good had he left and carried his crusade against communism abroad. Historians Joyce Kolko and Gabriel Kolko wrote that Mindszenty was a powerful Hungarian leader who advocated the return of the traditional order, including restoring the Hapsburg throne, the great estates, and the role of the privileged few. He opposed communism but also the liberal Protestants who were concerned about landless peasants and laborers. As an advocate of dispossessed landlords and aristocrats and the restoration of a landholding church, he became less appealing to the cause of freedom and democracy.[46]

44. Holborn, *Refugees*, 397.
45. Weinstock, *Acculturation and Occupation*, 31.
46. Marton, *Forbidden Sky*, 193; Joyce Kolko and Gabriel Kolko, *The Limits of Power: The World and U.S. Foreign Policy, 1945–1954* (New York, 1972), 213.

However, it does not appear that much consideration was given to understanding this enigmatic refugee beyond his role as refugee par excellence. In the United States, Mindszenty's heroic stature was enhanced by his relationship with the popular Cardinal Spellman of New York and by his position as the religious leader of the Hungarians in exile. In his memoirs, Eisenhower mentions Mindszenty as a possible leader emerging from the Hungarian revolution, before the Soviet intervention. With Mindszenty remaining at the American embassy until 1971, his role in his country was reduced to obstructing the normalization of U.S.–Hungarian relations for several years.[47]

As Hungary's southern neighbor, Yugoslavia posed an interesting aspect for American foreign policy. Independent and exemplary of the many roads to socialism, Yugoslavia was in an untenable situation after the Hungarian revolution. Tito's government stood the chance of being affected by the reestablishment of Soviet hegemony in Hungary and in the general region. Robert Murphy recalled that Leo Males, Yugoslavia's ambassador to the United States, was clearly upset by the possibility of American confrontation with the Soviets over Hungary. "He believed his country was trembling on the thin edge of war against the Soviet Union, and he urged that everything be done to confine the conflict to Hungary."[48]

Reports indicate that Yugoslavia turned back refugees from Hungary at first. This action may have demonstrated its loyalty to the Soviet Union and avoided the suspicion of complicity with the Hungarian rebels. Eventually, Yugoslavia received 20,000 refugees and, from all accounts, treated them well. It is possible that Yugoslavia was able to be generous only after it received assurances that the United States was not going to intervene in Hungary. The United States found itself in the curious position of cooperating with Tito's communist government in assisting the refugees. Resettlement from Yugoslavia was complicated because Yugoslavia was not a member of the ICEM and American immigration and refugee policies at the time made it difficult to resettle refugees from first asylum countries that were communist. Murphy pointed out that, actually, the U.S. Department of State was inclined to work with Yugoslavia because of its independence from

47. Eisenhower, *Waging Peace*, 82; Marton, *Forbidden Sky*, 193.
48. Murphy, *Diplomat Among Warriors*, 430.

Moscow but also because "we hoped President Tito might have a liberalizing effect on other Communist countries."[49]

By the summer of 1957, the Hungarian refugee crisis appeared to be over. The borders were sealed once again, and few refugees were arriving in Austria and Yugoslavia. All but about 30,000 refugees had been resettled abroad; many of those remaining in Austria were slated to be resettled elsewhere or to be integrated into Austrian society. The United States had taken in 38,000 refugees and had spent $71 million, including $20 million from private sources, on the refugee problem.[50]

Although the United States could claim to have resettled more refugees and spent more money than any other country, these statistics do not tell the whole story. When the resettlement is figured on a per capita basis, it is clear that ten other nations took more refugees and donated more financially. In addition, except for the 6,130 refugees who received permanent visas, the remaining refugees who came to the United States were parolees until July, 1958, when they were finally granted formal immigrant status by Congress. Parolee status conferred a degree of uncertainty for these Hungarians and precluded employment in certain sectors. Considering its wealth, power, and promises, many critics at home and abroad felt the United States could have done more. Those supporting a liberal policy for the Hungarians and also for the 160,000 European refugees from other communist-dominated countries included Senator Hubert Humphrey. The senator criticized the gap between rhetoric and reality, declaring that the numbers of Hungarians actually admitted constituted a miserable failure. Humphrey commented, "A far cry, isn't it, from what we preach." New York *Herald Tribune* columnist Roscoe Drummond pointed out the obvious humanitarian aspect of assistance to refugees, but he also mentioned the offering of haven as "one of the vital tools of the Cold War." Concerning refugees residing in camps, Drummond wrote that "the Soviets point to these camps as visible proof that Free World asylum is a delusion and a trap and use this evidence of the unfinished job to discourage others who would like to make the break to freedom."[51]

49. Lasky (ed.), *Hungarian Revolution,* 314; Murphy, *Diplomat Among Warriors,* 427.
50. Library of Congress, "Chronology of Hungarian Refugee Program," 4.
51. Bursten, *Escape from Fear,* 126; U.S. Congress, *Congressional Record,* 85th Cong., 2nd Sess., CIV, Pt. II, 1473, and Pt. XIII, 1631.

The response of the United States to the Hungarian refugee problem was motivated by humanitarian concern but also by national interests, bringing to mind Niebuhr's maxim that nations act out of self-interest, enlightened at best. For the United States, a magnanimous response based on the ideals of American democratic tradition was something the world had logically come to expect. However, in terms of American self-interests, if the Hungarian refugees had been added to the 160,000 displaced persons already in Europe, they would have been an additional burden to American allies, who were instrumental in the West's defense against the Soviet Union. If the refugees had been left in neutral Austria and independent Yugoslavia, they might have had a destabilizing effect on the border situations of the iron curtain countries. Propaganda credits accruing to the free world because of the Soviet intervention in Hungary would have been forfeited if the West had not responded to the refugee crisis. For their part, the Soviet Union and the new Kadar regime in Hungary lost no time in criticizing the lack of cooperation in repatriation efforts and family reunification, the selective screening process, and the ceilings placed on resettlement, especially by the United States. In the larger context of the Cold War, the refugees served foreign policy interests, as the United States capitalized on the refugee crisis in its moral crusade against the Soviet Union, exemplifying Kennan's observation that the United States is prone to cloak power and interest with moralism.

The decision of the United States not to intervene in Hungary conflicted with its Cold War pronouncements. Similarly, when the Eisenhower administration announced its intended refugee program, presumably based on humanitarian ideals, it promised more than it could deliver. The practical actions the government took to help the refugees fell short of the expectations the United States had helped to foster by idealizing and symbolizing the refugees' plight as part of its Cold War rhetoric. This example of the inherent conflict between idealism and realism in American foreign policy is explained by Thompson and other realist thinkers, who point out that foreign policy based on ideals and ideas of what the world ought to be in theory, without an honest appraisal of interests and what in fact is possible, often deteriorates into moralizing and eventually into hypocrisy. If the image of the Soviet Union suffered in the eyes of the world because of its brutality in Hungary, the failure of the United States to carry out in practice what it had rhetorically promised tarnished the image of the West. Leslie Bain judged that "the Hungarian Revolution underlined the bankruptcy of the cold war both as a tactical and as a moral weapon."[52] The idealization of the refugees as freedom fighters gave way to disillusionment, precluding an understanding and appreciation of who the refugees actually were and why they had fled. Ironically, both the domestic concerns of restrictionism and the foreign policy that pitted the State Department against restrictionists in Congress shared a similar goal; both sought security for the United States, as the Cold War heightened the perceived threat of the spread of communism by an aggressive Soviet Union. In the end, the American response was stymied by the classic dilemma in refugee crises: the right to flee persecution in one country is not automatically complemented by the right to asylum and nationality in another.

This case study of American national interests related to the Hungarian refugees provides the historical background against which we can view other refugee crises. Turning now to a more recent, more complex, and larger refugee phenomenon, the next chapters address the problem of nearly two million Indochinese refugees. These chapters examine the significant national interests that contributed to the Indochina refugee problem, providing us an opportunity to explore the similarities and differences in the two events.

52. Bain, *Reluctant Satellites*, 197.

II

National Interests and the

Roots of the Exodus

April, 1989, marked the fourteenth year of the ongoing refugee exodus from Indochina that has displaced more than two million people since the fall of Saigon. Although the Vietnam War ended in 1975, problems and conflicts, especially the Vietnamese invasion of Cambodia at the end of 1978 and subsequent hostile Sino-Vietnamese relations, have continued to plague the region of Southeast Asia. Only in 1988 did tensions start to ease somewhat with the beginning of Vietnamese troop withdrawals from Cambodia. Refugees from Vietnam, Laos, and Cambodia, who have sought and continue to seek asylum in neighboring ASEAN countries and in Hong Kong, affect and are affected by strategic, political, social, and economic national interests of the Southeast Asian states. In the larger context of international balance-of-power politics, the Indochina refugee issue is also related to the interests of other nations, including the United States, the Soviet Union, and the People's Republic of China.

The complexities of the Indochina refugee problem are compounded when humanitarian concerns for the refugees are added to the multiplicity of national interest factors. The various programs and policies involving several nations in rendering assistance and protection to the refugees directly or via international agencies may be judged reasonably successful. They reflect to considerable degree the concept of international burden sharing. For the most part, this cooperative effort is evident when national interests and humanitarian concerns coincide. The inability actually to resolve this refugee dilemma—

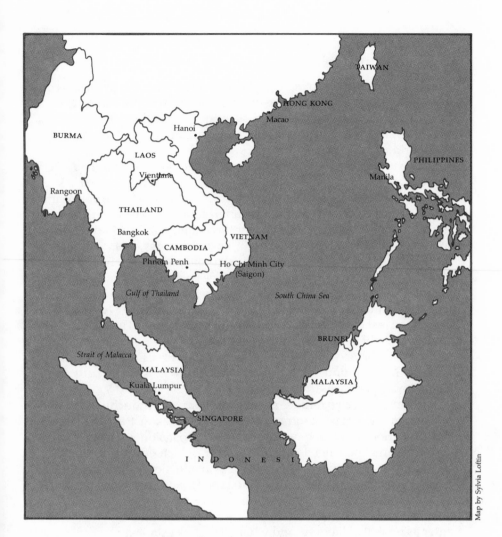

Southeast Asia

the nations' tendency to manage rather than address root causes—can be attributed, however, to the clash between national interests and human rights, with the power of such interests ultimately superseding, but perhaps being influenced by, humanitarian concerns in a political world.

In several respects, the Hungarian refugee problem foreshadowed characteristics that are intensified in the Indochina refugee issue. Chapter I showed how national interests influenced refugee policy and colluded and collided with humanitarian concerns. The willingness of the West, especially the attempt by the United States to admit large numbers of Hungarian refugees in 1956 and 1957, was, in part, a manifestation of the American foreign policy objective in the post–World War II era to focus on the deficiencies of communism by offering liberal democracy as a viable alternative to those who voted with their feet. The United States hoped that this visible response would not be lost on the rest of the world, especially the developing Third World.[1] A continuation of this motivation in overall refugee policy can be found in the welcome accorded refugees from other East European nations and the Soviet Union, then the refugees of the massive exodus from Cuba, and now those from Indochina.

However, the two refugee events, Hungary and Indochina, are also marked by important contrasts. Refugee policies in the post–World War II period coincided with economic expansion in resettlement countries and their need for skilled labor, which educated refugees, including the Hungarians, provided. A distinction can be made between old refugees, such as the Hungarians, and new refugees, such as the Indochinese, who, by contrast, are ethnically and culturally different from the Western countries of resettlement, which they often enter as unskilled laborers and where they lack established ethnic and cultural support systems. The more obvious differences in the two events, however, show up in the sheer size and the ongoing nature of the Indochina exodus in contrast to the Hungarian one.[2]

The conflict between humanitarian values and national interests poses a dilemma for the Indochina refugee case, just as it did for the Hungarian refugee problem of 1956 and 1957. We sometimes make the

1. Suhrke, "Global Refugee Movements," 15.
2. *Ibid.*; Barry N. Stein, "The Refugee Experience: Defining the Parameters of a Field of Study," *International Migration Review*, XV (Spring-Summer, 1981), 329–30.

assumption, even after the Hungarian experience, that American refugee policies, and by inference the refugee policies of other nations, are and should be based solely on a strong moral and humanitarian commitment. Given the dimensions of the human tragedy, we may need to believe this. The facts that the United States has resettled more than half of the Indochinese refugees (over 883,000), continues to pledge generous annual admissions (46,500 for fiscal year 1989), and is the major source of refugee relief funding are ample testimony to American compassion and magnanimity. By extending opportunities for freedom to those oppressed, the American response to these refugees fits well in both Judeo-Christian tradition and democratic ideology. Addressing a congressional committee in August, 1977, when asking for an increase in Indochinese refugee admissions at the beginning of the exodus, then assistant secretary of state Richard C. Holbrooke eloquently declared, "The motivation is simple: the deep humanitarian concern which has for so long been a distinctive part of our national character."[3]

Despite Holbrooke's eloquence, his assessment of American motivation is too simplistic, if not self-righteous, as evidenced by the earlier description and analysis of the American experience with Hungarian refugees. Holbrooke may have been appealing to the heartstrings of Congress, but both Congress and the State Department probably had other motivations. It is reasonable to assume that the American response, and the responses of other nations, to the Indochinese refugees included and continues to include elements of vested interest.

Kenneth Thompson's warning that an exclusively idealistic approach is often incapable of finding feasible solutions to political problems is illustrated in the following incident. Appearing at a press conference in 1979, when the Indochina refugee issue was at its height, to respond to accusations that his country had forcefully turned away refugees, Home Minister Mohammed Ghazali Shafie of Malaysia said he was weary of humanitarian handwringing by Western nations. Going further, he defined what he considered to be his government's primary role: "This government is responsible first and foremost to the

3. "Southeast Asian Refugee Arrivals in the United States by Nationality, FY 75–88," *Refugee Reports*, IX (December 16, 1988), 10; "Planned Adjustments to FY 89 Funded Regional Refugee Admissions Ceilings," *Refugee Reports*, X (January 27, 1989), 16; *House Documents*, 95th Cong., 1st Sess., No. Y4.J89/1:95-42, pp. 32–58.

people of this country. . . . Please write that down." At the other extreme, policies devoid of values—policies that do not reflect a nation's principles and beliefs—become calculated strategies that can be dehumanizing. In fact, some critics of American refugee policy claim the United States is too self-serving, because its policy at times fails to incarnate American ideals, such as unconditional regard for human rights. The Indochinese refugee issue ought to be viewed with an awareness of the tension between idealism and realism. Neither extreme is entirely responsible for policies and decisions; rather, as Niebuhr suggested, policies and decisions are the acting out of the interplay between humanitarian concerns and national interests.[4]

As was the case with the Hungarian exodus, journalists have made significant contributions to the study of the Indochina refugee crisis by offering detailed descriptions and analyses of events. *The Boat People,* by Australian diplomat and columnist Bruce Grant, who utilized extensive reportage by foreign correspondents of the Australian newspaper *The Age,* sympathetically tells the dramatic and tragic story of the boat people from Vietnam, revealing the extent of their persecution and describing the ordeal of exodus, the problems of trafficking in refugees, and the world community's reaction to the crisis. Grant's work, which was published in 1979, was one of the first accounts to appear on the subject, and it raised international consciousness about the human tragedy. His book ends with the Geneva conference held in July, 1979, convened to bring the international community at last to address the refugee problem formally. Grant correctly interpreted the refugee crisis as related to the larger political context, especially to the instability of Southeast Asia. He found that in addition to Vietnam, the United States and China also share responsibility for the problem, and in his study he asserts that any solution will have to address the overall political strife. Frustrated by the agony of the refugees, Grant was prone to be critical of governments as causative and exploitative agents in the issue. While recording the significant events of the years 1975–1979, Grant's work assigns "liability and responsibility," precisely as D'Souza said has been the tendency in the Indochina debate.[5]

4. Barry Wain, "Malaysia Fears Social Upheaval from Refugees," *Asian Wall Street Journal,* June 23, 1979, p. 5; Thompson, *Ethics, Functionalism, and Power,* 26–27.

5. Bruce Grant, *The Boat People: An "Age" Investigation* (New York, 1979); D'Souza, *Refugee Dilemma,* 5.

In a similar vein, *The Refused: The Agony of the Indochina Refugees,* by *Asian Wall Street Journal*'s Barry Wain, is critical of the world's response to the plight of the refugees and implicates the United States and China, though the author strongly blames Hanoi for forcibly expelling refugees, profiting from the refugee traffic, and polarizing Southeast Asia into two hostile blocs, ASEAN and Indochina.[6] Wain perceived the need for attention to human rights, bold political leadership, and imaginative solutions that move beyond treating only symptoms of the problem. *The Refused* addresses the plight of the land refugees, too, by discussing the Vietnamese who fled to Thailand and also the Cambodian and Laotian refugees.

A third and more recent work, *The Quality of Mercy: Cambodia, Holocaust and Modern Conscience,* by British journalist William Shawcross, examines the world's response to the murderous exploits of the Pol Pot regime in Cambodia from 1975 to 1979, the famine conditions that coincided with the Vietnamese invasion and occupation of Cambodia in late 1978, and the sudden influx of refugees into the area near the Thai-Cambodian border. Shawcross' study discusses the influence of the Jewish Holocaust in the world's response to Cambodia but also the human phenomenon of short memory, as issues such as the Cambodian tragedy are eclipsed by more immediate calamities. *The Quality of Mercy* chronicles the frustrations and is critical of international humanitarian relief organizations that become inextricably caught up with the policies of nations. Direct access by relief agencies to refugees who are in need of protection and assistance is compromised in such politically charged events when nations intervene to influence relief activities and when the refugees themselves are living among and are controlled by resistance forces. Food relief at the Thai-Cambodian border fed and continues to feed the resistance forces opposing the Vietnamese-supported Heng Samrin government in Cambodia. The major group in this coalition of resistance forces is a remnant of the ousted communist Khmer Rouge, which committed atrocity after atrocity against the Cambodian people. Humanitarian aid reaching the civilian refugee population, as well as the resistance forces in their midst, contributes to the effort to undermine the Vietnamese occupation in Cambodia. Shawcross comments that throughout one of the largest relief efforts in

6. Wain, *The Refused.*

history, "nearly all the governments involved used humanitarianism as a fig leaf for either the poverty or the ruthlessness of their politics."[7] Shawcross, along with Grant and Wain, shared the frustration of Niebuhr over the vexing problem of man. Each of the three accounts is highly judgmental of governments and, in Shawcross' case, also of humanitarian organizations that allowed themselves to be exploited for political ends.

Rice, Rivalry, and Politics: Managing Cambodian Relief, by Linda Mason and Roger Brown, who analyzed their experiences as relief workers at the Thai-Cambodian border, isolates three important relationships in relief work: relief organizations' relationships to one another, to refugees, and to political institutions. It is the last relationship that is specifically relevant to this study, for the authors identify and describe the interests of various governments, including Thailand, the United States, Cambodia, and Vietnam. Mason and Brown insist that though ethical dilemmas are evident for relief organizations in highly politically charged events, it is crucial that one be aware of the larger context within which the relief efforts must necessarily operate. The book concludes that relief organizations, rather than remaining powerless, should enter the political arena and that they have more power than they realize, often underutilized.[8]

Two important studies address the national interests of the ASEAN nations, especially Thailand, Indonesia, and Malaysia, vis-à-vis the Indochinese refugees. In several instances these papers validate and supplement my own firsthand observations, made during my field study in Southeast Asia. Astri Suhrke's *Indochinese Refugees: The Impact on First Asylum Countries and Implications for American Foreign Policy* was commissioned in 1980 by the Joint Economic Committee of the U.S. Congress. In it, she states that since the ASEAN states are economically, strategically, and politically important to the United States, American refugee policy needs to consider the interests of these first asylum countries. With the consolidation of communism in the Indochina nations, ASEAN has "become a focus for American efforts to promote stability in the region." However, the American goal to pro-

---

7. William Shawcross, *The Quality of Mercy: Cambodia, Holocaust and Modern Conscience* (New York, 1984), 416.

8. Linda Mason and Roger Brown, *Rice, Rivalry, and Politics: Managing Cambodian Relief* (Notre Dame, 1983).

vide an alternative to communism for the refugees is not shared by ASEAN. ASEAN is more concerned about the political impact of refugees and will provide asylum only if the United States and other countries guarantee permanent resettlement for the refugees. Suhrke's study emphasizes that ASEAN perceives the refugee exodus to be an American problem.[9]

Suhrke makes a case here for the existence of pull, as well as push, factors that affect Indochinese refugees. Recognizing that refugees, especially the first waves, were indeed pushed out of Indochina, she argues that we need to acknowledge pull factors, too, such as the existence of internationally funded refugee camps in Southeast Asia and liberal resettlement opportunities in the West. This appreciation of pull factors differs from the traditional interpretation of refugee behavior found in "The Refugee in Flight: Kinetic Models and Forms of Displacement," by Egon F. Kunz, which strongly emphasizes push factors.[10] Suhrke goes on to describe the various national interests of ASEAN and the United States that American refugee policy should take into account.

The second important study addressing national interests is a doctoral dissertation by Abdul Hadi Derani entitled "Refugees from Indochina, 1975–1980: Their Impact on the International Relations of Southeast Asia." It records the historical experience of refugee exoduses in the region, the destabilizing effect the refugees have on ASEAN, and the polarization of ASEAN and Vietnam caused by the exodus of refugees. Derani, who was able to interview high-ranking officials in his own country of Malaysia and in other ASEAN states, points out in this work that the refugee crisis has tended to strengthen ASEAN unity and respectability, as evidenced in particular at the Geneva conference in 1979, convened specifically to address the Indochina refugee crisis. He is critical of those, especially the UNHCR, who insist on emphasizing only the humanitarian aspects of the problem when ASEAN is faced with the important and immediate political realities of the situation.[11]

9. Astri Suhrke, *Indochinese Refugees: The Impact on First Asylum Countries and Implications for American Policy*, prepared for the U.S. Congress, Joint Economic Committee (Washington, D.C., 1980), 3.

10. Egon F. Kunz, "The Refugee in Flight: Kinetic Models and Forms of Displacement," *International Migration Review*, VII (Summer, 1973), 125–46.

11. Abdul Hadi Derani, "Refugees from Indochina, 1975–1980: Their Impact on the

Charles Benoit's "Vietnam's Boat People" and Pao-min Chang's "The Sino-Vietnamese Dispute over the Ethnic Chinese" provide thorough analyses of the forces that led to the expulsion of the ethnic Chinese, or "Hoa," from Vietnam—forces that implicate China as well as Vietnam. As Vietnam focused on the task of nation building and the socialist transformation of the south, the loyalty of the unassimilated Hoa, who had traditionally occupied middle-class entrepreneurial positions in Vietnamese society, came into question, a situation exacerbated by growing tensions between China and Vietnam. Benoit's and Chang's research corresponds to the work on refugee theory by Edna Bonacich and Barry Stein, who found that minorities, especially sojourners like the Hoa, are often victimized during times of nationalistic ferment. Benoit's work goes on to point out the obvious discrepancy between the concern for human rights, including the right to flee, and the international community's effort to stem the flow of refugees by pressuring Vietnam to prevent further exoduses.[12]

The relationship of refugees to national interests is most acutely demonstrated by the protracted dilemma along the Thai-Cambodian border, where 300,000 refugees mingle with resistance forces of the Coalition Government of Democratic Kampuchea (CGDK) in a "no man's land" frequently attacked by the Vietnamese military, who have occupied Cambodia since late December, 1978. Writings by Justus M. van der Kroef, including "Kampuchea: Diplomatic Gambits and Political Realities" and "Kampuchea: Southeast Asia's Flashpoint," discuss how the Cambodian refugees affect and are affected by the national interests of ASEAN and Indochina, and also of the United States, China, and the Soviet Union. The refugees are held hostage at the border by political forces beyond their control, a human buffer waiting for a resolution of the stalemate.[13]

Finally, in late 1986, two works by veteran journalists appeared,

International Relations of Southeast Asia" (Ph.D. dissertation, University of London, 1981).

12. Charles Benoit, "Vietnam's Boat People," in David W. P. Elliott (ed.), *The Third Indochina Conflict* (Boulder, 1981), 139–62; Pao-min Chang, "The Sino-Vietnamese Dispute over the Ethnic Chinese," *China Quarterly*, XC (June, 1982), 195–230; Stein, "The Refugee Experience," 321.

13. Justus M. van der Kroef, "Kampuchea: Diplomatic Gambits and Political Realities," *Orbis*, XXVIII (Spring, 1984), 145–62, and "Kampuchea: Southeast Asia's Flashpoint," *Parameters*, XIV (Spring, 1984), 60–70.

both of them significant contributions to the general understanding of political events in Southeast Asia, including the refugee issue. *When the War Was Over: The Voices of Cambodia's Revolution and Its People,* by former Washington *Post* reporter Elizabeth Becker, is an insightful study of Cambodia, "looking in history for the roots of today's turmoil." *Brother Enemy: The War After the War,* by Nayan Chanda of the *Far Eastern Economic Review,* who is reputed to be "the best-informed observer of Indochina since the fall of Saigon," is a careful analysis of the causes and complexities of the third Indochina conflict, a depiction of regional and superpower interests.[14]

It may never be known whether USIA propaganda efforts in Vietnam in 1956 and 1957, which highlighted the Hungarian refugees' plight and warm reception by the United States, in any way influenced those fleeing Indochina twenty years later. However, the refugee experience itself was not new in Vietnam when 130,000 Vietnamese either were airlifted from Saigon, along with American military and diplomatic personnel, or left by boat in the spring of 1975. Derani cites evidence from the first through the nineteenth century of people reaching asylum from China to what is now Vietnam and from Vietnam to Thailand. During the first Indochina conflict, from 1946 to 1954, when Vietnamese nationals fought French colonial rule, as many as 80,000 fled to Thailand. Perceived by Thailand to be Vietminh agents colluding with Thai Communist party insurgents in the rural areas, the refugees posed a serious security threat. Instances of racial violence between the local Thai population and the refugees occurred, straining Thailand's relations with Hanoi. Repatriation efforts in the 1960s resulted in the return of 40,000 refugees to North Vietnam, but the program was abruptly halted by Hanoi in 1964, apparently in retaliation for Thai support of the growing American presence in Saigon.[15]

In 1954, as a result of the Geneva accords, which allowed for the migration of Vietnamese between north and south, an estimated one million to two million Vietnamese, mostly Catholics led by their clergy and with assistance from the U.S. Navy and the Voice of America, left the north in fear of persecution. Many of these refugees became loyal

14. Elizabeth Becker, *When the War Was Over: The Voices of Cambodia's Revolution and Its People* (New York, 1986); Nayan Chanda, *Brother Enemy: The War After the War* (New York, 1986).

15. Derani, "Refugees from Indochina," 18–23.

supporters of and workers for the South Vietnamese government. Derani believes that a significant number of ethnic Chinese were part of this migration and that Hanoi was pleased to be rid of those who might resist the socialist transformation efforts in the north. The Saigon regime seized on the migration as proof that the Vietnamese people opposed communism, for a much smaller number made the migration from south to north.[16]

Historian Guenter Lewy, making use of previously classified materials, reports in his book, *America in Vietnam*, that during the Vietnam War, or second Indochina conflict, untold thousands of people in the south were dislocated not only for humanitarian reasons but also for political and military ones. Lewy writes, "Between 1964 and 1969, as many as 3.5 million South Vietnamese, over 20 percent of the population, had been refugees at one time or another." Villagers were often moved in order to avoid civilian casualties in the exasperating effort by the American military to discern the enemy, who employed the guerrilla tactic of "clinging to the people." Lewy's study concludes that people were inclined and encouraged to dislocate and to seek protection from American and South Vietnamese military forces, thereby "voting with their feet" in favor of the anticommunist war effort. Pacification programs to secure politically sections of the south involved the relocation of Vietnamese from traditional homes to new hamlets. In the last days of the war, as the North Vietnamese forces swept across the south toward Saigon, the ensuing panic and confusion generated a million more refugees, which prompted the cordoning of Saigon against the influx on April 3, 1975. Former high commissioner for refugees Sadruddin Aga Khan assessed the general state of mind of the Vietnamese people in this way: "[They] became conditioned to moving from place to place as offensive and counter-offensive prolonged the rootlessness of vast numbers who spent their lives in a succession of refugee camps created for them, not knowing whether or not their homes were still standing. For many, having to acquiesce in constant involuntary relocation to taking a decision to leave the country altogether would be a relatively short step."[17]

16. *Ibid.*, 25–26; Guenter Lewy, *America in Vietnam* (Oxford, Eng., 1978), 10.

17. Lewy, *America in Vietnam*, 108–14, 140, 226–30; Frank Snepp, *Decent Interval* (New York, 1977), 301; Sadruddin Aga Khan, *Study on Human Rights and Massive Exoduses*, prepared for the United Nations, 38th Sess. (December 31, 1981), E/CN.4/1503, Annex II, p. 29.

Barry Wain reported that in Laos, by 1973, an estimated 700,000 people were internally displaced by the effects of a war that included heavy American bombing. William Shawcross observed that in Cambodia a growing number of refugees were evident, though they were ignored by American authorities in Phnom Penh when the American diplomatic corps was evacuated in April, 1975. Former American ambassador to Cambodia Emory C. Swank noted that as early as September, 1973, the capital city of Phnom Penh was "alive with refugees, its population swollen to 1.5 million."[18]

Perhaps one of the most tragic events involving refugees at the eleventh hour was "Operation Baby Lift." U.S. Ambassador to South Vietnam Graham Martin was pained by the growing refugee situation before the takeover of the south by North Vietnam, and he saw an opportunity to shore up American support for South Vietnam by arranging for the transfer of orphans to the United States. Former CIA officer Frank Snepp recounted the story: "[Martin] hoped that the spectacle of hundreds of Vietnamese babies being taken under the American wing would generate sympathy for the South Vietnamese cause around the world. The White House apparently shared this sentiment, for on 2 April, AID officials in Washington announced 'Operation Baby-lift,' an emergency program whereby over two thousand orphans were to be flown to foster homes under a new immigration 'parole.'" It was Snepp's opinion that these children were not refugees and that it was unlikely they would suffer at the hands of the Communists in the takeover. A half-hour after leaving Saigon, "Operation Baby-lift's C-5A crashed killing almost everyone aboard, one of the worst accidents in aviation history."[19]

In the final days of April, 1975, President Gerald Ford, Secretary of State Henry Kissinger, and others continued their attempts to secure additional military aid from Congress for South Vietnam but without success. In the end, the administration requested humanitarian aid and the revision of law in order to allow the president to use American forces to evacuate Americans and Vietnamese nationals from South Vietnam. In a study of the foreign policy debate between Congress and the Executive over the fall of South Vietnam, political analyst P. Ed-

18. Wain, *The Refused*, 57; William Shawcross, *Sideshow: Kissinger, Nixon, and the Destruction of Cambodia* (New York, 1979), 223, 273; Emory C. Swank, "The Land In Between: Cambodia Ten Years Later," *Indochina Issues*, XXXVI (April, 1983), 1.

19. Snepp, *Decent Interval*, 301–305.

ward Haley found that some congressmen had worried that if they allowed the use of American forces ostensibly to assist refugees, a "too broad grant of authority to use force would be misused by the President to try to save what was left of South Vietnam, starting American participation in the war once more." Those critical of the war effort saw humanitarian assistance for evacuation and for refugees as a possible political ploy.[20]

Similar to the refugees' situation in Europe prior to their exodus from Hungary in 1956 and 1957, the Indochinese refugees were also familiar with the experience of dislocation prior to the collapse of South Vietnam. Although a person must flee across national boundaries in order to be assigned legal refugee status, according to international law as defined in the UN Convention and Protocol documents, many Indochinese had known internal displacement as a result of war. Often these population movements were politically interpreted as people voting with their feet. The humanitarian aspects of refugees had already become bound up with national interests, setting the stage for the large exodus that was to follow in the next few years. After the Vietnam War, refugees would continue to follow U.S. and South Vietnamese government and military personnel beyond the borders of Indochina, much the way they had within Indochina during the war years. However, it should be noted that conditions within Vietnam, Laos, and Cambodia as the new governments tightened their hold on all of Indochina were, and still are, major reasons for the exodus.

In 1956 and 1957 the United States attempted to aid the Hungarian refugees for a variety of humanitarian and national interest reasons. In 1975, as the United States disengaged from Vietnam, Kissinger reportedly wanted to evacuate as many refugees as possible "for the sake of America's global honor and prestige," according to Snepp in his highly critical account of the bungling of the evacuation of Americans and South Vietnamese in April, 1975, as the North Vietnamese invading forces closed in on Saigon. Snepp reveals how in the confusion many of the wrong people were airlifted out of Saigon or fled by boat at the last minute, while those who truly feared persecution because of their affiliations with the American and South Vietnamese governments

20. P. Edward Haley, *Congress and the Fall of South Vietnam and Cambodia* (Rutherford, N.J., 1982), 99–107.

were left behind, along with undestroyed lists of names detailing exactly who they were. Congress and the Department of Justice finally cooperated with the Ford administration to waive immigration restrictions in order to allow 130,000 high-risk refugees to enter the United States. Indeed, the press of the emergency situation, as in 1956 and 1957, precluded careful screening of the refugees by the INS, as a report to Congress indicated.[21]

After the emergency evacuation was over and the initial wave of refugees subsided, there was no great alarm about refugees, and many were thankful that the blood bath predicted after the takeover of the south by Hanoi did not materialize. Since 1975, the Vietnamese government but also American reporters, academics, and officials have maintained that a blood bath did not occur. However, recent research supports a disturbing thesis conservatively estimating deaths that calls into question the former supposition: "At least 65,000 persons were executed for political reasons between 1975 and 1983. . . . More than two-thirds of the deaths reported occurred in 1975–1976."[22] This new interpretation of events after the war helps to explain the fear of persecution many Vietnamese must have felt, a fear that eventually would influence their decision to flee the country.

Migrations expert Aristide Zolberg cites the exodus of a defeated opposition as a common occurrence after revolutionary conflict and during fervent nation building. The migration of potentially disloyal or dissident groups may facilitate political unity and allows the new government to concentrate on other important tasks. If some have interpreted the exodus from Vietnam as an indictment of the new socialist regime, Hanoi contends that those who left and continue to leave are "soft," spoiled by years of exposure to American capitalism and materialism and South Vietnamese corruption. Hanoi explains the exodus by saying that those who leave are not ideologically committed to the rebuilding of a new social, political, and economic order.[23]

However, the majority opinion is that intolerable conditions, political and economic, forced people to leave then and still influence refu-

21. Snepp, *Decent Interval*, 331, 565–67, 411, 413; U.S. Comptroller, *A Report to the Congress: U.S. Provides Safe Haven for Indochinese Refugees*, No. ID75-71 (June 16, 1975), 20, 24–25.
22. *Wall Street Journal*, April 22, 1985, p. 29.
23. Zolberg, "International Migrations," 24.

gees' decisions to flee. After the war Vietnam faced enormous nation-building tasks. Some experts claim that more destruction occurred during the war than has been admitted by Hanoi. Natural disasters, including cold, drought, and then flooding during 1976 and 1977, curtailed food production. Postwar population growth compounded problems, adding to already overcrowded conditions and unemployment, especially in urban areas. To these factors were added the harsh measures of totalitarianism, including the detention of political prisoners in reeducation camps, dubbed "Vietnam's gulags," and the execution of thousands of "high ranking officers of the former regime . . . and antigovernment resisters."[24] By 1977, the Vietnamese government decided to go ahead with plans to implement in the south a full-fledged socialist economic system that included the collectivization of agriculture and the abolition of private business. Some refugees, spared the reeducation camps, fled Vietnam because of forced assignments to new economic zones in the rural areas. Although Hanoi justified this policy because of its need to increase the acreage under cultivation, many refugees perceived punitive aspects in a policy that moved them to barren lands without adequate assistance for survival.

Coinciding with these internal conditions and adverse measures, large numbers of refugees began appearing in 1978 on the shores of the ASEAN countries and in Hong Kong, reaching a peak in 1979. Sadruddin Aga Khan wrote that Vietnam's burdens of rehabilitation and reconciliation were indeed "monumental" after 1975: "With the disappearance of the life support system of the country, no government could have been expected to reanimate the economy and restore its social fabric without massive external aid and the active support of all sectors of the population. The new government, however, was deprived on the one hand of the reconstruction aid it had expected, and on the other introduced a socialist system to a population ill equipped to accept and adapt itself to the new stringent measures."[25]

It appears not only that refugees escaped from Vietnam but that many were pushed out in 1978 and 1979 with the knowledge and even

24. U.S. Senate, Committee on Foreign Relations, *Vietnam's Future Policies and Role in Southeast Asia*, 97th Cong., 2nd Sess., No. 90-866-0, pp. 10–22; *Wall Street Journal*, April 22, 1985, p. 29.
25. Aga Khan, *Study on Human Rights*, 30.

the assistance of the Vietnamese government. There is evidence of Vietnamese complicity with chartered freighters that took out thousands of refugees in exchange for lucrative payments in gold. For the most part, these refugees were ethnic Chinese, who were directly affected by internal conditions and government policies but also by larger political tensions in Sino-Vietnamese relations. Vietnam area specialist Charles Benoit wrote that if the Hoa had not been targeted by Vietnamese policies, refugees still would have fled for political reasons, but never would the problem have reached the unmanageable proportions it did by 1979. In essence, the massive exodus of refugees from Vietnam has been the result of the expulsion of the ethnic Chinese population.[26]

Traditionally, Vietnam has lived with the threat of Chinese domination. Some attribute Vietnam's strong sense of independence to its long-standing opposition to Chinese hegemony. At times in history Vietnam was a reluctant part of China. At best, it retained a tributary status toward its more powerful northern neighbor and was subjected to periodic invasions and occupations. Control of Chinese immigration was one way Vietnam tried to limit China's influence; not unknown in this regard were anti-Chinese feelings and even riots vis-à-vis the Hoa, when the loyalty of this group, some of whom avoided assimilation and declined offers of Vietnamese citizenship, came into question. Examples of concern about the Hoa can be found in both the Hanoi and Saigon governments between 1954 and 1975.[27]

As the Vietnam War era closed, the Sino-Vietnamese unity forged by a common communist ideology was undermined by nationalistic forces in both China and Vietnam, and the third Indochina conflict, between China and Vietnam, began. The Hoa in Vietnam were caught in the escalation of Sino-Vietnamese tensions that eventually aligned Vietnam with the Soviet Union and China with the United States.[28]

In the power vacuum left by the withdrawal of the United States from Indochina, China was interested in promoting a balance of power in its favor. Its effort to offset Soviet influence in the region, however, affected Sino-Vietnamese relations. China policy analyst Robert Sutter marks May, 1978, as the time when Vice-Premier Teng Hsiao-ping

26. Wain, *The Refused*, 86; Benoit, "Vietnam's Boat People," 140.
27. Chang, "Sino-Vietnamese Dispute," 196.
28. *Ibid.*; Benoit, "Vietnam's Boat People," 144.

became decidedly more assertive in China's foreign policy, against Soviet expansion, Vietnamese expansion, and Soviet-Vietnamese relations. Even earlier, China's new economic and foreign policies, appearing after the removal of the "Gang of Four," included overtures to the overseas Chinese, a term used to refer to any Chinese outside China, for possible contributions to China's modernization efforts. Rhetoric concerning the overseas Chinese, in particular the Hoa in Vietnam, raised their status in January, 1978, when a Chinese official stated that the overseas Chinese were "part of the Chinese nation with their destiny closely linked with that of the motherland." In February, 1978, Premier Hua Guofeng stated that China was "duty-bound to protect those who decided to keep their Chinese citizenship." The exodus of ethnic Chinese from Vietnam followed both the more assertive Chinese foreign policy and the appeal to the overseas Chinese.[29]

Meanwhile, in Vietnam in late 1976 a split occurred in the Vietnamese Communist party, which then saw the ascendancy of a pro-Soviet faction in 1977. Pao-min Chang reported that China began to curtail certain aid to Vietnam and that it sided with Pol Pot in Vietnam's border dispute with Cambodia. The Soviet Union in turn sided with Vietnam and agreed to give it generous financial support. The Hoa, especially those concentrated in Sino-Vietnamese border areas, apparently posed a serious security threat for Vietnam. Amid the growing tension, by late 1977 and early 1978, refugees were crossing the border into China. At the same time, socialist efforts were implemented to transform the south economically, directly affecting many Hoa who traditionally had comprised the urban, middle-class, private entrepreneurs. By April, 1978, increasing numbers of refugees were leaving the south by boat; in contrast to the previous waves of boat people, they were mostly ethnic Chinese. By July, 1978, 160,000 had crossed by land into China.[30]

Pao-min Chang indicated that up until mid-1978, the exodus was largely a spontaneous event, brought about by contagious panic among the ethnic Chinese concerning their economic and political future. However, at that point Hanoi seized control of the situation in a

29. Robert G. Sutter, "China's Strategy Toward Vietnam and Its Implications for the United States," in David W. P. Elliott (ed.), *The Third Indochina Conflict* (Boulder, 1981), 164–65; Chang, "Sino-Vietnamese Dispute," 204–205.
30. Chang, "Sino-Vietnamese Dispute," 201–207.

negative way: it did nothing to prevent the outflow but rather encouraged distress and fear and actually expelled the Hoa, extracting huge sums of money in the process. So lucrative was the refugee traffic that it soon replaced the coal industry as Vietnam's primary source of foreign exchange. By mid-1978, too, Vietnam had dubbed China its main enemy, planned an invasion of Cambodia, expanded its military, revamped the economy along military lines, sought even closer ties with the Soviet Union, and reconsidered its relations with ASEAN and the United States. The threat of impending conflict, combined with internal conditions, generated thousands of refugees.[31]

China and Vietnam accused each other of causing the exodus. China helped bring the international community's attention to Hanoi's abuses of human rights, whereas Vietnam blamed China for encouraging the ethnic Chinese to leave. China charged Vietnam with deliberately expelling the refugees in order to destabilize the ASEAN countries by imposing severe economic and social burdens on these countries of first asylum. By mid-July, 1978, China closed its border with Vietnam to curtail the overland refugee flow into China. Vietnam alleged that China was exploiting the Hoa as a "fifth column" inside Vietnam and warned ASEAN to beware of the political impact this fifth column would have in their own ethnically sensitive countries.[32]

In late December, 1978, Vietnam invaded Cambodia, precipitating the demise of the Pol Pot regime, now allied with China. In February, 1979, the Chinese engaged the Vietnamese in a border war, brought on by the destabilizing effect of the massive flow of refugees into China in addition to other factors, including Soviet influence in the region, Vietnamese expansion into Cambodia, and perhaps, directly or indirectly, ostensible American support for China's effort vis-à-vis Vietnam. The brief border war, for the Chinese, stopped the flow of refugees into China, where they presented potential economic and social burdens. However, the conflict also probably influenced the decisions of thousands of refugees who left by boat and who, if they survived the high seas, landed on the shores of ASEAN nations and in Hong Kong, their numbers reaching 300,000 by mid-1979. For Vietnam, Robert Sutter wrote, the Sino-Vietnamese border war steeled it in its resolve to

31. *Ibid.*, 211–12, 228; Senate Foreign Relations Committee, *Vietnam's Future Policies*, 65–66.
32. Chang, "Sino-Vietnamese Dispute," 217–27.

oppose China.[33] The ensuing chaos brought on by the Vietnamese invasion and occupation of Cambodia and by the ouster of Pol Pot's Khmer Rouge regime generated a refugee outflow in another direction. Fleeing Cambodian refugees, Khmer Rouge among them, began to arrive at the Thai-Cambodian border in mid-1979, bent on seeking asylum in Thailand.

An ironic twist found more than a quarter of a million refugees resettled on state farms in China, probably similar to the ones they might have been assigned to had they remained in Vietnam. A few have fled from China, making their way to Hong Kong, where they were denied asylum and chances of resettlement in the West and returned to China, along with other illegal Chinese immigrants, through the cooperation of the Hong Kong and Chinese governments.

In a recent report, the U.S. Committee for Refugees estimated that more than 1,000,000 refugees had left Vietnam since 1975. A decline in the flow until recently has been attributed to tighter security measures by the Vietnamese authorities, a shortage of boats, limited resettlement opportunities abroad, piracy, and the prospects of long internment in austere camps in the ASEAN countries and in Hong Kong. However, during 1987 the largest number of asylum seekers since 1982 left the country; despite deterrents, over 28,000 Vietnamese arrived in first asylum countries. In fiscal year 1988, the exodus climbed to over 50,000 and was accompanied by alarming incidences of missing persons and of violence, including pushbacks, death, rape, and abduction.[34]

Until 1987, most refugees made the perilous journey by sea. A smaller number, about 10,000 since 1984, have made their way overland from Vietnam, through Cambodia, to the Thai border. This land route involved grave risks, including "crossing military lines, checkpoints and minefields," followed by "rough treatment in camps among antagonistic Cambodian refugees." By 1987, many asylum seekers were trekking across Cambodia to the western port city of Kompong Som, where charter boats would clandestinely shuttle refugees the short distance to eastern Thailand's Trat Province. The going price for

33. Ibid., 229–30; Sutter, "China's Strategy Toward Vietnam," 164.

34. Virginia Hamilton (ed.), World Refugee Survey: 1987, 51; "Amerasians in Vietnam: New Climate of Hope, but Problems Remain," Refugee Reports, IX (August 12, 1988), 8; Wall Street Journal, June 29, 1988, p. 18; "Indochinese Refugee Activity," Refugee Reports, IX (December 16, 1988), 7.

the trip from Ho Chi Minh City to Thailand was reported to be $4,000 in gold. Continued repression and worsening poverty in Vietnam, coupled with a lessening of the government's control of corruption and with rumors of an impending phasing out of resettlement opportunities, were cited as reasons for the latest upsurge in asylum seekers.[35]

Another reason for the recent increase in the exodus could be the refugees' disillusionment with the ODP, always bureaucratically sluggish and erratic. Until 1986, the growth of the ODP reflected an acceptance of the program as a safer, legal, and more assured means of resettlement abroad for those wanting to leave Vietnam. For example, in 1985 more refugees left Vietnam via the ODP than by escaping. The program seeks to regularize migration and requires cooperation between Hanoi and the resettlement countries, primarily the United States. Since the program began in 1979 as a result of international pressure on Hanoi, over 150,000 people have left Vietnam via the ODP, including more than 60,000 to the United States. Many of the departing have been ethnic Chinese, but there have also been Amerasians and their relatives.[36]

The ODP has been fraught with problems related to political sensitivities in Washington, D.C., and Hanoi. In early 1986, for example, Vietnam suspended ODP processing indefinitely, with a backlog of well over 670,000 cases. Ostensibly, Vietnam was expressing dissatisfaction with the "slow processing of receiving nations." The United States has expressed concern that Hanoi uses the ODP to facilitate the outflow of ethnic Chinese, whom Hanoi considers undesirable, while ignoring the names the United States submits for high-priority processing. The American refugee policy goal has been to utilize the ODP to resettle Amerasians and their close relatives, estimated to be 30,000 people, and political prisoners from the reeducation camps.[37]

35. Virginia Hamilton (ed.), *World Refugee Survey: 1985 in Review,* U.S. Committee for Refugees (Washington, D.C., 1986), 19–20, and *World Refugee Survey: 1986 in Review,* U.S. Committee for Refugees (Washington, D.C., 1987), 56; *Christian Science Monitor,* September 25, 1987, p. 12; New York *Times,* January 30, 1988, p. 4; *Wall Street Journal,* June 29, 1988, p. 18.

36. Wain, "Orderly Departure?," 6; "Amerasians in Vietnam," 7; "U.S. Shifts 7,000 Refugee Numbers from Asia to the Soviet Union," *Refugee Reports,* X (January 27, 1989), 10.

37. Virginia Hamilton (ed.), *World Refugee Survey: 1985,* 55, and *World Refugee Survey: 1987,* 51; "Amerasians in Vietnam," 1–5.

The ODP resumed the processing of new applicants as a result of an unanticipated announcement by Hanoi in July, 1987. Officially, Hanoi reported that it was satisfied that the United States had "completed the processing of its stalled Vietnamese ODP caseload." However, speculation is that the gesture was yet another overture in the thaw in U.S.-Vietnam relations.[38]

The topic of political prisoners in Vietnam has long been a contentious issue. Since 1975, as many as half a million people may have been incarcerated for a time in reeducation camps. In 1984, Vietnam responded to American complaints of human rights violations by offering to release prisoners on condition that the United States accept all the prisoners, without selective screening, for resettlement. After attempts at negotiating the release of the prisoners, Secretary of State Shultz reported, "Hanoi has indicated that it is backing off from its earlier announced willingness and commitment to allow these people to be resettled in the United States." Possibly related to its position was Hanoi's expressed concern about anticommunist activities among refugees resettled abroad. These Vietnamese resistance groups in the United States denied that they receive American military or financial assistance, and they are not thought to be very powerful. They do admit, however, that such aid has been offered by China.[39]

In 1987, Vietnam announced the beginning of periodic releases of political prisoners. By July, 1988, it indicated that 11,000 former political prisoners and 40,000 of their relatives would be allowed to leave for the United States. Hanoi's action was seen as yet another example of the thaw in U.S.-Vietnam relations that has focused primarily on humanitarian issues. This development, in large part, has been the result of talks between the special presidential envoy, retired general John Vessey, and Vietnam's foreign minister, Nguyen Co Thach. In talks during June, 1988, "the United States reassured Vietnam that it had no intention of allowing the resettled Vietnamese to engage in any activities hostile to Hanoi." However, 1988 saw few political prisoners allowed to leave, and the agreement appeared stalled. In another thaw-related development, in January, 1988, Hanoi agreed to cooperate in the migration of all Amerasian children and their families over

38. "Amerasians in Vietnam," 1–5.
39. U.S. Department of State, *Proposed Refugee Admissions for 1986*, 3; New York *Times*, January 7, 1985, p. 11.

the next two years. The announcement followed a visit to Hanoi by Congressmen Robert Mrazek and Thomas Ridge and coincided with the passage in December of 1987 of the Amerasian Homecoming Act, which created a separate immigration category and funding for the Amerasians.[40]

Increasingly since 1980, ASEAN officials but also Western observers have cited growing numbers of economic migrants among the Vietnamese refugees who seek opportunities abroad and are lured by the refugee asylum camps in Southeast Asia and resettlement possibilities in the West. Others, however, have expressed the opinion that those who escape now are more likely to be bona fide refugees, desperate enough to face serious dangers and fearful of working directly with Vietnamese government authorities via the ODP. As one reporter chided, "Observers who still assume that most boat people are essentially economic migrants would do well to remember that a large segment of the Vietnamese population has either experienced persecution personally or has detailed knowledge of others who have, up to and including the ultimate form of political repression, execution."[41]

Vietnam, with one of the lowest Gross National Products (GNPs) in the world, still "wages a grim struggle for subsistence." Diplomatically isolated in terms of foreign aid, except from the Soviet Union, the Vietnamese are still coping with the effects of their leadership's economic mismanagement, which brought "chaos and near catastrophe" to the country during the period of the "disastrous 1976–1980 five year plan." In 1988, despite reform efforts, the country continued to experience runaway inflation as well as a second year of crop failure due to typhoons and insects. The crisis triggered a call for international food aid, to which the UN Food Program and the Soviet Union responded, though most western nations did not, "because of their opposition to Hanoi's nine year old occupation of neighboring Cambodia." The situation holds little hope for change because population growth in Vietnam today continues to outpace food production, leaving 25 percent of the children malnourished. Vietnam ranks as the world's "12th most populous country," with over 62,000,000 people, 45 percent of whom

40. Washington *Post*, July 17, 1988, p. 19; "U.S. Shifts 7,000 Refugee Numbers," 7; "Amerasians in Vietnam," 1–7; Washington *Post*, January 21, 1988, p. 1.
41. *Wall Street Journal*, April 22, 1985, p. 29.

are under the age of sixteen. An alarmingly high birthrate puts the projected population at 168,000,000 by the year 2100.[42]

Observers such as Nayan Chanda report that the large contingent of refugees now resettled abroad is proving to be lucrative for the Vietnamese economy, because many refugees send money and packages to relatives in Vietnam. Items are reportedly sold on the black market at a time when Vietnam is still suffering from severe economic woes brought about by international isolation in terms of foreign trade and aid and by serious internal corruption and mismanagement. Alleged extortion involving Vietnamese government agents who compelled citizens to request money from relatives now living in the United States was reported in 1984.[43]

These chronic problems only fuel the refugees' desire to leave. Although the ODP shows signs of improving, it still has many problems. Even if it should operate at an optimum level, this program clearly cannot accommodate all those who want to leave Vietnam. For example, the United States set the ceiling for ODP admissions at 19,500 for the fiscal year 1989. Barry Wain reports that for an estimated 1,000,000 determined Vietnamese, "escape remains the only hope."[44] The exodus from Vietnam is ongoing, related to root causes still unresolved.

Situated to the west of Vietnam, the Lao People's Democratic Republic maintains an intense solidarity with Vietnam and consequently with the Soviet Union, thus influencing its relationships with ASEAN, China, and the United States. The presence of as many as 20,000 Vietnamese troops in Laos is evidence of this tiny country's status as a satellite of Hanoi. Like Vietnam, Laos has also been a source of refugees. Approximately 3,400 Lao fled in 1975 with the American withdrawal from Indochina. Since the Pathet Lao Communists officially took control on December 2, 1975, about 360,000 refugees, representing one-tenth of the total population, have fled to Thailand. The out-

42. Paul Quinn-Judge, "Hanoi's Bitter Victory," *Far Eastern Economic Review,* May 2, 1986, pp. 30–34; *Washington Post,* May 13, 1988, p. 27, June 10, 1988, p. 30; Stewart E. Fraser, "Vietnam Struggles with Exploding Population," *Indochina Issues,* LVII (May, 1985), 1; "Population and Family Planning," *Indochina Chronology,* V (April-June, 1986), 8–9.

43. Remarks by Nayan Chanda, Washington Correspondent, *Far Eastern Economic Review,* at the Asia Society, January 31, 1984; *Washington Post,* September 22, 1984, p. 1.

44. Wain, "Orderly Departure?," 6.

flow has been associated with internal conditions similar to factors influencing the refugees who leave Vietnam: the devastation of war, especially from heavy bombing by the United States, the poor state of the economy, food shortages, repression, reeducation camps, and government policies of socialist economic transformation, including agricultural collectivization. The exodus was at its height in 1979, when approximately 6,000 refugees, including ethnic Chinese, left Laos per month. Lao ethnic affiliation with the Thai people and a long tradition of crossing the Mekong River border into Thailand with apparent ease, plus the lure of economic opportunities abroad, have also apparently influenced the flow.[45]

Anticommunist resistance groups in Laos, some trained and funded by the Americans as special guerrilla units, especially the Hmong, have been part of the refugee exodus. Traditionally a fiercely independent mountain tribe resisting any governmental control, the Hmong, which translates "free men," were perceived to be most vulnerable to persecution by the new communist regime in Laos. Clearly associated with the CIA during the Vietnam War, the Hmong thought themselves earmarked for extinction. They presented economic and social, as well as security, problems for the new communist government, as they resisted efforts to transfer from slash-and-burn agriculture and opium growing in the hills to wet rice farming on agricultural cooperatives in the lowlands. Barry Wain reported that the communists feared the Hmong, along with other resistance groups, would remain a formidable force if allowed to flee to Thailand, where they would be rearmed. Led in exile by Vang Pao, who communicates by tape from California, over 58,000 Hmong are in camps in Thailand, including nearly 35,000 at Ban Vinai, a refugee camp in northern Thailand, twelve miles from the Thai-Laotian border. Vang Pao estimated that as many as 40,000 to 50,000 Hmong have died in fighting or in flight since 1975.[46]

The Hmong have also figured in allegations of biological and chem-

45. "Laos Chronology," *Indochina Chronology,* VIII (January-March, 1989), 12; Murray Hiebert, "Indochina Back Door," *Far Eastern Economic Review,* January 15, 1987, p. 26; New York *Times,* November 24, 1987, pp. 1, 12; Virginia Hamilton (ed.), *World Refugee Survey: 1986,* 52; Wain *The Refused,* 76.

46. Library of Congress, *Indochinese Refugees: Issues for U.S. Policy,* No. IB79079 (July 10, 1979, January 5, 1982), 8; Wain, *The Refused,* 58, 81–82; "Indochinese Refugee Activity," *Refugee Reports,* IX (December 16, 1988), 6.

ical warfare or "yellow rain." Although Laos, Vietnam, Cambodia, and the Soviet Union have been accused of waging war with mycotoxins against the Hmong and the Cambodians, to date such reports remain inconclusive, and the issue is unresolved. In 1981 and 1982, then secretary of state Alexander Haig accused Hanoi of such exterminating efforts. In Thailand, U.S. refugee official William Stubbs thought the evidence was still insufficient to prove the existence of yellow rain. However, a reputable refugee worker claimed to have seen an illness among Hmong refugees in northeast Thailand that doctors could not diagnose. She believed these refugees were suffering from some form of contamination by mycotoxin. In March, 1984, a UNHCR officer in Thailand thought the entire yellow rain issue had been exaggerated and exploited by the United States to discredit the Indochina and Soviet governments.[47] Little discussion of the issue has appeared in recent years.

As of late 1988, nearly 80,000 refugees from Laos were living in Thai refugee camps. Perhaps as many as 50,000 more were living secretly outside the camps. It was the opinion of Thai authorities that many of those arriving from Laos were economic migrants, since most of the truly persecuted had already left. Amnesty International estimated in 1987 that 5,000 Laotians might still be held in reeducation camps or living in restricted internal exile. As of late 1987, an ODP to regularize the exodus from Laos was only in the planning stages. Those now attempting to enter Thailand clandestinely risk violent pushbacks, a reflection of continued tensions along the Thai-Laotian border. A screening program, begun by Thailand in June, 1985, with UNHCR assistance, is intended to separate bona fide refugees from economic migrants.[48]

Many believe the exodus from Laos has had a serious, negative effect on the country's recovery and overall economic development.

47. Library of Congress, *Indochinese Refugees*, 8; John W. Garver, "The Reagan Administration's Southeast Asian Policy," in James C. Hsiung (ed.), *U.S.-Asian Relations: The National Security Paradox* (New York, 1983), 115; interviews with William Stubbs, Director, Refugee Section, U.S. Embassy, Bangkok, March 13, 1984, and Rob Burrows, Public Information Officer, UNHCR, Bangkok, March 14, 1984; anonymous interviews, Bangkok, March 13–15. For both sides of the debate, see Sterling Seagrave, *Yellow Rain: A Journey Through the Terror of Chemical Warfare* (New York, 1981), and Grant Evans, *The Yellow Rainmakers: Are Chemical Weapons Being Used in Southeast Asia?* (London, 1983).

48. "Indochinese Refugee Activity," 6; Virginia Hamilton (ed.), *World Refugee Survey: 1985*, 53, and *World Refugee Survey: 1987*, 47, 50.

Those who fled constituted the majority of the educated middle class. According to journalist and historian Martin Stuart-Fox, "The Lao economy would not be in such a poor state, nor Laos so dependent on foreign aid and expertise, if so many educated Lao had not fled the country since 1975." The government of Laos cited Thai asylum and American resettlement policies as deliberate pull factors, "designed to weaken the social fabric and undermine the economy of Laos" by enticing its citizens to leave. However, Stuart-Fox and others also blamed the exodus on Lao policies, including socialist transformation and forced collectivization, and on citizens' fears of denunciation and arrest. Packages and money from refugees abroad also benefit the national economy in Laos, one of the poorest countries in the world, a distinction it shares with Vietnam and Cambodia.[49]

Although the peak of the exodus occurred in 1975, in fiscal year 1988 over 19,000 refugees from Laos arrived in Thailand, up from approximately 9,000 in 1987. The 1988 figures include 3,625 lowland Lao and 15,626 highlanders. According to the U.S. Committee for Refugees, the future of asylum seekers from Laos remains uncertain as the Thai screening process denies more and more people refugee status, as camps remain crowded and unsanitary, as forced repatriations occur from time to time, and as resettlement offers from the United States are expected to drop considerably.[50] Asylum seekers from Laos have been called the "least noticed" of the Indochinese refugees. As with those who flee Vietnam, their case continues, unresolved.

If turmoil in Indochina precipitated a series of sad human events, the story of Cambodia is the most tragic. An estimated 1,000,000 to 2,000,000 people died in the decade after the fall of the Lon Nol government in April, 1975. The fanatical policies of Pol Pot's Khmer Rouge regime, which resulted in "disease, forced migration, slave labor, and assassination," were followed by the invasion and occupation of Cambodia by Vietnam in December, 1978, and famine conditions that finally brought Cambodia to the world's attention.[51]

49. Martin Stuart-Fox, "Politics and Patronage in Laos," *Indochina Issues*, LXX (October, 1986), 4–6; *Asia 1984 Yearbook, Far Eastern Economic Review* (Hong Kong, 1984), 207; Carlyle A. Thayer, "Laos in 1983," *Asian Survey*, XXIV (January, 1984), 51.
50. "Indochinese Refugee Activity Since April 1975," *Refugee Reports*, IX (December 16, 1988), 7, and VIII (December 18, 1987), 8; Cerquone, *Refugees from Laos*, 1–22.
51. Swank, "Land In Between," 2.

The Vietnamese invasion and occupation of Cambodia presents a complex dilemma, because by the same action Vietnam liberated Cambodia from the odious Pol Pot and also stands condemned of aggression by China, ASEAN, and the United States. Vietnam's actions "induced China to support the sporadic insurgency that remnants of Pol Pot's forces wage from jungle enclaves near the Thai border," said former U.S. ambassador to Cambodia Emory Swank.[52]

Since April, 1975, an estimated half-million Cambodians have fled the violence in their homeland. Near the end of the Lon Nol government in 1975, William Shawcross observed the growing refugee problem in and around the capital city of Phnom Penh, dislocations brought about by the extension of the Vietnam War into Cambodia, civil war, and the impending takeover by the Khmer Rouge. During the reign of Pol Pot, from April, 1975, to January, 1979, 150,000 refugees found their way to Vietnam and 33,000 fled to Thailand to escape brutal persecution, disease, and food shortages. Soon after the Vietnamese invasion, in the ensuing chaos from January to September, 1979, more than 100,000 sought asylum in Thailand. According to a congressional report, Thailand did not recognize the refugee status of these Cambodians and discouraged their entry into Thailand, turning many away. ASEAN members, and Thailand in particular, "feared that a depopulated Kampuchea would sooner or later be colonized by Vietnam." More to the point, a populated Cambodia would be a buffer zone in the interest of Thailand's security.[53]

In June, 1979, 42,000 Cambodian refugees were forcibly repatriated with many casualties, finally prompting international dismay. At this time, other refugees denied entrance to Thailand began to gather in makeshift camps along the border. Reaching Thailand in October, 1979, was another wave of refugees, along with retreating Khmer Rouge, the result of spreading famine conditions and a Vietnamese offensive in west and southwest Cambodia against the remaining Khmer Rouge. In cooperation with the UNHCR and voluntary organizations, Thailand provided temporary holding centers inside its borders for nearly 200,000 Cambodian refugees and held the rest at the border. Eventually, these UNHCR holding centers in Thailand were

52. *Ibid.*; Library of Congress, *Indochinese Refugees*, 6.
53. Virginia Hamilton (ed.), *World Refugee Survey: 1986*, 51; Shawcross, *Sideshow*, 223, 273; Library of Congress, *Indochinese Refugees*, 6.

consolidated and reduced to one at Khao-I-Dang, as nearly 200,000 Cambodians were resettled abroad and Thailand relegated those refugees arriving after 1980 to the unprotected border camps. Frustrated by this long-term refugee problem and the failure of the United States and other nations to resettle all the holding center residents, Thailand announced the closing of Khao-I-Dang, a "symbol of hope," in late December, 1986. Refugees there were expected to be moved to the border camps. At the end of 1988, over 17,000 Khmers still remained at Khao-I-Dang, their future uncertain.[54]

There are still some 300,000 Cambodians who have been denied formal asylum in Thailand and who live in camps just inside Thailand, near a two-hundred-mile stretch of the ill-defined Thai-Cambodian border. They were evacuated here from encampments strung along the border when the Vietnamese launched a major offensive beginning in late 1984 against the refugee camps, which doubled as border bases for Cambodian resistance fighters.

A coalition of resistance forces, the CGDK, emerged from the border camps to challenge the Vietnamese occupation of Cambodia. The CGDK is recognized as the legitimate representative of Cambodia at the UN, to the satisfaction of ASEAN, China, and the United States, but to the consternation of Vietnam and the Heng Samrin government it supports in Cambodia.

The strongest of the coalition's three factions is Democratic Kampuchea (DK) with an estimated force of 35,000 well-equipped and trained soldiers. The DK is the former Khmer Rouge organization, led still by Pol Pot, and is supplied and supported by China, with the cooperation of Thailand. The other two factions are the anticommunist Khmer People's National Liberation Front (KPNLF), led by former premier of Cambodia Son Sann, with approximately 10,000 soldiers, and the Moulinaka (Mouvement de Libération Nationale du Kampuchea), led by former Cambodian ruler Prince Norodom Sihanouk, with about 12,000 to 15,000 followers. A major issue in the fate of the Cambodian refugees is their intricate relationship to the interests of various na-

54. Library of Congress, *Indochinese Refugees*, 6; Virginia Hamilton (ed.), *Cambodians in Thailand: People on the Edge*, U.S. Committee for Refugees (Washington, D.C., December, 1985), 10–15; New York *Times*, December 30, 1986, p. 1; "Cambodia: Peace at Last or the Return of Pol Pot?," *Refugee Reports*, IX (July 15, 1988), 1–8; "1988 Statistical Issue," *Refugee Reports*, IX (December 16, 1988), 3.

tions. The border refugee camps have been sources of recruits and of military staging bases for the CGDK's anti-Vietnamese effort. For example, 32,000 Cambodians who live at Site 8, a Khmer Rouge–run camp, "are within walking distance—sometimes forced marches—of their war." However, it has also been suggested that the CGDK's responsibility for the defense of the refugees in their midst may pose a liability, limiting its military effectiveness.[55]

The yearly dry-season attacks on the border camps by the Vietnamese in an effort to rout the resistance forces were evidence of Vietnam's concern about this floating refugee population. Most observers agree that realistically the CGDK could never defeat the Vietnamese forces. Rather, the resistance movement has served to undermine the legitimacy of the Vietnamese occupation of Cambodia and of the Heng Samrin government. The intense and sustained Vietnamese attacks on the resistance forces within the refugee border camps from fall, 1984, to spring, 1985, confirmed speculation that the Vietnamese wanted to mop up the border area once and for all.[56]

The Vietnamese offensive did destroy the border bases, but it also brought other changes. The refugees are temporarily safer at emergency evacuation sites inside Thailand. However, the human buffer of refugees along the Thai-Cambodian border is gone. According to M. K. Sukhumbhand Paribatra of Chulalongkorn University in Bangkok, "Now Thai and Vietnamese troops face each other 'eyeball to eyeball' along the length of the border." Occasional Vietnamese forays aimed at destroying the resistance forces now take place clearly inside Thailand, not at the ambiguously defined border. Additionally, the resistance forces inside Thailand may benefit from better protection. From Thai staging bases, they are now capable of guerrilla forays well into Cambodia. For example, such activity by the Khmer Rouge was reported in provinces close to Phnom Penh in early 1986 during the dry season, when the "Vietnamese army usually has the upper hand."

55. Library of Congress, *Cambodian Crisis: Problems of a Settlement and Policy Dilemmas for the United States*, No. IB89020 (January 9, 1989), 11; Virginia Hamilton (ed.), *Cambodians in Thailand*, 13–17; van der Kroef, "Kampuchea: Diplomatic Gambits," 146–47; New York *Times*, January 17, 1988, p. 14.

56. See press coverage, November, 1984–March, 1985: for example, New York *Times*, January 10, 1985, p. 4; Washington *Post*, February 15, 1985, p. 30; and Garver, "Reagan Administration's Southeast Asian Policy," 113.

Although not a serious threat, the rebel attacks tend to raise anxiety, curb development, and lower morale in Cambodia. Some observers noted that since 1979, the Khmer Rouge resistance forces at the border have managed to establish "extensive arms caches" well inside Cambodia. Congressman Chet Atkins warned that the Khmer Rouge are "poised and ready for a second takeover of Cambodia." Such a prospect further clouded the cautious optimism during 1988 regarding the announced military withdrawal by Vietnam from Cambodia and the efforts to resolve the Cambodian issue. By late 1988, the Khmer Rouge allegedly were moving thousands of refugees to strategic sites closer to the border and even to points inside Cambodia in preparation for a return to power after the Vietnamese withdrawal from Cambodia, which is scheduled to be completed by late 1989.[57]

In addition to the ethical dilemma posed by recognition of the CGDK, whose strongest component is the communist Khmer Rouge faction, aided by China, pressures on the United States by ASEAN and others to give direct aid to the Son Sann and Sihanouk noncommunist groups forced a foreign policy debate concerning American involvement in Southeast Asia for the second Reagan administration. A significant development of this debate was the congressional authorization of $1.5 million to $5 million beginning in fiscal year 1986 for not only economic but also direct military assistance to the CGDK's noncommunist forces. The inherent conflict in this action had been expressed by Jerry M. Tinker, an aide to Senator Edward Kennedy: "Concerning the Khmer problem, we seem to be acquiescing to the policy of our ASEAN allies, and the Thais and Chinese, in using Khmer displaced persons as a human buffer in support of their anti–Phnom Penh guerrilla campaign. This means one arm of the United States Government is working in complicity with those who help fuel the fighting inside Kampuchea and which produces the refugees, while the other arm pleads on their behalf and urges some be resettled in the United States." Although the Reagan administration decided to provide only nonlethal aid to the noncommunist forces, the issue of direct military assistance heightened early in the new Bush administration. The ad-

---

57. Paribatra, "Can ASEAN Break the Stalemate?," 85–106; Murray Hiebert, "Cambodia: Guerrilla Attacks Curb Development," *Indochina Issues*, LXIX (September, 1986), 1–2; "Cambodia: Peace at Last?," 1–8; Murray Hiebert, "The Khmer Rouge Regroups," *Far Eastern Economic Review*, December 1, 1988, pp. 34–35.

ministration's covert arms plan is an attempt to enhance the bargaining position of the noncommunist factions, particularly the position of Prince Sihanouk, in impending negotiations with Vietnam and the Heng Samrin regime it backs in Phnom Penh, regarding the future of Cambodia. In addition, the strengthening of Sihanouk is clearly an eleventh-hour effort to limit the role of the Khmer Rouge in Cambodia's future. However, as of June, 1989, the issue was still being hotly debated, especially in Congress.[58]

Despite intractable and volatile conditions, international relief to refugees at the border area, especially during 1979 and 1980 but continuing to the present day at evacuation sites, is certainly commendable though problematic. Denied formal refugee status and the legal UNHCR protection and the services that such designation confers, the displaced Cambodians receive humanitarian assistance from a special office, the United Nations Border Relief Operation (UNBRO) and those very few agencies under its auspices. This international aid effort has perhaps unavoidably included assistance to rebel forces living in the midst of civilian refugees. When humanitarian aid falls into the hands of the Khmer Rouge faction of the CGDK, human rights concerns become especially embroiled with political agendas. Refugee assistance was effectively cut off completely for the refugees, as many as 17,000, who were forced by the Khmer Rouge to move to strategic sites in late 1988.[59]

Possibly compounding the plight of the displaced Cambodians was the financial crisis in 1987 at the United Nations, which caused what was feared to be a serious downgrading of the UN's relief effort. The Economic and Social Commission for Asia and the Pacific (ESCAP) assumed responsibility for humanitarian assistance in 1987 as the special office for Cambodian relief was phased out. Most disturbing was the coinciding of this action with the announced closing of Khao-I-Dang and reported abuses at the border encampments.[60]

58. Library of Congress, *Vietnam-U.S. Relations: Issues for U.S. Policy*, No. 86-35F (February 10, 1986), 11–12; U.S. Senate, Committee on the Judiciary, *U.S. Refugee Program in Southeast Asia: 1985*, 99th Cong., 1st Sess., No. 47-710-0, p. 40; Washington *Post*, June 13, 1989, p. 24.

59. Washington *Post*, January 20, 1989, p. 27. For an in-depth discussion of assistance problems, see Shawcross, *Quality of Mercy*, and Mason and Brown, *Rice, Rivalry, and Politics*.

60. *Christian Science Monitor*, January 9, 1987, pp. 11–12; "Cambodia: Peace at Last?," 6.

Clearly, the problems of the Cambodian refugees, aptly described as "people on the edge," are not over. The resettlement of nearly 200,000 Cambodians has been a partial solution at best, but resettlement processing for Cambodians is now virtually over. Although "the majority of those massed along the border want to go home," the present situation inside Cambodia precludes such a move. Even as the Cambodian stalemate begins to show signs of change, all sides must take into account the displaced Cambodians, whose fate remains inextricably bound up with any future developments. As with the exoduses from Vietnam and Laos, the issue of Cambodian refugees remains unsolved.

Since the communist takeover in Vietnam in 1975, relations between the United States and Vietnam "have remained essentially frozen." Although signs of a thaw were evident beginning in 1987, relations were, and still are, characterized by strong mutual distrust, which has had implications for the Indochina refugee issue. For example, during 1975 and 1976 the relationship consisted only of American demands to know what Hanoi intended to do in the south and Vietnam's continued and unsuccessful requests for postwar aid from the United States.[61] Vietnam has accused the United States of promoting the international isolation of Vietnam. American vindictiveness, say some critics, has seriously curtailed the foreign aid Vietnam needs to rehabilitate itself and has driven the Vietnamese further to their only source of assistance, the Soviet Union. During the Ford administration the United States blocked Vietnam's admission to the UN, and it has worked to prevent UN recognition of Cambodia's Heng Samrin government, which is supported by Vietnam.

The issue of U.S. servicemen missing in action (MIAs) has been a constant source of ill will between the two countries, with many Americans appalled by Hanoi's ghoulish use of the remains of Vietnam War soldiers as political bargaining chips from time to time. For example, in February, 1985, after a U.S. team searched and found the remains of some missing American servicemen in Laos, hopes for future search missions were dampened by Hanoi's reminder that the normalization of U.S.-Vietnam diplomatic relations is a prerequisite to Vietnam's cooperation in such projects. To date, approximately 2,400 Americans

61. Library of Congress, *Vietnam-U.S. Relations*, 6.

remain unaccounted for in Indochina. In April, 1986, as the remains of 21 American soldiers were formally turned over to U.S. authorities at the Hanoi airport, an official of Vietnam's foreign ministry warned that Hanoi's efforts to resolve the MIA issue are impeded by "statements that vilify or discredit Vietnam in Washington."[62]

The American retreat from Southeast Asia precipitated a power vacuum in the region. After the withdrawal of the United States from Indochina, the resettlement of 130,000 Vietnamese refugees in the United States in 1975 and 1976, the subsequent unification of north and south as the Socialist Republic of Vietnam (SRV), and the establishment of communist regimes in Cambodia and Laos, it was American policy to avoid substantial involvement in Southeast Asia. This disengagement accompanied an effort to repair the political, social, and psychological fragmentation the war experience had brought about at home. In 1976, the United States withdrew its military forces from Thailand, considered a withdrawal from its bases in the Philippines, and reduced aid to the ASEAN nations, in particular Thailand. A conflict of interests soon emerged between the two communist superpowers as the Soviet Union appeared interested in lessening the impending influence of China in Southeast Asia and China warned of "the Soviet tiger entering Southeast Asia through the back gate as the American wolf was driven from the front door."[63]

At first, refugees were leaving Vietnam but in small numbers, so not much notice was paid them. By the end of 1976, excluding the 130,000 refugees who were evacuated and fled in 1975, the number of refugees reached 5,247. By 1977, however, ominous signs were evident. Economic mismanagement, severe drought, cold, and then typhoons caused rice shortages in Vietnam; border disagreements between Vietnam and Cambodia increased; and tensions between China and Vietnam over the subject of the ethnic Chinese living in Vietnam and over other questions became apparent. That year, there were over 15,000 refugees from Vietnam.[64]

In 1977, President Jimmy Carter called for "healing the Vietnam War scars." Some trade restrictions were lifted, ships and planes bound

62. Washington *Post*, February 15, 1985, p. 27; "Vietnam Chronology," *Indochina Chronology*, V (April-June, 1986), 3.
63. Senate Foreign Relations Committee, *Vietnam's Future Policies*, 1, 37.
64. Wain, *The Refused*, 42; Chang, "Sino-Vietnamese Dispute," 101–107.

for Vietnam were allowed to refuel in the United States, travel restrictions expired, mailings resumed, and Vietnam was admitted to the
UN on July 20, 1977, without an American veto. Progress reached an
impasse, however, when Vietnam continued to demand aid as a precondition for normalizing relations.[65]

In 1978, as the threat from China grew, Vietnam dropped that
precondition for normalizing relations· with the United States. This
new policy was perceived as an attempt to reduce the significance of
impending Sino-U.S. ties, to limit China's role in Vietnam's conflict
with Cambodia, to improve Vietnam's image with ASEAN, to
strengthen the Vietnamese economy, and to provide leverage in Vietnam's relations with the Soviet Union. By this time, however, the
United States was no longer pursuing better relations with Vietnam.
The Vietnam War experience still made the possibility of diplomatic
ties unpopular in the United States. Some believed Vietnam had designs on other countries in Southeast Asia. The increased exodus of
refugees, especially the expulsion of the ethnic Chinese, was also a
negative factor. What is more important, the United States had decided
to pursue better relations with China, not Vietnam, as the key to
stability and a favorable balance of power in Southeast Asia. Some
critics have accused the United States of deliberately stalling any rapprochement with Vietnam because it was secretly negotiating with
China during this time.[66]

By 1978, certain factors had led the United States to reconsider its
involvement in Southeast Asia in accordance with its own national
interests. First, the escalation of rivalry between China and the Soviet
Union grew in direct proportion to the exodus of refugees from Vietnam, and Hanoi was preparing to invade Cambodia, thereby increasing the role of Southeast Asia in the relations of the United States with
China and with the Soviet Union. Second, the United States was developing closer relations with China, in part as a means to check what
appeared to be the unbridled expansion of the Soviet Union, particularly in the Third World. The United States thus sided with China in its
disputes with the Soviet-backed Vietnamese in Southeast Asia. Third,
the United States became increasingly aware of a security threat as sea

65. Senate Foreign Relations Committee, *Vietnam's Future Policies*, 64–68.
66. *Ibid.*, 66; Sutter, "China's Strategy Toward Vietnam," 186–87. For an in-depth
discussion, see Chanda, *Brother Enemy*.

lanes used to transport Middle Eastern oil through Southeast Asia to Japan and other allies were threatened by the expansion of the Soviet Union's air and naval power, which began to utilize bases in Vietnam. As a result, China, Japan, and ASEAN all advocated a more active American presence in the region. Fourth, "the publicized plight of Indochinese refugees brought Southeast Asia back into the consciousness of Americans."[67]

The Carter administration and Congress responded to these events by retaining bases in the Philippines, increasing the activity of the Seventh Fleet, expanding military sales to Thailand, including airlifting arms to Thailand in emergencies, and assisting Indochinese refugees directly. At this time, the foreign policy of the United States concerning Asia was to rely on increased cooperation with China in order to confront the Soviet challenge. On December 15, 1978, the United States agreed to establish diplomatic ties with China. The new Sino-U.S. relations, coupled with ASEAN-U.S. relations, became the foreign policy strategy of the United States in Southeast Asia and reflected American interests.[68]

The new balance-of-power relationships quickly fell into place. Just prior to the announcement of normalization, Vietnam signed a friendship treaty with the Soviet Union in November, 1978. In early December the United States sided with Cambodia in its dispute with Vietnam. On December 25, Vietnam launched its invasion of Cambodia. In late January, 1979, China's vice-premier Teng Hsiao-ping visited the United States.[69]

Asian policy analyst Robert Sutter found the United States, in particular presidential adviser Zbigniew Brzezinski, "publicly associated with China's harder line toward Vietnam." For example, the United States facilitated a meeting between Teng and Cambodia's Prince Sihanouk in Washington, D.C. Soon after, Sihanouk announced that China was funneling military assistance to the Khmer Rouge already grouped along the Thai-Cambodian border. A few days later, Presi-

67. Senate Foreign Relations Committee, *Vietnam's Future Policies*, 1; interview with Robert Sutter, Senior Specialist in Asian Affairs, Foreign Affairs and National Defense Division, Congressional Research Service, Library of Congress, Washington, D.C., September 5, 1985.

68. Senate Foreign Relations Committee, *Vietnam's Future Policies*, 1, 67; interview with Robert Sutter, September 5, 1985.

69. Sutter, "China's Strategy Toward Vietnam," 187.

dent Carter confirmed American support for Thailand if it was threatened by Vietnam. In February, 1979, China invaded Vietnam. "Meanwhile, the exodus of refugees from Vietnam grew and was seen in the U.S. as one of the worst violations of human rights in the 20th century." The continued occupation of Cambodia by Vietnam and the invasion of Afghanistan by the Soviet Union in December, 1979, another event with a refugee component, seemed to reinforce the validity of American policy in Southeast Asia.[70]

The United States has remained cautious about its reentry into Southeast Asia, influenced by what some call the "Vietnam syndrome," a term used to indicate American reluctance to become involved ever again in an experience like the Vietnam War. In 1984, Evelyn Colbert, deputy assistant secretary of state for East Asian and Pacific affairs from 1978 to 1980, explained that the role of the United States in the region has been confined to leading the refugee relief effort but otherwise following the lead of ASEAN, thus displaying its interest in supporting ASEAN as the "major factor for East Asian peace and stability and an influential voice in the Third World." Therefore, the United States maintains its security commitment to Thailand and gives modest military assistance to the rest of the ASEAN nations. ASEAN as a unit has emerged as the seventh largest trading partner of the United States, and it strategically commands "the straits connecting the Pacific and Indian Oceans." One of its member nations, the Philippines, allows important U.S. air and naval bases on its soil. Colbert astutely observed that this somewhat low profile American policy involves little cost and does not meet with significant opposition at home.[71]

Similar to 1956, when the United States concluded that Hungary was important but not vital to its national security, as evidenced by its nonintervention there, after 1975 the United States would deem Southeast Asia important but not vital to its interests. It would be content with maintaining a secondary role in the region's political affairs, in marked contrast to the major role it played during the Vietnam War. As

70. *Ibid.*, 165, 187–88; Senate Foreign Relations Committee, *Vietnam's Future Policies*, 67.

71. Evelyn Colbert, "Stand Pat," *Foreign Policy*, LIV (Spring, 1984), 139–55; Library of Congress, *Vietnam–U.S. Relations: The Missing in Action (MIAs) and the Impasse over Cambodia*, No. IB87210 (December 8, 1988), 6.

in 1956 and 1957, the United States would focus on the refugee issue, offering assistance to the first asylum countries by funding refugee relief and by providing permanent resettlement for the refugees.

In American foreign policy in Southeast Asia, the Reagan administration appeared to have followed its predecessors: it played the China card and followed the lead of ASEAN, resulting in a low profile for the United States in the ASEAN–China–United States strategy vis-à-vis Indochina and the Soviet Union. In October, 1981, John H. Holdridge, assistant secretary for East Asian and Pacific affairs, said that American foreign policy objectives were to preserve the security of ASEAN, in particular of Thailand, to seek the withdrawal of Vietnam from Cambodia and foster Cambodian self-determination, and to reduce Soviet military influence in Indochina. Pursuit of these objectives involved U.S. support of ASEAN's lead in the Cambodian situation, which meant supporting UN efforts and ASEAN aid to the noncommunist factions of the CGDK. In addition, the United States continued to emphasize diplomatic, economic, and military pressures on Vietnam, including a denial of foreign aid, an embargo on trade, and military support to Thailand and other ASEAN states.[72]

A reflection of these goals can be found in American refugee policy for the resettlement of Indochinese in the United States, as admissions levels for refugees are related to ASEAN-U.S. relations and to the isolation of Vietnam. Appearing before the Senate Subcommittee on Immigration and Refugee Policy in late 1984, Secretary of State Shultz proposed admission of 50,000 Indochinese refugees for fiscal year 1985, pointing out that generous American resettlement offers had been a major stabilizing factor in Southeast Asia since 1975 by helping to avoid "potentially destructive economic, social, and political pressures" in first asylum countries. Shultz went on to blame the continuing exodus on Vietnam's oppressive policies.[73]

Various political observers concurred that recent American foreign policy objectives in Southeast Asia serve U.S. interests. As Colbert observed, the low-profile policy of following the lead of ASEAN and playing a leadership role only in refugee matters costs little and meets

72. U.S. Department of State, *Recent Developments in Indochina*, No. 334 (October 22, 1981), 1–2.

73. U.S. Department of State, *Proposed Refugee Admissions for FY 1985*, No. 610 (September 11, 1984), 3.

little opposition at home. Paul Kattenberg, a former foreign service officer who traveled to Indochina in 1983 and met with officials there, thought American policy toward Vietnam to be guided by attitudes of embarrassment and humiliation as a result of the Vietnam War. He cited evidence of an American cold war with Hanoi as the United States plays a secondary role in Southeast Asia. This cold war consists of pressuring and isolating Vietnam by focusing on the plight of refugees and the violations of human rights, by putting an embargo on trade, by denying foreign aid, and by offering a conditioned normalization of relations that involves the withdrawal of Vietnam from Cambodia, an offer that is unlikely to entice Hanoi. Kattenberg agreed with Colbert that the United States, with few interests in Indochina, would have little to gain from a change in its present policy. For example, normalizing relations with Hanoi might come at the expense of jeopardizing relations with China and ASEAN.[74]

Anthony Lake, a former State Department official in the Carter administration, questioned the importance of the United States in the region. He wrote that any U.S.-Vietnam rapprochement would not necessarily foster the American goal of drawing Vietnam away from the Soviet Union, since that issue is more directly related to Sino-Vietnamese relations. Yet an obvious conflict exists between American efforts to assist refugees and a foreign policy objective that highlights human rights abuses in Vietnam. Lake pointed out that a policy pursuing international isolation of Indochina by restricting trade and assistance, even at the private, humanitarian level, might perpetuate, even exacerbate, conditions in Vietnam, Laos, and Cambodia that contribute to the refugee flow.[75]

Until recently, at the superpower level, then, there has been contentment with the status quo. The United States has enjoyed a low profile at a time when its interests in Southeast Asia have been eclipsed by events elsewhere, in the Middle East and in Central America. The Soviet Union has continued to maintain important strategic benefits in exchange for its costly support of Vietnam. Soviet economic aid to

74. Paul M. Kattenburg, "Living with Hanoi," *Foreign Policy,* LIII (Winter, 1983–84), 131–49.
75. Anthony Lake, "Dealing with Hanoi: What Can Washington Do?," *Indochina Issues,* XLIX (August, 1984), 1–7, and "Normalization: Only Cautious Steps Now," *World Policy Journal,* III (Winter, 1985–86), 143–55.

Vietnam is estimated to be $2.5 billion annually; the Soviets have given "over $4 billion in military aid since 1979." Recent reports indicate a Soviet squadron of fourteen MiG-23 interceptor jet aircraft is in place at Cam Ranh Bay in south Vietnam. According to Richard L. Armitage, assistant secretary of defense for international security affairs, "The port and airfield facilities in Cam Ranh Bay in Vietnam are an important forward base for deployed Soviet naval forces." China appears to have been content, with American approval, to "bleed" Vietnam in Cambodia and at home by encouraging Vietnam's international isolation and its harassment by the CGDK resistance forces, thus ensuring that Vietnam remains subordinate to China in the region. Its anti-Vietnam stance has put China in a more favorable position with ASEAN, especially with Thailand, though some ASEAN members remain wary of what China's long-range intentions would be if Vietnam becomes totally weakened. China's policy, however, has been strengthened by its relationship with the United States. Compounding the dilemma, according to Lake, continued Vietnamese dependence on the Soviets has precluded any improvement in Hanoi's relations with China and the United States.[76]

Complacency over the situation in Southeast Asia, especially the Cambodian stalemate, appeared to be waning by 1986. Small signs that year, with notable diplomatic activity involving several nations at the superpower and regional levels beginning in 1987, pointed to some flexibility on all sides. This new concern for resolving the deadlock over tensions in Southeast Asia portends consequences for the refugees from Vietnam, Laos, and Cambodia as well. As one astute observer noted, "The reason for the optimism and enthusiasm is that finally, doing something to end the turmoil in the troubled region appears to be in everybody's interest."[77]

Leadership changes in Vietnam and in the Soviet Union, its staunch ally, signaled a loosening of rigid positions. In December, 1986, long-awaited and perhaps significant leadership changes were announced at the sixth congress of the Communist party of Vietnam.

76. Library of Congress, *Vietnam-U.S. Relations*, 6; Washington *Times*, January 9, 1985; "Vietnam Chronology," *Indochina Chronology*, V (January-March, 1986), 7; Lake, "Dealing with Hanoi," 5.

77. Rochelle L. Stanfield, "Eyeing Indochina," *National Journal*, January 14, 1989, p. 100.

General Secretary Le Duan, who died in July, 1986, was reportedly instrumental in the estrangement between Vietnam and China. Nguyen Van Linh, a known reformer, was named the new party chief. Although Vietnam observers have remained cautious about predicting change, either internally or in Vietnamese foreign policy, they greeted with some optimism the surprise announcement in May, 1988, that Vietnam planned to withdraw militarily from Cambodia by 1990. An estimated 50,000 Vietnamese troops allegedly were withdrawn by the end of 1988, with an accelerated withdrawal plan slated to remove all troops by September, 1989. Speculation regarding the reasons for the proposed withdrawal included the worsening of Vietnam's domestic problems, which have been exacerbated by the occupation of Cambodia. Too, an estimated 35,000 Vietnamese soldiers are said to have died in Cambodia since 1978. The occupation, which has contributed to Vietnam's isolation from the international community, prevents Vietnam from receiving the outside technical and economic assistance it sorely needs. However, pressure from the Soviet Union may also have influenced the shift in position.[78]

Under the leadership of President Mikhail Gorbachev, the Soviet Union's foreign policy has shown marked change. The new approach can be seen in efforts to curtail Soviet commitments to costly clients abroad and to reverse the Soviet Union's "international isolation caused by the Brezhnev-era decision to use military power and assistance to spread Soviet influence in such third world areas as Afghanistan, Angola, and Indochina." Soviet interest in limiting its substantial financial aid to Vietnam and in prodding Vietnam to withdraw from Cambodia figures in its effort to foster a rapprochement with China.[79]

Efforts at easing tensions between the Soviet Union and China, with implications for Vietnam, commenced with Gorbachev's speech on the matter at Vladivostok in July, 1986. In August, 1988, talks between China and the Soviet Union, which included the issue of Cam-

78. William J. Duiker, "Applying the Lessons of Vietnam: The View from Hanoi," *Indochina Issues*, LXVIII (August, 1986), 6; Murray Hiebert, "A New Gerontocracy," *Far Eastern Economic Review*, January 1, 1987, pp. 10–11; *Washington Post*, May 26, 1988, p. 14, May 4, 1988, p. 21, July 1, 1988, p. 14, July 2, 1988, p. 14; *Christian Science Monitor*, January 17, 1989, p. 3.

79. Library of Congress, *Cambodian Crisis*, 6–7.

bodia, took place in Beijing on the vice-ministerial level. These were followed by meetings in Moscow and Beijing in late 1988 and in early 1989 between Chinese foreign minister Qian Qichen and Soviet foreign minister Eduard Shevardnadze. The way was prepared, then, for a summit meeting in Beijing, in May, 1989, with Gorbachev and China's leader, Teng Hsiao-ping, the first such event involving China and the Soviet Union in over thirty years. Gorbachev, who is also interested in improving relations with ASEAN, has been thwarted in his initiatives by the thorny issue of the Vietnamese occupation of Cambodia, which is supported by Soviet military aid.[80]

In 1986, Vietnam quickly asserted that any improvement in Sino-Soviet relations would have no bearing on its own policies, including its policy toward Cambodia. Yet Nayan Chanda saw indications that Hanoi was "concerned about recent Moscow moves." In a similar vein, historian and former foreign service officer in Vietnam William J. Duiker asked how unstinting the Soviet Union's support of Vietnam is: "Wartime experience undoubtedly taught the Vietnamese that Moscow's interests in Southeast Asia do not always coincide with their own. As in the past, Soviet leaders may be tempted to reduce the level of their support for Vietnam if they must, in order to pursue other objectives." Indeed, a news analysis in early 1989 indicated that "both the Chinese and Soviets want to reduce tensions and the costs of the military security measures they prompt, and concentrate on modernizing their economies."[81]

In yet another development, Sino-Vietnamese talks took place in Beijing on the vice-ministerial level in late January, 1989. With these talks coming on the heels of the series of Sino-Soviet meetings, the Soviet Union appeared to have played a role in orchestrating this breakthrough, for it had been nine years since such high-level talks had occurred between China and Vietnam. With plans underway for more Sino-Vietnamese talks at higher levels in the spring of 1989, the Soviet Union's initiatives to promote a Cambodian settlement in order to forge its own ties with China seem to have been fruitful. Related to

80. Washington *Post*, July 1, 1988, p. 14, February 3, 1989, p. 22; interview with Robert Sutter, September 11, 1988.
81. Nayan Chanda, "Weather Eye on Moscow," *Far Eastern Economic Review,* October 26, 1986, p. 24; Duiker, "Applying the Lessons of Vietnam," 6; Washington *Post*, February 3, 1989, p. 22.

this issue, the Soviet Union's initial withdrawal of troops from Afghanistan in May, 1988, was soon followed by Vietnam's announcement that it would begin to remove its troops from Cambodia. Noticeable, too, was the lack of border conflict between Vietnam and China during the dry season in January, 1988. Such hostilities had been a regular annual occurrence since the 1978–1979 season.[82]

Some signs of a thaw in U.S.-Vietnam relations became apparent in 1987. Increased pursuit of fresh approaches in the area of humanitarian concerns perhaps influenced the appointment by President Reagan of John Vessey as special envoy to talks with Nguyen Co Thach in August, 1987. This important meeting was seen as a breakthrough on such humanitarian issues as MIAs, the ODP, Amerasians and reeducation camp prisoners, as well as a recognition of Vietnam's own war-related humanitarian concerns. A hopeful sign, the meeting was followed by a flurry of activity, including the visits of a few congressional delegations to Vietnam during late 1987 and early 1988.[83]

In the spring of 1988, a proposal by Senator John S. McCain, a former prisoner of war, and Congressman Thomas Ridge to create "interest sections," or low-level diplomatic offices, in Hanoi and Washington, D.C., generated further discussion of U.S.-Vietnam relations. Observer Frederick Z. Brown noted that an "attitudinal barrier may have been dented" in the long-frozen U.S.-Vietnam relationship by the debate over the interest sections idea.[84]

That dent in the attitudinal barrier may be spreading in the United States. Although the Reagan administration remained cool to the idea of high-level, formal rapprochement with Vietnam, firmly reiterating the condition that Vietnam withdraw completely from Cambodia first, the issue of Cambodia was raised at the U.S.-Soviet summit conference in June of 1988. Also, quietly, private American humanitarian assistance to the Vietnamese people was allowed to resume, albeit at a low level, with "administrative blessing." Those who argue against promotion of improved American ties with Vietnam point to the low

82. Washington *Post,* January 21, 1989, p. 18, June 4, 1988, p. 21, January 22, 1988, p. 14.

83. New York *Times,* January 11, 1988, p. 1; Washington *Post,* January 21, 1988, p. 1, June 10, 1988, p. 30.

84. Frederick Z. Brown, "Sending the Wrong Signal to Hanoi," *Asian Wall Street Journal,* April 18, 1988, p. 16.

level of national interest in the region, the need to remain firm with Vietnam, and a general satisfaction with the status quo. Those who argue for improved relations, however, suggest the United States is an important, if not a lead, player in the region of Southeast Asia, especially with regard to Cambodia. One observer noted that the task of an improved relationship with Vietnam will be left to a new American president and perhaps will present an opportunity for the next administration to effect change. It is noteworthy that in his inaugural address in January, 1989, President George Bush asked the American people to put behind them the Vietnam War, which began more than a quarter of a century ago. Only days later, Vietnam's ambassador to the UN Trinh Xuan Lang declared, "It's time for bygones to be bygones."[85]

As the United States ponders whether to alter its policy vis-à-vis Vietnam significantly, more immediate concerns related to the future of Cambodia are evident. With Vietnam's apparent flexibility regarding a political settlement of the Cambodian conflict and its own military withdrawal have come "a great promise and extraordinary peril for the Cambodian people," said Congressman Stephen Solarz. The specter of a "second holocaust" is raised by fears that unless safeguards are arranged, the Khmer Rouge will return to power once the Vietnamese leave Cambodia. This fear colors peace negotiations, which commenced with symbolic, if not-so-fruitful, talks between resistance leader Prince Sihanouk and Cambodian prime minister Hun Sen in Paris in December, 1987. These were followed by the first Jakarta Informal Meeting (JIM talks) in late July, 1988, when representatives of the three resistance groups that make up the CGDK sat down with a representative from the People's Republic of Kampuchea (PRK) and Vietnamese foreign minister Nguyen Co Thach. Little progress was made toward a settlement at this and subsequent meetings in October, 1988 (Paris), and February, 1989 (Jakarta), as the various parties wrestled with how to share power after the Vietnamese withdrawal. However, the continuation of such meetings scheduled during 1989 held forth the possibility of a breakthrough.

85. *Ibid.*; Washington *Post*, June 10, 1988, p. 30; Stanley Foundation, *Report of the Twenty-eighth Strategy for Peace, U.S. Foreign Policy Conference*, Warrenton, Va. (October 22–24, 1987), 14; Frank Tatu, "U.S. and Vietnam: Converging Interests?," *Indochina Issues*, LXXXI (May, 1988), 2; New York *Times*, January 24, 1989, p. 7; Washington *Post*, January 27, 1989, p. 18.

While some observers looked to the Sino-Soviet summit conference in May, 1989, for help in finding a solution, some also looked to the United States to assume a more active role. For example, Prince Norodom Ranariddh, a representative of the noncommunist resistance forces and a son of Sihanouk, thinks the United States has much to contribute to the peace negotiations and has urged it to provide military aid to the noncommunist resistance forces. The vested interests of the Cambodian factions, as well as the interests of several regional powers and of the superpowers, are caught up in any attempts to resolve the Cambodian issue. Clearly, more than just the future of 300,000 displaced Khmers in limbo just inside Thailand is implicated in any deliberations. The shifting of positions at all levels would appear to have ramifications for Cambodian refugees and possibly for refugees from Vietnam and Laos as well.[86]

Any discussion of the political situation and refugees in Southeast Asia also needs to consider the interests of those countries that bear the brunt of the refugee exodus. The member nations of ASEAN and Hong Kong, in close proximity to Indochina and as countries of first asylum, are affected by any escalation in the regional conflict and by increases in the refugee outflow from Vietnam, Laos, and Cambodia. These nations repeatedly voice concern over dwindling international attention to the refugee problem, the continual arrival of asylum seekers, and the possibility of their being left with large numbers of residual refugees who are not resettled abroad. The national interests of ASEAN nations and of Hong Kong and what impact the refugees have on these countries of first asylum form the topics of the next two chapters.

86. "Cambodia: Peace at Last?," 1–8; Washington *Post*, July 8, 1988, p. 14; Library of Congress, *Cambodian Crisis*, 3–4; Washington *Post*, February 22, 1989, p. 26.

III

Thailand as a First
Asylum Country

The dilemma of international migrations, acutely evident in refugee exoduses, is the disparity between the individual's freedom to exit a country and the state's right to control access to asylum within its borders. The individual versus society tension that generates refugees also causes tension between sending and receiving nations. As explained by migrations expert Aristide Zolberg, in a world defined by national affiliations, the individual right of movement exists alongside the perception that statelessness is deviance from the norm. Although there are readily apparent inequalities among nations in regard to strategic, political, and economic power, nations strictly adhere to the concept of equality among all when it comes to respecting the regulation of migration and the control of borders according to national interests, except during war. It is usually with reluctance and according to a principle of selectivity, then, that nations receive refugees and offer asylum and resettlement. Hannah Arendt observed that the stateless are robbed of their humanity as nations expel and others accept or reject these displaced according to political, social, and economic attributes related to national interests.[1]

According to former UN High Commissioner for Refugees Sadruddin Aga Khan, "the consequences of mass exodus situations may be measured in terms not only of human suffering but also of threats to national or regional peace and stability."[2] In the case of the Indochina

1. Zolberg, "International Migrations," 6, 10, 19.
2. Aga Khan, *Study on Human Rights*, 53.

refugees, purely humanitarian considerations have been compromised by the reactions of nations receiving the direct impact of the exodus. The ASEAN states and Hong Kong, in close proximity to Indochina, are unavoidably the areas where refugees seek first asylum. Because they affect refugee policies, the national interests of these first asylum states are important and bear examination here.

When the refugee exodus reached crisis proportions in 1979, the foreign ministers of the ASEAN nations issued a joint communique on June 30, 1979, declaring that their countries would no longer permit refugees to enter their borders and would take strong measures to send out those refugees then residing in camps. This denial of asylum, already evident in the *refoulement* (forced repatriation) of 42,000 Cambodian refugees by Thailand in June of 1979 and in the push-offs of Vietnamese refugee boats approaching Malaysia, prompted an international conference, held in Geneva, in July, 1979, under the auspices of the UN.[3] The results of the meeting were a call for burden sharing and the promulgation of a clear message that ASEAN nations and Hong Kong would continue to offer temporary first asylum only insofar as other nations would honor their commitments to resettle refugees at a sufficient rate so as to limit the buildup of refugee populations in Southeast Asia. Responding to the call, the United States, for humanitarian reasons coupled with foreign policy interests, emerged as a leader in refugee relief aid and resettlement.

Before 1975, ASEAN was little more than a regional cooperative endeavor whereby the member states—Thailand, Malaysia, Singapore, Indonesia, and the Philippines—met annually to discuss common economic interests. After the Vietnam War, however, ASEAN distinguished itself from the Southeast Asian Treaty Organization (SEATO), long associated with American interests, by becoming an independent regional organization, interested in assessing "the full implications of the new political order in Indochina." Concerned at first about Vietnam's fervent ideological commitment to foster communist revolution throughout Southeast Asia and later about the growing exodus of refugees, ASEAN recognized the possibility of its own exploitation by Vietnam if it failed to present a unified stance.[4]

3. *Ibid.*, 4.
4. Derani, "Refugees from Indochina," 195–96.

From 1975 to 1978, Vietnam's policy toward the ASEAN nations was sometimes hostile and did actually encourage communist revolution in those states. At an ASEAN Bali conference in 1976, Vietnam dubbed ASEAN "a Washington backed scheme of intervention and aggression against Communist governments in Southeast Asia."[5] However, by mid-1978, influenced by increasing tensions with China, it altered its policy. In order to distance ASEAN from China, Vietnam highlighted the superpower's threat to the region, including China's overtures to its overseas populations. This policy was especially directed toward racially sensitive Malaysia and Indonesia, where the ethnic Chinese had long been part of a web of deep-seated animosities. Vietnam also sought to split ASEAN unity, in effect, by emphasizing the growing relationship between Thailand and China. Coinciding with its new ASEAN policy was Vietnam's more conciliatory approach toward the United States.

Although Vietnam curtailed its support for communist insurgency in the ASEAN states (except in Thailand), its invasion of Cambodia and the threat that posed to ASEAN member Thailand, coupled with the massive flow of refugees to the ASEAN states in 1978 and 1979, seem to have thwarted Vietnam's objectives and fostered ASEAN unity. Vietnam's approach had been to deal with the noncommunist nations of Southeast Asia individually, one on one. Abdul Hadi Derani has concluded from his research, however, that Vietnam's decision in July, 1979, to curb the flow of refugees signaled its recognition, in part, of ASEAN cohesiveness regarding this problem. In addition, ASEAN's overall response to the refugee problem and its continued insistence on the restoration of an independent and neutral Cambodia have served not only to establish unity but also to enhance its international respectability.[6]

According to Singapore's ambassador to the UN, Khishore Mahbubani, ASEAN-U.S. relations constitute a success story for American foreign policy, important for American credibility in the Third World. Besides participating in annual ASEAN meetings, the United States maintains bilateral economic and political relations with each ASEAN nation and has treaty obligations with two, Thailand and the Philip-

5. Senate Foreign Relations Committee, *Vietnam's Future Policies*, 53.
6. *Ibid.*, 54–59; Derani, "Refugees from Indochina," 287–88.

pines. By 1984, American trade with ASEAN nations, who are rich in minerals, reached $23 billion, making ASEAN rank fifth among the trading partners of the United States, and investment in them reached $8 billion. During the 1973 oil crisis, Indonesia declined to participate in the OPEC boycott and delivered on its American contracts. Commanding significant sea straits, especially along the Indonesian archipelago, and housing U.S. military bases in the Philippines, the ASEAN nations figure significantly in the strategic interests of the United States. Along with China, ASEAN is important to U.S. foreign policy goals in order to balance Vietnamese and Soviet influence in Southeast Asia.[7]

In 1981, Assistant Secretary of State John Holdridge remarked that the political stability and economic progress of ASEAN are at the heart of American policy toward the entire region. Cited by political observer John W. Garver as threats to ASEAN stability are the Soviet presence in Southeast Asia, Vietnam's threat to Thailand by way of its continued occupation of Cambodia, Vietnamese support for communist insurgency, and the large numbers of refugees.[8]

Along these lines, political scientist Astri Suhrke has indicated that ASEAN views the refugee crisis as a political, not a humanitarian, issue and, concomitantly, as essentially an American responsibility connected with the involvement of the United States in the Vietnam War. Equally important, ASEAN does not share with the United States a need to offer refugees an alternative to life under communism. Attentive to ASEAN's concerns and following its lead, U.S. Undersecretary of State Walter J. Stoessel in 1981 indicated that large refugee populations in the ASEAN countries are indeed destabilizing elements where they threaten internal security by providing recruits for communist insurgency groups, where they retard economic growth in these developing countries, where they cause political unrest among local populations, and in the case of the ethnic Chinese refugees, where they could possibly foster the adoption of anti-Chinese and pro-Vietnamese foreign policies in Malaysia and Indonesia.[9]

7. Khishore Mahbubani, "The Kampuchean Problem: A Southeast Asian Perspective," *Foreign Affairs*, LXII (Winter, 1983–84), 421–22; Garver, "Reagan Administration's Southeast Asian Policy," 86–91.

8. Garver, "Reagan Administration's Southeast Asian Policy," 92.

9. Suhrke, *Indochinese Refugees: The Impact*, 3; Garver, "Reagan Administration's Southeast Asian Policy," 107.

Secretary of State Shultz, in a report to Congress in September, 1984, stressed that the resettlement of large numbers of Indochinese refugees in the United States has been a key element in promoting stability in Southeast Asia. Suhrke warned that any change in American refugee policy signaling a reduction in U.S. assistance to refugees could jeopardize relations with ASEAN. From the opposite perspective, Garver stated that the spectacle of Thailand and other ASEAN states rejecting refugees might erode American public support for ASEAN and, therefore, undermine American foreign policy objectives.[10]

Former ambassador to Thailand Morton Abramowitz remarked that the role of the United States in the refugee crisis was "insufficiently understood and grossly underestimated." Besides "saving countless lives . . . it has also contributed fundamentally to the security of every nation" in the Southeast Asia region.[11] The reaction of the United States to the Indochina refugee exodus, then, appears to be related to humanitarian concern for the refugees and to the foreign policy objective of internationally isolating Vietnam, but also to American interests in the ASEAN nations.

In general, the refugee exodus engendered fear among the ASEAN states regarding Vietnam's intentions in the region—fear that was further exacerbated by the Vietnamese takeover of Cambodia. The ASEAN nations reacted with criticism of Vietnam for causing the outflow but also with criticism of non–Southeast Asian countries for their lack of resettlement offers. ASEAN was trapped between Vietnam, the instigator of the exodus, and Western humanitarianism, which called for ASEAN to accept the refugee burden. In January, 1979, the ASEAN foreign ministers' meeting in Bangkok noted the severe problems the refugees were causing in Thailand and Malaysia and the threat to regional stability they posed.[12]

In all the first asylum countries, national interests are intertwined with the effects of the influx of refugees on the security, the politics, the

10. U.S. Department of State, *Proposed Refugee Admissions for 1985*, 3; Suhrke, *Indochinese Refugees: The Impact*, 2; Garver, "Reagan Administration's Southeast Asian Policy," 106–107.

11. Wain, *The Refused*, 255.

12. Library of Congress, "ASEAN Reaction to Indochinese Refugees, January 1–15, 1979" (Typescript, September 4, 1979), 1–3.

economics, and society itself in each nation. For example, national security concerns are clearly evident in Thailand, where the largest numbers of refugees have sought asylum, arriving by land and sea from all three Indochina states. Security concerns are also evident in Malaysia and Indonesia, where existing racial tensions are affected by the arrival of large numbers of ethnic Chinese refugees from Vietnam. In Thailand, Malaysia, Indonesia, and the Philippines, refugees are perceived to affect development programs adversely and to tax economic systems. In Hong Kong and Singapore, high-density populations pose problems if refugees are allowed to compete with host populations for limited physical space, employment, and services. Although the ASEAN nations and Hong Kong as a group share some similar concerns regarding the Indochina refugees, each state's reaction to the problem reflects the difference in impact the refugees have on those countries. This next section examines the reaction of Thailand to the Indochina refugee issue in light of that country's national interests.

A front-line first asylum country, Thailand has helped more Indochinese refugees than any other Southeast Asian nation. According to refugee officials, Thailand has had "a good track record" overall, having assisted nearly 1,000,000 refugees from all three Indochina states since the exodus began in 1975. Almost a decade and a half later, the refugee problem continues for Thailand. In mid-1988, over 108,000 refugees remained in Thai refugee camps. Of this number, almost 69,000 were long-term residents, having lived in the camps for more than three years. Arrival rates are down considerably from what they were in the period 1979–1982, yet during fiscal year 1988, almost 33,000 refugees sought asylum in Thailand. In addition, well over 300,000 displaced persons from Cambodia remain at evacuation sites just inside Thailand, close to the Cambodian border. A UNHCR public information officer in Bangkok explained that refugee arrivals replace those resettled abroad, making it difficult to solve the refugee problem in Thailand. A New York *Times* correspondent noted that "there seems to be no end to the flow of refugees out of Indochina into Thailand."[13]

13. Interview with William Stubbs; "Indochinese Refugee Activity," *Refugee Reports,* IX (August 12, 1988), 16; U.S. Department of State, *Indochinese Refugees and Relations with Thailand,* No. 1052 (February 24, 1988), 1; "Indochinese Refugee Activity Since April

An official explanation of Thai refugee policy invariably mentions the past burdens and hardships imposed on Thailand by refugees, including 32,000 Burmese nationals settled along the western border, 25,000 nationalist Chinese in the north, and 50,000 Vietnamese from the period 1945–1954 who were never repatriated. As recently as September, 1988, an estimated 5,000 to 10,000 Burmese dissidents fled to the Thai border in the wake of disturbances in Burma. Prasong Soonsiri, secretary general of the National Security Council in Thailand and leading refugee policy maker, remarked, "The old and new problems are combined in a bad way for Thailand." Examination of Thailand's recent history proves Prasong's statement. From 1975 until 1978 approximately 228,000 refugees, mostly from Laos, sought asylum in Thailand. Beginning in 1978 and during 1979, however, the country was inundated by the various refugee exoduses, as boat people arrived from Vietnam, increased numbers of Laotians crossed the Mekong River border, and Cambodians, including the Khmer Rouge fleeing in the wake of Vietnam's invasion of Cambodia and impending famine conditions, moved toward Thailand. According to former U.S. Bureau for Refugee Programs official Frank Sieverts, "Refugees are the continuation of war by other means."[14]

Thailand's refugee policy over time has been responsive to the size and duration of the exodus and to assistance from other nations, especially to offers of resettlement abroad. However, Thailand was only reluctantly inclined toward a liberal refugee policy when the United States emphasized the need for first asylum, which coincided with increased Vietnamese and Soviet power in the region after 1975. Thus, Thai refugee policy seems to have been responsive to the importance of good U.S.-Thai relations for security reasons. In addition, for Thailand the importance of its good relations with China was reinforced by the Vietnamese invasion of Cambodia in late 1978. Sensitivity to the repercussions of any violation of international humanitarian principles re-

---

1975," *Refugee Reports*, IX (December 16, 1988), 7; interview with Rob Burrows; New York *Times*, March 3, 1985, p. 3.

14. *Refugee Reports*, IX (November 11, 1988), 8; Thailand, "Statement by Squadron Leader Prasong Soonsiri, Secretary General of the National Security Council, at the Annual Conference on Indochinese Displaced Persons in Thailand" (Bangkok, July 7, 1983), 7; Thailand, Embassy, "Refugee Problems in Thailand" (Typescript, Washington, D.C., n.d.), 1–2; interview with Frank Sieverts.

garding refugees and, by 1979, generous international refugee relief assistance also influenced Thai refugee policy. Although these foreign policy concerns are the major part of the refugee issue in Thailand, they converge with national security issues and political, social, and economic factors to influence Thai refugee policy, which can be characterized as a general reluctance to accept refugees.[15] Its basic objective is to reduce the numbers of asylum seekers in Thailand, which it pursues in two ways: deterrence measures designed to discourage entry and resettlement abroad to reduce the numbers of refugees already in the country.

The Indochinese who seek refuge in Thailand are classified as illegal immigrants or displaced persons, not as refugees, as Thai officials are very careful to indicate. The pressure of national interests seems to preclude Thailand's signing the UN Convention and Protocol documents, international legal instruments designed to protect refugees. To sign the documents or to assign official refugee status to the Indochinese would formally obligate Thailand to be a cooperative and responsible protector of the refugees and perhaps place humanitarian concerns in conflict with its national interests. Thailand has, however, permitted the UNHCR access to many, if not all, of the asylum seekers within its borders in order to render protection and relief services and to seek durable solutions to the problem.

UNHCR guidelines generally offer three durable solutions to refugee situations. Voluntary repatriation, with the emphasis on voluntary, is the most favored, but this approach has met with little success in either Thailand or elsewhere in Southeast Asia. The second solution, local integration, has been clearly rejected by Thailand for several reasons, including traditional ethnic antagonisms (especially between Thais and Vietnamese and Cambodians), fear of communist infiltrators among the refugees, desire to avoid an expansion of the ethnic diversity of the population, limited resettlement resources, and other political and economic burdens already imposed on this developing country. Resettlement, the least favored and costliest alternative, has been an important, if problematic and partial, solution to relieving Thailand's refugee burden. Thus far, over 575,000 Indochinese refugees have left Thailand to be resettled elsewhere.[16]

15. Suhrke, *Indochinese Refugees: The Impact*, 7–8.
16. U.S. Department of State, *Country Reports on the World Refugee Situation: Report to*

Thailand agreed to shoulder the humanitarian burden of temporary first asylum if other nations did their fair share by permanently resettling the refugees in due time. Its growing dissatisfaction with this solution, however, stems from its dependency on a generosity from the resettlement countries that is not always forthcoming. It has long been the Thai perception that dwindling and selective resettlement offers, coupled with the ongoing nature of the exodus, result in a protracted refugee problem for Thailand. The concern that resettlement as a solution would be problematic was soon borne out by another fact: resettlement opportunities acted as pull factors, encouraging even more refugees to seek asylum in Thailand.

Consequently, though still relying on resettlement as a partial solution, Thai refugee policy has sought to limit the magnet effect of resettlement with alternative measures to reduce its refugee burden. Deterrence, official and unofficial, has been an important component of this policy.

The most shocking act to deter refugees occurred in June, 1979, when 42,000 Cambodians were forcibly repatriated, precipitating public outrage within Thailand and ending international indifference to the growing plight of Cambodians arriving at the Thai border. Even after the establishment of holding centers inside its borders for close to 200,000 Cambodians by late 1979, Thailand "officially ceased granting asylum to Cambodian refugees, hoping to stem the tide of people flowing across the border," the order effective in February, 1980. From that date on, displaced persons from Cambodia were relegated to the border areas, where they still remain until they can return to their homeland. The deterrence measures at the border area camps include the absence of both UNHCR protection and prospects for resettlement abroad, only minimal relief services, and human rights abuses.[17]

By 1981, Thailand also began to take steps to deter the influx from Vietnam and Laos. It applied a policy of humane deterrence to arrivals of lowland Lao in January, 1981, then to Vietnamese and hill tribe refugees from Laos. Humane deterrence is characterized by "indefinite detention in austere camps, denial of all but essential services required

---

the Congress for Fiscal Year 1984 (August, 1983), 3; U.S. Department of State, *Indochinese Refugees and Relations with Thailand*, 1.

17. J. Patrick Hamilton, *Cambodian Refugees in Thailand: The Limits of Asylum*, U.S. Committee for Refugees (Washington, D.C., August, 1982), 4; Virginia Hamilton (ed.), *World Refugee Survey: 1986*, 54.

for care and maintenance, and deferral or denial of access to third country resettlement processing." Thought to reduce the magnet or pull effect of asylum in Thailand, humane deterrence is modified from time to time in direct response to any liberalizing of admissions by the resettlement countries, especially the United States. For example, during 1986 refugees from Vietnam and Laos benefitted from one of these modifications.[18]

Expanding on its policy of deterrence, Thailand instituted a screening program in July of 1985 for asylum seekers from Laos. Intent on controlling borders, it screens arrivals, with UNHCR observance, for refugee status and, consequently, resettlement eligibility. Those accepted move on to the refugee camps, whereas those rejected are detained and await repatriation to Laos.

Other deterrence measures include efforts to lessen the refugee problem by closing and consolidating refugee camps. In 1986, four more facilities were phased out: Ubon Repatriation Center for Laotian refugees; Songkhla Receiving Center for Vietnamese boat people; Sikhui Detention Center for Vietnamese asylum seekers; and Khao-I-Dang, the last, and therefore highly symbolic, holding center for Cambodian refugees. By 1987, Khao-I-Dang's residents were being sent to the border camps to rejoin 300,000 fellow Khmers.[19]

Controversial, and at times unofficial, deterrents have long been associated with the refugee issue in Thailand. For Laotian refugees, pushbacks and forced repatriation have been recurring problems, with a marked increase in such actions against Hmong asylum seekers in 1987. For Vietnamese refugees, piracy in the Gulf of Thailand has long plagued boat people attempting to reach southern Thailand. Piracy incidents declined by 1986, but by late 1987 and during 1988, Vietnamese approaching the coast were met with a Thai naval and marine blockade, violent pushbacks to sea, and a dramatic increase in pirate attacks on those pushed away from the Thai coast. Over 500 boat people died in such incidents during 1988. For Cambodian refugees, the absence of protection at the border camps has resulted in serious human rights abuses.[20]

18. U.S. Department of State, *Country Reports*, 47; "Little Known Ethnic Lao Refugees Resettle in Record Numbers," *Refugee Reports*, VII (June 13, 1986), 1.

19. New York *Times*, December 30, 1986, p. 1.

20. Washington *Post*, March 3, 1987, p. 18, March 22, 1987, p. 21; New York *Times*,

Refugee personnel spoke of the overall attempts deliberately to "manage down" the Indochina refugee problem throughout Southeast Asia and especially in Thailand. The decrease in the numbers seeking asylum, before the upsurge in Vietnamese refugees in late 1987, was attributed to stricter surveillance of departures by the Indochina governments, a scarcity of boats in Vietnam, and the possibility that most of those who feared persecution had already left. However, several refugee personnel concurred that a major factor in the decrease in arrivals is the reduction of pull factors, including the reduced availability of safe first asylum and resettlement opportunities. In Thailand specifically, Joint Voluntary Agency official Dennis Grace pointed out that Thai refugee policies of deterrence have "forced the numbers down."[21] The harsh and violent treatment accorded Vietnamese boat people attempting to reach Thailand in late 1987 and during 1988 is a case in point. Clearly, the purpose of such policies is to discourage refugees by emphasizing the danger and hopelessness associated with seeking asylum in Thailand. The fact that refugees come despite such treatment underscores their desperation. However, the number of arrivals would no doubt be much higher without these restraints.

A general perspective shows that Thailand's refugee policy relies on resettlement abroad for many refugees already inside Thailand, on eventual repatriation for the Cambodians and those Laotians rejected by the screening program, and on deterrence measures to dissuade asylum seekers from entry. This policy reflects important concerns about the continuation and recent increase in the influx, about being left with a substantial residual population made up of those rejected for resettlement—a population that, from the Thai perspective, includes criminals, infiltrators, and the aged and infirm—and about waning international commitment as resettlement countries reduce admissions levels and apply more stringent criteria.

Although thousands of asylum seekers have been assisted by Thailand, the reaction of this country to the refugees raises questions about a host of humanitarian issues, as many of those fleeing persecution are obviously not met with open arms when they reach its borders

January 30, 1988; *Wall Street Journal*, June 29, 1988, p. 18; "Lawyers Committee Issues Report on Dangers to Refugees in Thailand," *Refugee Reports*, X (January 27, 1989), 15.

21. Interview with Dennis Grace, Director, Joint Voluntary Agency, U.S. Embassy, Bangkok, March 14, 1984.

and shores. Yet Thailand's response to the refugee problem cannot be seen as merely a reaction to an isolated human rights event. Rather, Thai refugee policy reflects, in addition to humanitarian concerns, a web of complex, interrelated national-interest factors, which are now discussed in relation to each refugee group.

The word *Thai* translates as "free," and freedom in Thailand is taken seriously in this highly nationalistic, Buddhist, mostly rural country of almost fifty million people. Concern for national security was evident to me firsthand in March, 1984, when the front-page headlines of the Bangkok press I read referred to an incursion into northwest Thailand by Burmese soldiers, to the arrest of alleged Communist party members in the capital city, and to tension in Thai-Vietnamese relations concerning the Cambodian border regions where resistance forces and refugees mingle. This siege mentality has historic roots: Thailand is the only country in Southeast Asia to have avoided colonization by either a Western or a regional power. Traditionally, Thailand served as a buffer between French and British hegemony in the region.

Longstanding ethnic animosities have plagued Thai-Vietnamese relations for centuries, often with Cambodia as a buffer. Along these lines, during the Vietnam War Thailand hosted important American air bases, from which attacks on Vietnam were launched. Although Thailand had its share of problems with the repugnant Pol Pot regime of Democratic Kampuchea from 1975 to 1978, Abdul Hadi Derani reported, eventually cordial relations led to the recognition of Vietnam as a common enemy by Thailand and the Khmer Rouge government and to sanctuary at the border area for the Khmer Rouge fleeing the invading Vietnamese in late 1978 and 1979.[22]

Thailand expresses real and immediate concerns for its national security. Until recently, some 160,000 to 180,000 Vietnamese troops occupied neighboring Cambodia, and there were allegations of the "Vietnamization" or colonization of Cambodia by the migration of up to 700,000 Vietnamese civilians to Cambodia. In addition, there were reportedly 40,000 Vietnamese troops in Laos. Northeast Thailand borders on Laos and on Cambodia where the population is ethnically similar to Lao. In 1981, Vietnam's foreign minister Nguyen Co Thach

22. Derani, "Refugees from Indochina," 166–67.

referred to the region as "the sixteen provinces of Laos currently under Thai administration." The overall security threat is heightened by indefensible, heavily forested, and mountainous border areas. Thailand's vulnerability to incursions by the Vietnamese, infiltrations by Vietnamese-backed communist insurgents, and refugee migrants is apparent. In early 1987, it was reported that the Thai army was preparing to rout out 500 Vietnamese soldiers "holding the hills where the borders of Laos, Thailand and Cambodia meet."[23]

Another important concern expressed by Thailand is the possible relationship between refugees and communist insurgency. Thailand has long been plagued by communist insurgency activities in areas far from the reaches of central government authority: in the south, which is ethnically and culturally different from central Thailand and where Vietnamese boat people arrive, and also in the north and northeast, where Lao refugees cross ill-defined borders into Thailand. Ministry of Interior official Mr. Thani said there was no doubt in his mind that an agent network connects all the refugee camps throughout the country. The initial wave of Indochinese refugees coincided with heightened concern about communist insurgency in Thailand, particularly in the border areas.[24]

In his research, Derani wrote of similar suspicions Thailand had of the Vietnamese refugees who came to Thailand from 1945 to 1954 and who are now settled in the northeast. Remaining aloof from Thai society, many were accused of being Vietminh agents in collusion with the Communist party of Thailand. Somboon Thawatcharmat, vice-governor of Nong Khai, where many refugees from Laos arrive, expressed his concern for security to a U.S. congressional fact-finding group in July, 1978, associating his distrust of the Vietnamese who arrived earlier with the possible influence they might have on the new refugees. Apparently, this security threat is also in the minds of some Americans. Appearing before the Senate Subcommittee on East Asian and Pacific Affairs in July, 1981, Richard Armitage, deputy assistant secretary for East Asian and Pacific affairs in the Department of Defense, expressed similar worries about the fifth column potentiality of the

23. Swank, "Land In Between," 5; Senate Foreign Relations Committee, *Vietnam's Future Policies*, 62; Washington *Post*, March 22, 1987, p. 21.

24. Suhrke, *Indochinese Refugees: The Impact*, 17; interview with Mr. Thani, Director, Welfare Section, Ministry of Interior, Bangkok, March 20, 1984.

earlier Vietnamese refugees in Thailand. In particular, he was concerned about the communist leanings of these Vietnamese in Thailand, who he believed had supported Ho Chi Minh and North Vietnam during the war. He testified the following:

I can state from personal experience and with a great deal of surprise that I had in 1969, in a visit to the then friendly border, when I visited some Vietnamese homes and saw pictures of "Uncle Ho" prominently portrayed. They did pay taxes during the war to support the Vietnamese. They do what they have to do to survive. My point is that they are very powerful economically and they can easily become a fifth column movement. I think this is a fact that is often overlooked when people deal with the Vietnamese threat.[25]

Historical ethnic animosities in combination with fears about communist infiltrators make Vietnamese refugees unwelcome in Thailand. Of special humanitarian concern are those asylum seekers from Vietnam who have trekked across Cambodia and young Vietnamese military defectors from the occupation army in Cambodia. When these so-called land refugees arrive at the border, they are taken to and held at the Site 2 border camp, where they suffer "physical assault, abuse and extortion threats" at the hands of hostile Cambodians whose cultural antipathy toward the Vietnamese occasionally overrides the fact that these refugees are fleeing the same enemy. Site 2, with nearly 175,000 residents, is administered by the noncommunist KPNLF, part of the CGDK coalition of resistance forces. There were over 4,500 Vietnamese asylum seekers at Site 2 in early 1989.[26]

In order to "limit the attraction of an overland route from Vietnam," officials long rejected efforts to move this vulnerable population to safer UNHCR camps. In July, 1988, Thai officials announced that these "land Vietnamese" would be moved to a new facility, an annex to Site 2. The new camp, Ban Thad, was built to accommodate the influx of Vietnamese refugees to Thailand's eastern shore from 1987 and 1988. In order to deter more asylum seekers, Thai officials decreed that those at Ban Thad would not be eligible for resettlement abroad. However, though Thailand administers the camp, the UNHCR is allowed to provide protective services to the refugees. This permission is an

---

25. Derani, "Refugees from Indochina," 22; U.S. House of Representatives, Committee on the Judiciary, *Indochinese Refugees: An Update*, 95th Cong., 2nd Sess., No. 35-721 0, p. 12; *Senate Documents*, 97th Cong., 1st Sess., No. 83-102-0, p. 35.

26. Virginia Hamilton (ed.), *World Refugee Survey: 1986*, 55.

important development, because the UNHCR has long been pre-vented from aiding refugees at the border area.[27]

Asylum seekers who leave by boat from Vietnam face an especially traumatic and violent journey to Thailand. Piracy, a problem endemic to the Gulf of Thailand over the centuries, has frequently and brutally victimized Vietnamese boat refugees since the exodus began. Tradi-tional cultural antipathies between Thais and Vietnamese, the exis-tence of a fleet of about 40,000 to 50,000 small, unregistered, Thai fishing boats in southern Thailand, far removed from central govern-ment control, and official priority given to curbing the refugee influx instead of to deterring pirates are all factors believed to have helped continue the high incidence of piracy attacks. In late 1978, reportedly two out of every three refugee boats were attacked. A critical report by the U.S. Committee for Refugees in 1984 found that an estimated 56 percent of refugee boats arriving in Thailand had been attacked, usu-ally more than once. These attacks are noted for their violence, includ-ing murder, rape, and abduction, "with women experiencing the worst of the violence." The first antipiracy attempt, one unarmed pa-trol boat supplied through the UNHCR to Thailand, was woefully inadequate. Despite the international financing of an antipiracy pro-gram by twelve nations in July, 1982, nearly a year later no pirates had been arrested, and piracy attacks continued unabated. Although the Vietnamese boat refugees have never constituted a major percentage of Thailand's Indochina refugee burden, piracy is generally thought to discourage boat people from seeking asylum in Thailand. Barry Wain reports that from the early days of the exodus, refugees have deliber-ately made the longer journey to other ASEAN states just to avoid Thai pirates, because the priority, even for the Thai navy, has been given to deterring refugees, not pirates.[28]

The U.S. Committee for Refugees' report concluded that Thailand's racial hostility toward the Vietnamese and its desire to limit its refugee burden might explain "Thailand's lack of concerted effort" to combat piracy. With the United States committing $5 million to the antipiracy

27. U.S. Department of State, *World Refugee Report* (September, 1986), 27; *Refugee Reports*, IX (August 12, 1988), 7–8; Murray Hiebert, "A Change of Heart," *Far Eastern Economic Review*, May 5, 1988, pp. 39–40.

28. Joseph Cerquone, *Vietnamese Boat People: Pirates' Vulnerable Prey*, U.S. Committee for Refugees (Washington, D.C., February, 1984), 1–18; Wain, *The Refused*, 42–43.

program for fiscal year 1984, Congressman Stephen Solarz noted that the horrors of pirate attacks on refugees and the ineffectiveness of the antipiracy program are unacceptable. In testimony before the U.S. congressional subcommittee on Asian and Pacific affairs in April of 1984, U.S. Committee for Refugees director Roger Winter criticized the United States for not taking a more active leading role in the antipiracy effort. Winter noted that it would take more than money to solve the problem but that American political interest in good U.S.-Thai relations precluded emphasis on the piracy issue. He recounted in his testimony the following conversation he had had with a U.S. government official: "As one government official said to me within the last couple of weeks. 'You can't expect us to do much more on piracy. Thailand is a frontline state in a geopolitical context. Our relations with them are exceedingly complicated. Therefore, piracy on the total agenda with Thailand must take a minor role.' "[29]

Political analyst Nguyen Manh Hung concurred, indicating that the United States is cautious about generating public opinion on the piracy issue because it does not want to strain relations with Thailand. According to two informants, an American official and a UNHCR representative, the United States prefers to internationalize the antipiracy program by acting through and pressuring the UNHCR on this issue, thereby limiting direct confrontation between itself and Thailand.[30]

Thailand responds to the piracy issue with defensiveness, noting that pirates can be of any nationality, that attacks occur in international—not Thai—waters, that Thai fishermen are also attacked by pirates, and that Thailand is not the sole party responsible for curbing piracy in the Gulf of Thailand. Pointing to Thai efforts at preventing piracy, Prasong Soonsiri also remarked that piracy occurs all over the world and that undue attention and criticism are directed at the Gulf of Thailand.[31]

The U.S. Committee for Refugees reported that between 1981 and 1986 pirate attacks were responsible for "758 deaths, 1,022 rapes, 643 abductions," and 1,210 missing persons from among 34,000 boat refu-

29. *House Documents*, 98th Cong., 2nd Sess., No. 35-654 0, pp. 51, 67.
30. Interview with Nguyen Manh Hung, Professor of International Relations, George Mason University, Fairfax, Va., February, 1984; anonymous interviews, Bangkok, March 14–15, 1984.
31. Thailand, "Statement by Prasong Soonsiri," 12–13.

gees sailing in the direction of Thailand. By 1986, the percentage of boats attacked was down, arrests were up, and reports of refugees receiving help from Thai fishermen were increasing. New land-based measures were effectively combatting the piracy problem. And a special antipiracy section at the U.S. Embassy in Thailand was cited as evidence that America was upgrading its commitment to the antipiracy campaign. Optimism remained guarded, however, for observers still complained that the United States was not pressuring Thailand enough about the piracy issue. Although actual attacks were down in 1985, statistics can be misleading. For example, 1985 was also "one of the worst years for violence," with 50 refugees dead as a result of an attack on just one boat. By 1988, cooperative efforts to reduce piracy rapidly deteriorated as an increase in the arrivals of Vietnamese boat people was accompanied by an alarming increase in violent pirate attacks.[32]

In addition to charges that Thai pirates close to the southern coast of Thailand seem to be permitted to attack with impunity, Thailand has also been criticized for alleged push-offs of refugee boats approaching its shores. A congressional report in 1978 indicated that refugee personnel in Thailand "speculated that all most recent boats had been 'pushed back to sea' by the Thai navy or marine police." The UNHCR's Poul Hartling accused the Thais of a push-off in January, 1984, that resulted in the drowning of 23 refugees. Although some refugee officials criticized the UNHCR privately for being undiplomatic, many agreed that the UNHCR, usually a cautious protector of refugees, probably did not issue the public complaint without careful and sufficient evidence. Just before the incident the UNHCR had been criticized in the Bangkok press for being too reticent in the protection of refugees. The public complaint created a national embarrassment but also a display of strong nationalism, especially by Thai secretary general Prasong Soonsiri. Some officials believed the issue was a setback for cooperation between the UNHCR and Thailand over the refugee issue. Again, an increase in violent push-offs was noted during 1987 and 1988.[33]

32. Virginia Hamilton (ed.), *World Refugee Survey: 1986*, 55; "The U.S. and Anti-Piracy Efforts: New Results but Violence Persists," *Refugee Reports*, VII (April 18, 1986), 1–5; *Refugee Reports*, IX (August 12, 1988), 8.

33. House Judiciary Committee, *Indochinese Refugees: An Update*, 7; interviews with

Before it closed in April, 1986, boat refugees from Vietnam were held at the Sikhui Detention Center, a humane deterrence camp, off limits to UNHCR officials and Western visitors. Harsh conditions and long detention at this camp were said to have contributed to desperation, even suicide. At Phanat Nikhom Holding and Transit Center, where refugees are a step closer to resettlement possibilities, the Vietnamese were cordoned off from the Lao, the hill tribe, and the Cambodian refugees, apparently for security reasons. As of late 1988, approximately 9,000 Vietnamese refugees were at Phanat Nikhom. The new Ban Thad Camp near the Thai-Cambodian border had 3,603 Vietnamese refugees as of September, 1988. According to UNHCR figures, 11,195 Vietnamese refugees were registered as arrivals in 1987, triple the figure for 1986. During 1988, 1,043 "land" refugees and 11,153 boat people from Vietnam arrived in Thailand.[34]

According to a Ministry of Interior official, the majority of Vietnamese in Thailand were thought to be economic migrants seeking opportunities in the United States. He cited similar American public opinion and mentioned the numbers of Vietnamese refugees in the United States who were reluctant to take jobs once they were resettled and who are now on welfare. The official was simply voicing the opinions and attitudes of the Thai people in general toward this particular group of refugees. The long-standing cultural antipathies, their past experiences with Vietnamese refugees, their fears of the relationship between refugees and communist insurgency, and the current state of Thai-Vietnamese relations all influence the Thai people's perceptions of the refugees from Vietnam. These factors have combined with their overall weariness of the continuing exodus, which has gone on for too long.

The case of the refugees from Laos presents an entirely different picture. In the northeast where refugees from Laos enter Thailand, the initial threat to Thai security appeared tempered by Lao, who are ethnically compatible and similar to the Thais, and by anticommunist

---

UNHCR official and anonymous others, Bangkok, March 13–14, 1984. Although the UNHCR remained adamant in its position, the officer who reportedly "blew the whistle" on this issue was quickly reassigned to another country.

34. "Indochinese Refugee Activity," *Refugee Reports*, IX (August 12, 1988), 16; United Nations, Office of the United Nations High Commissioner for Refugees, "Fact Sheet: Southeast Asia," II, no. 1 (April, 1988), 3; "Indochinese Refugee Activity," *Refugee Reports*, IX (December 16, 1988), 6–7.

sympathies among the refugee groups, especially the hill tribes. For example, the large, well-established Hmong camp at Ban Vinai did not seem to worry Thai officials, even though the Hmong until recently have not been interested in resettlement abroad. Abdul Hadi Derani wrote that in 1979 and 1980, as a goodwill gesture to relieve the refugee burden in Thailand, China took over 2,500 hill tribe refugees at a time when China was strapped with nearly a quarter of a million refugees of its own from Vietnam. Critics speculate that the refugees were to be trained to infiltrate Laos.[35]

Astri Suhrke reported in 1980 that the hill tribe and lowland Lao camps in Thailand aid resistance activities inside Laos by "providing free facilities, including medical services, and the Lao can move relatively freely in and out of the camp." American Friends Service Committee co–field director Ruth Cadwallader explained the phenomenon of "camp widows," prevalent in some Lao camps. Resistance members leave their wives and children in the camps, where they are protected, and return to visit periodically, between forays into Laos. An estimated 50,000 refugees from Laos live outside the camps among relatives and friends, because the government of Thailand turns a blind eye toward them. Refugee workers in northeast Thailand spoke of a devotedly anticommunist Catholic priest who cared for a small group of male Lao refugees outside the camp and near the Mekong River border. It was the consensus that these refugees were resistance fighters. It is not clear whether these groups act with any official government sanction, though refugee workers believed they have at least tacit local government approval. Their activities may also reflect the semiautonomy of the local regions far from central Thai control.[36]

These resistance activities have not been successful in undermining the government of Laos, yet they do seem to have exacerbated Lao-Thai tensions and to have heightened concern over the control of borders. For example, in June, 1986, Pathet Lao troops allegedly attacked an encampment of refugees from Laos six miles inside Thailand, killing 35 refugees and wounding several others. It remained unclear if "the Lao were resistance fighters, and their families, Lao army deserters, or some other group." Particularly vulnerable are the

35. Derani, "Refugees from Indochina," 178.

36. Suhrke, *Indochinese Refugees: The Impact;* interview with Ruth Cadwallader, Co–Field Director, American Friends Service Committee, Bangkok, March 20, 1984.

hill tribe Hmong, who were associated with the CIA's secret war in Laos. In December, 1986, Vietnamese soldiers attacked a group of Hmong fleeing to Thailand, killing 43 at the Mekong River. In February, 1987, a large group of over 500 hill tribe Hmong and Khmu were attacked by Pathet Lao troops as they attempted to cross into Thailand. Most made it to Nan Province, but 19 were killed.[37]

Although Thai concern about communist infiltration by refugees from Laos may be less than its concern about refugees from Vietnam, some worry does exist. For example, in April, 1986, the Thai Supreme Command reported it had received information that Laos was preparing to send 150 Buddhist monks to Thailand's border provinces as spies. Thai officials in Washington, D.C., connected the recent activity of communist insurgency groups in northeast Thailand with refugees from Laos. "Thailand has to be careful about people moving across the border into her territory," they warned. The Thai military also suspects that a group of Thai insurgents, Pak Mai, receive sanctuary in Laos. Border clashes continued during 1988.[38]

Refugees from Laos exacerbate issues of border control and security for Thailand but cause concern in other areas as well. Thailand has viewed the seemingly unending stream of asylum seekers, the Indochinese refugees "least noticed" by the international community, as a group of draft dodgers and economic migrants. The resettlement countries, including the United States, thus see these people as lacking a strong claim to refugee status. Officials originally thought humane deterrence camps, instituted for lowland Lao refugees in January, 1981, and for hill tribe Lao in March, 1983, would diminish the magnet effect for asylum seekers and alleviate many problems. However, deliberately poor camp conditions, made worse over time by camp closings and consolidations, have brought overcrowding, crime, including drug use, and high fertility rates, which not only have been extremely detrimental to the refugees but have fueled Thai public resentment as well.[39]

37. "Laos Chronology," *Indochina Chronology,* V (April–June, 1986), 12; *Refugee Reports,* VII (July 11, 1986), 10; Virginia Hamilton (ed.), *World Refugee Survey: 1986,* 53; *Refugee Reports,* VIII (February 20, 1987), 8.
38. "Laos Chronology," 11; Cerquone, *Refugees from Laos,* 12; Washington *Post,* March 22, 1987, p. 21; New York *Times,* January 7, 1988, p. 13.
39. Cerquone, *Refugees from Laos,* 1–2, 13–15.

The exodus from Laos is considered to have been influenced by a combination of push and pull factors. In 1984, liberal American resettlement admissions may have contributed to an increase in arrivals in Thailand. However, new taxes and military drafting in Laos were also cited as reasons for the increase. Refugee admissions to the United States in 1986 brought the warning that "once the U.S. finishes processing this group," the rate would decline. This incident is an example of how the lack of clear, predictable, and long-range resettlement admissions figures and policies makes the resettlement solution perplexing for both the refugees and Thailand. In 1987, severe drought in Laos, speculation that the Hmong had abandoned the resistance idea, and possibly the prospect of high American admissions rates for resettlement may have influenced the arrival rate.[40]

In mid-1985 Thailand, with UNHCR assistance, implemented a screening program to separate refugees from economic migrants and other adventurers. By the end of 1987, over 2,400 asylum seekers had been screened out. But this process has created another problem, for the screened-out numbers of Laotians are building. Since 1980, only 3,100 refugees from Laos have been voluntarily repatriated successfully. In 1987, only 200 returned to Laos. By late 1987, nine Laotians became the first of those screened out to return to Laos. A second problem associated with the screening program is the case of Hmong and other hill tribe people who enter Thailand secretly. Labeled illegal immigrants, they are then ineligible to enter the screening process, according to Thai authorities.[41]

Other deterrents to asylum in Thailand include *refoulement* and pushbacks, which prevent refugees from reaching the screening process. Incidents of this kind of deterrence increased in 1986 and 1987. On March 15, 1987, Thai authorities sent 38 Hmong tribesmen back to Laos. According to a U.S. State Department spokesman, the Hmong were in danger, "turned over to Lao officials who came in boats to the Thai side of the Mekong River to get them." Two days later, 97 Hmong were arrested as illegal immigrants and sent back to Laos. On March 30, 1987, a similar incident involved 20 Hmong attempting to enter Ban Vinai Camp. Yet another incident, this time involving 34 Hmong, oc-

40. "Little Known Ethnic Lao Refugees Resettle," 1; New York *Times*, December 27, 1987, p. 20.
41. Virginia Hamilton (ed.), *World Refugee Survey: 1987*, 47, 50, 53.

curred in November, 1987. In testimony before a congressional sub-committee, Roger Winter remarked on the scope of the problem: "In 1986, UNHCR documented 362 cases of pushbacks. The real number is undoubtedly higher." These incidents continued in 1988, with 200 Hmong reportedly pushed back in July.[42]

The increases in pushbacks and in involuntary repatriation reflect Thai impatience with the refugee problem and the problematic connection between refugee arrivals and border control. Such incidents also reflect Thailand's perception that resettlement is both an inadequate solution, dependent on third-country generosity, which is never sufficient, and a pull factor that only exacerbates the problem. Voluntary repatriation, desirable in theory, has not proven to be a viable option. Humane deterrence, though somewhat successful, creates problems in the camps and raises serious human rights issues. Abusive measures, such as pushbacks, in part may be calculated to bring to the attention of the international community the fact that the root causes of the exodus from Laos remain to be addressed.

Why are the Hmong especially targeted for these measures of late? A partial explanation may be that this group constitutes the largest refugee group from Laos and the one that has stayed the longest in Thailand. The Thai may be saying that because of their special ties to the United States, the Hmong are a special American responsibility. One reporter wrote, "The Thai are tired of pressure from the United States to provide sanctuary for these step-children of the U.S. War." Analysts speculate that Thailand's new tough response to resistance fighters, specifically the Hmong, may even be an attempt to improve Thai relations with Laos. Or the Thai may be pressuring the Hmong to remain in Laos, where they would be more inclined to fight the Vietnamese-backed government.[43]

As of late 1988, there were 19,004 lowland and 58,314 hill tribe Laotian refugees in Thai camps. For the nearly 400,000 refugees who have fled from Laos, Thailand has been the sole country of first asylum. Despite deterrence measures, 7,279 refugees from Laos arrived in

42. Washington *Post*, March 22, 1987, p. 21; *Refugee Reports*, VIII (April 17, 1987), 5; Virginia Hamilton (ed.), *World Refugee Survey: 1987*, 47; "House Subcommittee on Asian Affairs Holds Hearings on Refugees in Thailand," *Refugee Reports*, VIII (March 20, 1987), 10–11; *Refugee Reports*, IX (November 11, 1988), 8.
43. Washington *Times*, May 8, 1987, p. 9.

Thailand during fiscal year 1986, followed by 9,018 in 1987 and 19,251 during 1988.[44]

Just as Vietnamese and Laotian refugees are caught up in issues that compromise humanitarian concern, so too are those displaced from Cambodia. One refugee observer frankly noted that the "Vietnamese and Thais will fight to the last Cambodian," a comment unfortunately appropriate to the situation affecting more than a quarter of a million Cambodian refugees.

The present conflict has historical roots in centuries of border hostilities between Cambodia and Thailand. The ethnic animosity between them is evidenced by the following Thai attitude: "The Khmers are like snakes. If you put out your hand to feed them they bite you."[45] Such cultural antipathies compound the larger issues of Thai-Vietnamese hostility, especially the Vietnamese occupation of Cambodia, the related intrusions into Thailand in pursuit of resistance elements, and, of course, the Cambodian refugees.

Although Thailand expressed concern about the internal security threat posed by fleeing communist Khmer Rouge who were given sanctuary after the Vietnamese invasion of Cambodia in late 1978, this fear was seemingly overshadowed by foreign policy interests involving Vietnamese aggression. According to international relations specialist Nguyen Manh Hung, it is in the political interests of several nations not to resettle Cambodian refugees abroad. In Washington, D.C., Thai embassy official Mr. Sakthit noted that Thailand did not want an empty Cambodia, which would facilitate the continued Vietnamese occupation of Cambodia and future movement toward Thailand. The magnet effect of asylum for Cambodians in Thailand and of resettlement abroad would serve the interests of Vietnam by burdening Thailand with refugees and lessening the buffer effect between Vietnam and Thailand.[46]

This reasoning explains Thai reluctance to allow unlimited numbers of Cambodian refugees to enter UNHCR holding centers in 1979 and 1980. After February, 1980, by which time nearly 165,000 displaced

44. "Indochinese Refugee Activity," *Refugee Reports*, IX (December 16, 1988), 6–7, VIII (December 18, 1987), 8, and VII (October 10, 1986), 16.
45. Virginia Hamilton (ed.), *Cambodians in Thailand*, 2.
46. Interviews with Nguyen Manh Hung and with Mr. Sakthit, Minister-Counsellor, Embassy of Thailand, Washington, D.C., January 25, 1984.

Cambodians had been given asylum, legal entry into Thailand ceased, with an understanding given to the refugees that those who had entered would be resettled or eventually returned to the border. The issue of Cambodians clandestinely moving from the border area to the holding centers has been a security concern for Thailand from the beginning. As many as half a million Cambodians received international relief supplies at the border at the height of the crisis, in 1979 and 1980, with the flight of the Khmer Rouge and civilian populations, the Vietnamese invasion and occupation, and impending famine conditions. Although many returned to Cambodia, thousands remained at the border, where today they number 300,000.

Thailand agreed to allow the Khmer Rouge resistance forces to remain among the refugee population at the border for several reasons. The Khmer Rouge had decided to fight in Cambodia and not to flee inside Thailand, so they would not be a disruptive force. Also, ASEAN supported Thailand after the Vietnamese invasion of Cambodia, and other assurances of support from China were forthcoming. In effect, Thailand allowed the use of its border region by the resistance in exchange for protection and support from the United States, China, and ASEAN.[47]

This arrangement changed notably as a result of the attacks in 1984 and 1985 on the border camps by Vietnamese troops. These camps, strung along the ill-defined Thai-Cambodian border were controlled by the three resistance factions of the CGDK, including the Khmer Rouge. The attacks caused the evacuation of the displaced Cambodians a few kilometers inside Thailand, which has brought a new dilemma for Thailand. Now it has a huge refugee population and supports a resistance movement that includes remnants of the Pol Pot regime clearly inside its territory, no longer on some ambiguously drawn border. "The Cambodians who rushed to fill the evacuation sites . . . across the border inside Thailand were not escaping the war but bringing it along with them."[48]

The refugees near the border are also the source of recruits for the three-factioned CGDK, recognized by the UN as the legitimate representative of Cambodia. According to UNHCR official, "bodies give

47. Garver, "Reagan Administration's Southeast Asian Policy," 109.
48. Paribatra, "Can ASEAN Break the Stalemate?," 10; Virginia Hamilton (ed.), *Cambodians in Thailand*, 16.

credibility to the coalition." Justus van der Kroef wrote that the camps provide manpower and supplies and operational bases for the resistance. The value of the Cambodian refugees to the larger political context was evidenced when resistance forces at the border discouraged refugees from moving to the holding centers inside Thailand in 1979 and early 1980. Martin Barber, director of the British Refugee Relief Council and former UNHCR official in Thailand, reported that the resistance forces wanted the refugees to remain at the border to fight the Vietnamese. Another source spoke of members of the resistance forces coming to the holding centers to force refugees back to the border with possible Thai complicity. One such persuasion technique was the following reminder:

> Those who go back first will sleep in hammocks.
> Those who go back second will sleep on mats.
> Those who go back third will sleep in the mud.
> And those who return last will sleep under the ground.[49]

Refugee workers at Khao-I-Dang Holding Center for Cambodians spoke in March, 1984, of refugees from the border who would sneak into the camp at night to escape harsh and violent conditions at the border. Unregistered, they were ineligible for food rations and other services. The problem of illegal entrants plagued Thai authorities, and their surprise purges to remedy the problem instilled fear among the entire camp population. As late as March 4, 1987, Thai authorities in pursuit of illegal residents found "a network of crudely designed subterranean hideaways throughout the camp." Human rights observers have issued strong criticisms of these abuses, including a well-publicized report in 1986 by the Lawyers Committee for Human Rights.[50]

Most noticeable in a camp like Khao-I-Dang were large numbers of young refugees who had limbs missing, victims of mines they had encountered in the border area. Van der Kroef reported the existence of a "landmined and bamboo-studded trench" built by the Vietnamese;

49. Anonymous interview, Bangkok, March 13, 1984; van der Kroef, "Kampuchea: Southeast Asia's Flashpoint," 64; Martin Barber, "Trapped: Cambodians on the Border with Thailand," *Exile: Newsletter of the British Refugee Council*, III (May-June, 1983), 4–5; Kosol Vongsrisart (ed.), *The Indochinese Refugees, Thailand*, Federation of Asian Bishops' Conference (Bangkok, 1980), 96.

50. Virginia Hamilton (ed.), *Cambodians in Thailand*, 17–18; *Refugee Reports*, VIII (March 20, 1987), 5, and (February 20, 1987), 7.

dubbed "Vietnam's Berlin Wall," it was an attempt to seal off the border camp region and thus prevent refugees from both entering and leaving Cambodia. By May, 1983, it was reportedly already twenty-five kilometers long. After their large-scale attacks on the border camps in 1985, the Vietnamese continued this effort by building "a defense perimeter of free-fire zones, anti-tank and personnel traps and ditches, and permanent installations" to prevent reoccupation of the area by resistance forces.[51]

In an interview in March, 1984, Colonel Sanan Kajornklam of the Thai Supreme Command said that very soon those Cambodian refugees in Thailand not resettled would be transferred to the border area and the Khao-I-Dang Holding Center for Cambodians would be closed down. Colonel Sanan estimated that 25,000 Cambodians "would be joining their countrymen" at the border within a year.[52] In December, 1986, Thailand announced the phasing out of Khao-I-Dang and began transferring residents to the evacuation sites near the border. This action closed an important safe haven and symbol of hope for the Cambodian refugees, thus restricting their fate to the dangerous border region.

Singapore's ambassador Mahbubani noted that though life at the border is precarious, with little chance of moving into Thailand, "a Kampuchean refugee joining the Khmer Rouge is assured of clothes, shoes, a bowl of rice, rifle, and ammunition," perhaps far more than what he would receive in Cambodia.[53] However, refugees at the border are caught, hostage to the larger political dilemma over which they have no control. Not allowed to enter Thailand, they are tainted by association with the resistance and stand small chance of being allowed to return home without recriminations, including prison and death.

The thorny dilemma posed to refugee relief agencies and governments who attempt to assist Cambodian border refugees but who unintentionally also aid the resistance forces in their midst is chronicled by Mason and Brown and by Shawcross. American and other

51. Van der Kroef, "Kampuchea: Southeast Asia's Flashpoint," 64; Virginia Hamilton (ed.), *Cambodians in Thailand*, 15.
52. Interview with Colonel Sanan Kajornklam, Joint Operations Center, Supreme Command, Bangkok, March 14, 1984.
53. Mahbubani, "Kampuchean Problem," 414.

humanitarian aid to the border areas has been implicated in this issue; however, such aid to the resistance may in fact be intentional. According to Dick Clark, former ambassador for refugee affairs, "it appears that America, like China, is satisfied to bleed Vietnam into eventual submission by supporting a coalition that includes Pol Pot."[54]

By 1985, in the national interests of Thailand and the United States, direct American military assistance to Thailand reached almost $100 million, or three times the level of aid before the Vietnamese invasion of Cambodia. However, the United States seemed reluctant openly to increase its level of participation in the Cambodian deadlock specifically. Some modest funding was apparently forthcoming from the Carter administration for nonmilitary use by the noncommunist resistance groups. After meetings between President Reagan and Prince Sihanouk in September, 1984, American nonlethal aid to the noncommunist resistance doubled and is believed to have been between $6 million and $7 million. Journalist Paul Quinn-Judge reported that though U.S. aid is designated for nonlethal purposes, "few restrictions are put on the use of the aid." Since 1982, the CIA reportedly has funded these same groups, its contributions reaching $5 million by 1985. In 1988, a scandal erupted over the aid, with allegations that corrupt Thai military officers had skimmed over $3 million from the Reagan administration's $12 million aid program to the noncommunist resistance.[55]

Pressured by ASEAN but reluctant to become involved in "another Vietnam," according to Nayan Chanda, the United States has been provided by inventive bureaucratic terminology with a way to increase American financial assistance to Thailand in general and to the resistance specifically. The new term is "fungible," and fungible aid can refer to any commodity used to replace another, according to Chanda. He explains the process: "Money earmarked for humanitarian assistance, for example, is handed over to ASEAN countries who use an equivalent amount from their budgets to buy weapons and ammunition for the resistance." American humanitarian aid channeled through the UN and the International Red Cross increased from $9.5 million in 1983 to $14 million for 1984. Chanda reported that $5 million

54. New York *Times*, February 16, 1984, p. 27.
55. New York *Times*, October 12, 1984, p. 11; *Christian Science Monitor*, October 12, 1984, p. 13; Washington *Post*, July 8, 1985, p. 18, November 5, 1988, p. 15.

in American aid to Thailand to support Thai villagers affected by the turmoil along the border and experiencing the impact of refugees is "another fungible fund" meant for use by the resistance.[56]

In 1985, humanitarian aid from the United States was over $15 million. In addition to humanitarian aid, since 1985 Congress has annually appropriated over $3 million specifically for nonlethal use by the noncommunist resistance forces. Covert aid each year is thought to be "several times as much."[57]

According to Nguyen Manh Hung, Thailand and other countries have a practical interest in keeping the refugee issue alive at the border in that it serves to bring international attention to the resistance effort. The refugees give legitimacy to the "paper tiger" resistance. Van der Kroef concurred, pointing to the efforts of the United States, China, Thailand, and the rest of ASEAN to internationalize the Cambodian problem—efforts that often highlight the plight of the refugees. John Garver thought there must be some kind of mutual agreement that China would support the resistance militarily, especially the Khmer Rouge faction of the coalition, whereas the United States would give humanitarian aid to the refugees that would also benefit the resistance.[58]

With the phasing out of the last holding center inside Thailand, all Cambodians were to be moved to border evacuation sites. Conditions in these camps, politically administered by factions of the CGDK in cooperation with Thai military authorities, continue to raise serious concerns about the safety and well-being of the displaced Cambodians. According to one report, "Once refugees enter these political camps, their chances of going anywhere else, except into Cambodia to fight the Vietnamese Army—dwindle close to zero." Site 2, with a population of nearly 175,000 is run by the noncommunist KPNLF. Site B, also called Green Hill, with 42,000 inhabitants, is administered by the Sihanouk-led group. Site 8, with 30,000 people, is run by the Khmer Rouge. Smaller camps are located elsewhere in the vicinity.[59]

56. Nayan Chanda, "CIA No, U.S. Aid Yes," *Far Eastern Economic Review,* August 16, 1984, pp. 16–18; Washington *Post,* September 17, 1984, p. 23.

57. Washington *Post,* July 8, 1985, p. 18; U.S. Department of State, *World Refugee Report,* 30; Library of Congress, *Vietnam-U.S. Relations,* 11–12, and *Cambodian Crisis,* 8.

58. Interview with Nguyen Manh Hung; van der Kroef, "Kampuchea: Diplomatic Gambits," 155; Garver, "Reagan Administration's Southeast Asian Policy," 113.

59. *Wall Street Journal,* February 23, 1987, p. 25.

The refugees are difficult to protect, especially at night after relief workers leave. At Site 8, Vietnamese shelling killed 11 civilians on May 8, 1986. There was, however, a rumor that the shelling may have been the result of "factional fighting within the camp itself." A year earlier, violence had erupted at this same camp, presumably when Khmer Rouge soldiers had forced as many as 200 civilians to leave the camp for military service. Some of these may have been rounded up "to warn backsliders"—those who had lost their zeal for the Khmer Rouge struggle by showing signs of more interest in the other, noncommunist resistance groups. Conditions are even worse in the smaller camps closer to the border, which are also run by the Khmer Rouge and where another 30,000 refugees are totally "unreachable" by international relief agencies. Reports indicated that by 1988, thousands of refugees had been moved to points closer to the border and to sites inside Cambodia as part of Khmer Rouge strategy in preparation for a return to Cambodia once the Vietnamese withdraw. One such encampment, made up of more than 6,000 civilian refugees forced to leave the Ta Luan Camp near the southeastern Thai-Cambodian border, was shelled by Vietnamese artillery. Hundreds were reported killed and wounded, but the Khmer Rouge would not allow survivors to receive outside medical assistance.[60]

Reported abuses at the evacuation border camps have prompted calls for a UNHCR presence there. Conditions have also led observers to call for educational and other social programs, especially for the many children born in the camps, who comprise more than one-third of the displaced population. The border issue, already likened to the Palestinian situation, has generated efforts, in effect, to institutionalize the camps for humanitarian reasons. Thailand, on the other hand, has sought to limit such activities. With the closing of Khao-I-Dang, Secretary General Prasong Soonsiri warned, "There will be no new UNHCR camps." Morale in the border camps is reportedly at a psychological breaking point, with social problems—including crime, domestic violence, depression and alcoholism—on the rise. One refugee noted with despair, "The culture of the Cambodian people is breaking

60. "Thailand's Site 8 Shelled; 12 Killed, Scores Injured," *Refugee Reports*, VII (June 13, 1986), 7–8; Paul Quinn-Judge, "Knowing Thy Enemy," *Far Eastern Economic Review*, June 6, 1985, p. 6; Washington *Post*, November 25, 1988, pp. 1, 44, November 29, 1988, p. 19, January 20, 1989, p. 27; Hiebert, "Khmer Rouge Regroups," 34–35.

down." The refugees have long suffered the abuses of the infamous Task Force 80, the Thai military unit charged with security at the camps. In 1988, Task Force 80 was finally replaced by the Displaced Persons Protection Unit (DPPU), which has "taken on more of a social welfare role in the camps, winning praise from camp administrators, relief workers and refugees alike."[61]

Nearly a decade after these Cambodians fled, they are still being victimized by interests that compromise human rights. The Cambodians reportedly would like to return to their homeland. According to the deterrence principle, they are ineligible for resettlement, and camp conditions remain poor and dangerous, discouraging new asylum seekers. Wedged into a no man's land, the civilian population continues to figure in the resistance to the Vietnamese occupation of Cambodia according to the interests of the groups that control the camp and the foreign policy and security interests of Thailand and other nations. The displaced Cambodians attract aid that benefits the resistance elements as well, and they offer fresh military recruits, if involuntarily. A congressional report summarized the situation: "The present strategy of Thailand towards the Khmer is to keep them along the border. . . . For now, they appear satisfied that this human barrier is in their national interest as a buffer to Vietnamese forces inside Kampuchea, who are fighting Khmer guerillas who are mixed in and supported by the border population."[62] The situation for the displaced Cambodians remains particularly tenuous as the deadlock over the Cambodian issue appears to be changing with the announced withdrawal of Vietnamese troops by late 1989. For the refugees, anxiety about the future heightens as diplomatic activity regarding Cambodia increases. At this point, no clear negotiating plans that would safeguard the displaced Cambodians' future are evident.

There are a number of other issues related to the problem of refugees in Thailand. Thai officials cite, in particular, adverse political and economic effects from the Indochina refugees. Ministry of Interior official Mr. Thani mentioned a backlash, or a threat to government credibility, as local populations grow more resentful of government in-

61. *Washington Post,* March 3, 1987, p. 18; "House Subcommittee on Asian Affairs," 10; New York *Times,* December 30, 1986, p. 6; Washington *Post,* November 21, 1988, pp. 1, 20, November 28, 1988, p. 11.
62. Senate Judiciary Committee, *U.S. Refugee Program: 1985,* 35.

volvement in refugee assistance at the expense of attention to indigenous needs. Thani underlined the fact that Thailand is obligated to take care of its own people first. Secretary General Prasong echoed these ideas: "Thailand is a developing small country with scarce resources and confronted by many pressing problems and internal needs. . . . Taking care of its own citizens is the first priority of any government."[63]

Refugee camps and centers are often located in the rural border areas, where the local standard of living is low. Thai villagers there perceive a marked contrast between their own lives and the lives of the refugees, who receive free food and services in the camps. A UNHCR field officer noted also that the death rate for Thais is higher than it is for camp residents. At the other end of the spectrum, Thailand is also sensitive to high birth rates among the refugees. As early as 1978, this matter was broached by the vice-governor of Nong Khai during the visit of a U.S. congressional delegation. In March, 1984, refugee workers spoke of the use of a highly controversial birth control drug considered medically unsafe yet administered to refugee women in Thailand. The birth rate among the Hmong refugees is 5.9 percent; at the Cambodian border camps, the birth rate is estimated to be about 5 percent, or "twice the Thai rate."[64]

Awareness of the disparities between refugee and villager can be found in many quarters. The report of a Thai Catholic refugee program described the plight of the villagers in this way: "Many of their own people are living in conditions that make a refugee camp seem like a holiday resort to local villagers." The differences are noted from another Thai perspective in this way: "Millions of dollars have been spent to help the refugees. The money should have been spent to develop the poverty stricken areas in this developing country whose own people also need help." A Thai social worker said her father questioned her work among the refugees. He thought she should be helping her own people. UNHCR guidelines in Thailand reflect sensitivity to this issue: "The level of care provided to illegal aliens must not exceed that provided to Thai citizens in the same area."[65]

63. Interview with Mr. Thani; Thailand, "Statement by Prasong Soonsiri," 10.
64. Interview with Joan Edwards, Field Officer, UNHCR, Phanat Nikhom Holding and Transit Center, Thailand, March 23, 1984; House Judiciary Committee, *Indochinese Refugees: An Update,* 12; U.S. Senate, Committee on the Judiciary, *U.S. Refugee Program: 1985,* 13; *Wall Street Journal,* February 23, 1987, p. 25.
65. Kosol Vongsrisart (ed.), *Indochinese Refugees, Thailand,* 27; "Refugees: A Problem

Land for cultivation, and sometimes even water, is scarce in areas where refugee camps are located. Deforestation, a problem in Thailand, is believed to have been aggravated by the refugees. Officials say that Cambodian refugees, in their search for firewood, altered local ecology in the border regions, where deforestation has affected the ability of the soil to hold water. In the northeast, hill tribe refugees accustomed to slash-and-burn agriculture are a problem at a time when Thailand is seeking to curtail this farming method among its own hill tribes. Some refugee camps are located in national forestry zones that are off limits to Thai villagers, causing discontent among the villagers.[66]

Local economies have been disrupted as inflation and short supplies have adversely affected local Thai consumers. For example, prices in the border town of Aranyaprathet doubled as a result of the large Cambodian refugee population nearby. The refugee problem also seems to have invited corruption and graft by politicians and merchants. In early 1987, a U.S. State Department spokesman reported the possible "institution of open markets to deter criminal black market activities" at the Cambodian border camps. Today, legalized markets inside the camps are said to have reduced the black market economy considerably.[67]

Thailand's concern for an estimated 200,000 villagers, including 80,000 displaced, all of whom have been adversely affected by the refugee influx either along the Thai-Cambodian border or near the Lao border, led to its adoption of a special program in 1980. With international support of $80 million, 117 villages near the Cambodian border and 133 villages in the northeast near Laos were the recipients of a project that included, in addition to emergency relocation services, development focused on agriculture, water sources, education, community growth, public health, and road construction. By 1986, the Affected Thai Program had grown to assisting 170 villages near the Cambodian border and 242 villages near the border with Laos. In the period

Yet To Be Solved," *Focus on Thailand*, VIII (October, 1982), 1–2; U.S. Department of State, *World Refugee Report*, 26.

66. Suhrke, *Indochinese Refugees: The Impact*, 15, 18; Kosol Vongsrisart (ed.), *Indochinese Refugees, Thailand*, 57; U.S. Senate, Committee on the Judiciary, *Refugee Problems in Southeast Asia: 1981*, 97th Cong., 2nd Sess., No. 88-643-0, p. 26.

67. Suhrke, *Indochinese Refugees: The Impact*, 15; Derani, "Refugees from Indochina," 136–37; "House Subcommittee on Asian Affairs," 10; Washington *Post*, November 28, 1988, p. 11.

1980–1986, the United States contributed $32 million, with additional donations coming from Germany, Japan, Canada, and UN agencies.[68]

As the emergency situation was winding down after 1982, voluntary organizations associated with refugee relief became increasingly sensitive to and were reminded of the needs of local populations and began to provide programs and services. In 1983, the Committee for the Coordination of Services to Displaced Persons in Thailand (CCSDPT) noted the wide range of relief projects, water, health, and sanitation programs, skills-training programs, and agricultural and community development projects then already underway for the Thai people by voluntary agencies.[69]

Thai officials report that their country is burdened with the costs of land, facilities, administration, and security for the refugees, which have not been reimbursed. In addition, personnel are assigned to refugee matters at the expense of other programs, including the military. In fiscal year 1983, Thailand spent an estimated $6.5 million on the refugee program. During the same year, outside assistance from the UNHCR, the World Food Program (WFP), UNBRO, the International Committee of the Red Cross, and private voluntary organizations came to about $72 million in Thailand. In addition, nations made significant bilateral contributions. In 1985, outside contributions again totaled over $72 million.[70]

There are indications that the refugee problem's adverse effects are offset somewhat by benefits, though these are minimal and difficult to substantiate. According to a U.S. refugee report, UNBRO represents a "net foreign exchange gain for Thailand," and "the impact of refugee camps in other parts of the country does not affect the economy one way or another."[71] This report seems to refer to the national economy, not to local economic impact.

Refugee workers, at one time representing over sixty voluntary

68. Thailand, Joint Operations Center, Supreme Command, "Indochinese Displaced Persons" (Typescript, Bangkok, June, 1983), 12, 18; U.S. Department of State, *Country Reports*, 49; U.S. Department of State, *World Refugee Report*, 30.

69. Committee for the Coordination of Services to Displaced Persons in Thailand, *Perspectives: The CCSDPT Monthly Newsletter* (February, 1986), 4.

70. U.S. Department of State, *World Refugee Report*, 26; U.S. Department of State, *Country Reports*, 48.

71. U.S. Department of State, *Country Reports*, 48.

agencies who bought locally, are seen as a plus for local economies. One refugee agency director felt certain that Thailand regularly makes a profit by siphoning off UNHCR funds. In March, 1984, refugee workers spoke of a stand-off between the UNHCR and government-approved food contractors, who allegedly inflated prices to as much as twice the normal price for the food that was purchased for Phanat Nikhom Holding and Transit Center. Another group of refugee personnel noted that when the influx began, provincial governors lobbied the central government in order to have refugee camps located in their districts because of anticipated profits. Another refugee field worker claimed that the refugee camps helped to create a false economy, which would then quickly collapse when the camps closed.

One refugee worker believed that Thailand makes the refugee issue into a scapegoat in order to cover up the government's own failure to meet the needs of the rural poor with adequate social and economic policies and programs. Others share these criticisms of Thailand's responses to the refugees. An American refugee official said the Thais' complaints about the refugees are for public consumption; they thereby give the impression that the government is doing something about the refugee problem. Another American official remarked that Thailand's forced repatriation attempts "are popular with the Thai public," even though they cause an international outcry. Along these lines, another American official noted that Thailand complains even though the problem is only a fraction of what it was.[72]

The refugee issue presents the horns of a dilemma. On the one hand, Thailand has responded to humanitarian concerns for the refugees and out of necessity has been dependent on third-country resettlement. A UNHCR officer noted that without the United States, "the Thais would never have gotten rid of the refugees."[73] On the other hand, Thailand would like to manage its own affairs without outside interference. The refugee crisis induced large-scale involvement by outside governments, international organizations, and over sixty voluntary relief agencies. The overwhelming emergency refugee situation in 1979, especially the Cambodian refugees who came to the border,

72. Anonymous interviews, Thailand, March 13–22, 1984; Suhrke, *Indochinese Refugees: The Impact*, 17.
73. Anonymous interview, Bangkok, March 14, 1984.

followed by increasing numbers from Vietnam and Laos, brought sorely needed and welcomed outside assistance, but it also carried with it interference that appears at times to conflict with and undermine local Thai control and to affect national pride.

In *The Quality of Mercy,* journalist William Shawcross details the major involvement of the United States in the refugee problem when the crisis was at its height in 1979 and 1980. He describes then ambassador to Thailand Morton Abramowitz as an aggressive refugee advocate who believed that America was responsible for what had happened in Cambodia, feared the extinction of the Cambodian people, was highly critical of both international relief organizations and the Thai government and who himself lobbied extensively for more generous resettlement by the United States. Abramowitz was supported in his efforts by a contingent of senior embassy officials who had a "compassionate commitment to the cause of Indochinese refugees." Shawcross writes that the ambassador "was constantly arguing with his own government for increased resettlement of refugees and was trying to bully both Thai and international officials into doing more and more." Abramowitz, who is credited with being one of the foremost champions of refugees, apparently did not endear himself to Thai authorities with remarks such as the following: "The Thais have contributed a generous share of the difficulties. Their indifference, preoccupation with the Vietnamese threat, callousness, and lack of attention to planning and detail create enormous problems for us all."

By contrast, the removal of Abramowitz and his replacement by Ambassador John Gunther Dean, who was appointed by the Reagan administration in 1981, installed a decidedly different approach to refugee affairs in the embassy. Dean announced he "would be ambassador to Thailand, not to refugees." Sources in Bangkok reported in 1984 that Dean was highly regarded in Thailand. Coming to Bangkok after the worst was over, he restored and improved relations between the United States and Thailand—relations that had been damaged somewhat by a focus on the human rights of refugees, with too little attention given to the impact of the exodus on Thailand.[74]

In a discussion of the refugee issue, specifically the crisis regarding Vietnamese boat people seeking asylum in Thailand in early 1988,

74. Shawcross, *Quality of Mercy,* 178–83, 411.

then-ambassador William H. Brown noted that humanitarian concerns such as refugees need to be considered within the broader context of U.S.-Thai relations. Referring to interests in the areas of security, narcotics trafficking, and trade, the ambassador indicated that "when difficulties arise in one sphere, the spill-over impact on other dimensions of our relationship is often instantaneous and sometimes severe."[75]

The end of the Abramowitz era also brought a serious curtailment in resettlement that was alarming to Thailand. By 1981, the INS was stringently screening refugees for admission to the United States, rejecting and deferring thousands. This change also influenced Thailand's adoption of humane deterrence policies. A UNHCR official said that "western nations turn a blind eye to deterrence" because such measures coincide with their own desires to limit resettlement. This lack of expressed concern about Thai deterrence policy was perhaps an uneasy decision by Washington to encourage at least some form of "continued refugee asylum" in Thailand.[76]

Several refugee workers remarked that the presence of many voluntary agencies in Thailand has presented a problem in several respects. Resentment by the Thai population as refugees receive goods and services denied them has been somewhat alleviated by international aid to local Thai villages. One refugee worker noted, however, that the "Thais want autonomy" in managing the refugee problem. Another said, "No one can tell the Thais how to run their government." Refugee personnel explained how recent camp closings and consolidations by the Ministry of the Interior were efforts by Thailand to increase its control of the refugee situation. A UNHCR field officer also remarked that in 1979 and 1980 too many voluntary agencies and workers may have been attempting to help. An American refugee official noted that voluntary agencies representing constituencies back home who wanted to help created a magnet effect in attracting refugees, which may have promoted, inadvertently, institutionalization of the problem. A refugee report indicated Thai sensitivity to Western tourists who come to gape condescendingly at this "Asian problem" of refugees. It also noted that the Thais resented refugee workers who

75. U.S. Department of State, *Indochinese Refugees and Relations with Thailand*, 1.
76. Interview with Rob Burrows; Cerquone, *Refugees from Laos*, 7.

did not understand Thai culture, the preponderance of Christian organizations in a Buddhist country, and the failure of voluntary organizations to employ many Thais in refugee relief work.[77]

Thailand has been notably sensitive to outside interference in the form of any criticism of its response to the refugee problem. This sensitivity is related to genuine concern in Thailand and elsewhere among the first asylum countries that they are caught between Indochina as the source of the exodus and Western humanitarianism. At its height, from 1978 until 1982, the pressure of the emergency gave publicity to the humanitarian aspects of the refugee problem at the expense of addressing root causes and the serious negative effects the influx was having in Thailand and elsewhere. To the point, Thailand in particular thinks the resettlement countries have not done their fair share to relieve the refugee burden in Thailand. This source of tension is particularly evident when the resettlement countries voice complaints about alleged abuses by Thailand, especially incidents related to piracy, pushbacks, and forced repatriation. Thailand feels unjustly maligned at these times, for it has already done much to assist refugees.

Secretary General Prasong has commented on the noticeable discrepancies between Western nations' humanitarian pronouncements and their actual practice regarding refugee resettlement. Recalling that Thailand agreed to offer asylum to refugees based on humanitarian principles, without selectivity, in exchange for resettlement commitments made by other nations, Prasong noted the "immigration principle" of the resettlement countries, whereby selective admissions criteria mean rejected refugees remain as Thailand's burden. He cited the "humanitarian principle" of freedom preached to refugees as a motivating factor that influences them to "risk their lives in fleeing their lands." In response to lower-than-expected resettlement rates, he warned, "We in Thailand cannot uphold the humanitarian rule much longer while the rest of the world has begun to lose faith in it."[78]

Another Thai official said that Thailand's refugee policy of humane deterrence was needed to discourage new asylum seekers and that it

77. Anonymous interviews, Thailand, March 13–22; Kosol Vongsrisart (ed.), *Indochinese Refugees, Thailand*, 58.
78. Thailand, "Statement by Prasong Soonsiri," 8–13.

ensured Thailand would take care of those already in the camps. Ministry of Interior official Thani remarked that refugees should be resettled according to when they arrived, with the earliest arrivals being the first resettled. He expressed concern that the ODP unfairly discriminates against refugees who have been in the camps for a long time, that long-term refugees in Thailand are passed over in favor of those the program has leave directly for resettlement from Hanoi. An American refugee official concurred that the ODP conflicted and competed with efforts to resettle those refugees who are in Thailand. For example, the projected quota of 50,000 refugees for resettlement in the United States requested for fiscal year 1985 by the Department of State earmarked 10,000 specifically for the ODP. Projected admissions to the United States for fiscal year 1988 were 32,000, including 8,500 for the ODP. For 1989, the projected refugee admissions ceiling was set at 46,500. Specifically, 19,500 places were allotted for the ODP and 27,000 to accommodate all admissions from Thailand and the other countries of first asylum. Although the figures for 1989 reflected an increase over the previous year, there were still over 108,000 refugees in Thailand at the end of 1988. Thus, the generous American support of the ODP seems to have come at the expense of efforts to lessen Thailand's refugee burden.[79]

In February, 1985, a complaint by Senator Mark Hatfield that Thailand was "forcibly turning back refugees from neighboring Laos," prompted an angry reply from Secretary General Prasong, who claimed that the Thai border forces had not fired, that in fact those attempting to cross were not real refugees. "He compared the turning back of 'illegal entrants' from Laos to the repatriation of Mexicans and Cubans by the United States." The secretary general reiterated Thailand's serious concern about the ongoing and growing problem with refugees from Laos, remarking that resettlement countries are accepting fewer refugees than before. Weary of the refugee burden, Thailand often threatens to repatriate, forcibly if necessary, those not accepted by other countries for permanent resettlement. William

79. Interview with Mr. Thani; anonymous interview; U.S. Department of State, *Proposed Refugee Admissions for 1985*, 3; U.S. Department of State, *Proposed Refugee Admissions for 1988*, 2; "Indochinese Refugee Activity," *Refugee Reports*, IX (December 16, 1988), 6; "Planned Adjustments to FY 89 Funded Regional Admissions Ceilings," *Refugee Reports*, X (January 27, 1989), 16.

Stubbs noted, by contrast, that the frequent forced repatriation of illegal entrants from China by the Hong Kong police goes unnoticed.[80]

Complaints by the United States about the forced repatriation of 38 Hmong refugees that took place on March 15, 1987, again exposed "deepseated Thai sensitivity to any western criticism of its handling of Indochinese refugees." Thailand called for the large-scale resettlement of Hmong by the United States "if the U.S. is so concerned with the human rights of 38 Hmong." In Washington, D.C., Thai ambassador Arsa Sarasin responded predictably to the interference: "[It is] uncalled for. . . . We resent it very much. . . . We don't want to be a client state."[81]

Reacting to Western criticism of the closing of Khao-I-Dang Holding Center, a Bangkok newspaper editorial in turn criticized the resettlement countries for not resettling the holding center's long-term residents. Many at Khao-I-Dang had been screened and rejected for resettlement in the United States. The editorial made its point succinctly: "Khao-I-Dang is not a gymnasium for idealistics to practice their nebulous virtue. The refugee question is one in which compassion and idealism should be translated into action."[82]

A refugee officer at the U.S. Embassy in Bangkok expressed the view that Thailand complains about the refugee problem in order to raise world consciousness about the problem. Another official noted that those governments "screaming loudest" get results. He recalled that in 1979 and 1980, refugee quota numbers were shifted from Hong Kong to Malaysia for precisely that reason. And the "managing down" of the refugee problem can be seen as a deliberate attempt by Thai authorities to take control. Perceptions of dwindling international burden sharing, the never-ending stream of refugees, the magnet effect of hospitable asylum, including possible resettlement, all continue to make the refugee issue a problem for Thailand.[83]

80. *Washington Post*, February 2, 1985, p. 26; interview with William Stubbs.
81. *Washington Post*, March 22, 1987, p. 21.
82. New York *Times*, February 22, 1987, p. 3.
83. Interviews with William Stubbs and with Carl Harris, Bureau for Refugee Programs, U.S. Department of State, Washington, D.C., February 3, 1984.

IV

Other First

Asylum Countries

Although Thailand has been the country of first asylum for many refugees from Indochina, other Southeast Asian nations, especially Malaysia, Indonesia, Singapore, and the Philippines, as well as Hong Kong, have shared the burden. In addition, refugee processing centers for all Indochinese groups en route to resettlement are located in the Philippines and, until recently, Indonesia. Refugees arriving in these countries are primarily Vietnamese boat people. This chapter discusses the responses of these important countries to the refugee issue, in light of their respective national interests.

Malaysia

A small country of 13,000,000 people, Malaysia has been the temporary refuge for more Vietnamese boat people than any other country has taken in; over 235,000 refugees have arrived at its shores. Malaysia took the lead among ASEAN nations in expressing the urgency of the refugee problem, prompted by dramatic increases in refugee arrivals in 1978 and 1979. An American refugee official in Malaysia at the time recalled how upset, scared, and unprepared the country was for the influx. The arrival of the *Hai Hong*, a freighter carrying over 2,500 refugees, in November, 1978, was considered a flashpoint influencing Malaysia's outspokenness, issuing in criticism not only of Vietnam for generating the problem but of resettlement countries for not doing their share and prompting a hard-line refugee policy. This policy refused refugee boats permission to land in Malaysia, and the Malaysian navy simply towed approaching boats out to sea. Since the July, 1979, Geneva conference, Malaysia has cooperated with humanitarian efforts to protect and care for refugees. It has permitted first asylum, with the understanding that resettlement countries would assume responsibility for moving the refugees out of Malaysia. Its position underlines the view that the refugee issue is not solely an ASEAN concern but an international problem requiring burden sharing. More to the point, since it was not involved in the Vietnam War, Malaysia believes it should not be burdened with what it sees as the aftereffects of war, namely, the refugees.[1]

The Malaysian response to the influx of refugees is clearly related to the national interests often articulated by the popular and foremost spokesman for refugee policy, Home Minister Mohammed Ghazali Shafie. The home minister has reminded the international community that the focus on humanitarian aspects of the refugee problem should not preclude attention to the legitimate national concerns of first asylum countries. The home minister has pointed out that his government's first responsibility is to the people of Malaysia, not to refugees.[2] Although foreign policy interests in the refugee issue are not as important for Malaysia as they are for Thailand, nonetheless, they combine with important security issues and political, economic, and cultural factors to influence Malaysian reactions to the problem.

Malaysia has had experience with refugees besides those arriving from Vietnam. About 2,500 refugees from Burma, 7,000 Cham from Cambodia, and, most recently, 70,000 to 200,000 Filipinos sent to the island of Sabah all appear to be integrating without major problems. In each of these cases, the refugees are Muslim, reflecting the state religion of Malaysia. On Sabah, the refugees are also welcomed laborers. The ongoing exodus from the Philippines is reportedly played down to defuse tension between the two ASEAN states. However, discord is more evident the longer the Filipinos remain on Sabah. The Christian-

1. "Indochinese Refugee Activity Since April 1975," *Refugee Reports*, IX (December 16, 1988), 7; Virginia Hamilton (ed.), *World Refugee Survey: 1986*, 53, and *World Refugee Survey: 1987*, 50; interview with Dan Sullivan, Director, Refugee Section, U.S. Embassy, Singapore, March 30, 1984; Derani, "Refugees from Indochina," 141–42, 152.
2. Wain, "Malaysia Fears Social Upheaval," 5.

dominated Sabah United party would like to see the refugees repatriated. Some Filipinos were implicated in the riots that occurred prior to the April, 1986, elections. By contrast, the refugees from Vietnam have been mostly ethnic Chinese posing more complex social, economic, and political problems, with the remedy of local integration out of the question. An estimated 60 to 70 percent of the boat refugees have been ethnic Chinese, though some indicate the number may be as high as 80 percent.[3]

In Malaysia, deep-seated ethnic animosities vis-à-vis the refugees color other issues as well. This is especially apparent in the area of security. The refugee problem comes under the authority of a special government agency called Task Force Seven (VII), whose numerals were unofficially referred to as an acronym for "Vietnamese Illegal Immigrants." According to Task Force Seven's deputy director Tuan Haji Mohammed Som, the refugees pose a serious security threat related to the larger context of Sino-Malaysian relations. Many refugees, including former soldiers, arrive armed, perhaps for their own protection, yet how can we tell "who among them are Vietcong?" queried the deputy director. What is more important, the problem of the largely ethnic Chinese communist insurgency in Malaysia since 1948, ethnic hostilities, the role of the Malaysian Communist party in the quest for independence, racial riots in 1969, and the popular perception that all the refugees are Chinese are all factors heightening the security problem. Although official relations between China and Malaysia are cordial, evidence of China's continued support of communist insurgents and its refusal to call off communist party-to-party relations increase the fear that some refugees are infiltrators. The discovery of Malaysian identity cards among refugees in 1979, later found to be local forgeries, only increased concern.[4]

Malaysia blames Vietnam as the source of the exodus, and according to Tuan Haji Mohammed Som, Vietnam is continuing to expel refugees deliberately. Yet wariness of China's designs for the region also colors Malaysia's reactions to the refugee problem. Abdul Hadi

3. Office of the UNHCR, "Fact Sheet," II, no. 1 (April, 1988); anonymous interview, Singapore, March 30, 1984; Wain, *The Refused*, 132; Derani, "Refugees from Indochina," 153.

4. Interview with Tuan Haji Mohammed Som, Deputy Director, National Task Force Seven, Kuala Lumpur, March 28, 1984; Derani, "Refugees from Indochina," 150.

Derani wrote that the flood of refugees exasperated Malaysia to the point that it impaired relations with Vietnam, to the benefit of China. Bad experiences with China in the past have not been forgotten, however, and may undermine a solid ASEAN unity regarding China and Vietnam.[5]

Malaysian diplomatic official Hamidah Yusoff indicated that this small and vulnerable country is threatened by both Vietnam and China but that the fear of China's intentions looms larger. Yusoff also mentioned Malaysia's concern about the increasingly closer relations between the United States and China that may be at ASEAN's expense. Ethnic Chinese refugees who were disloyal citizens in Vietnam are perceived as a potential fifth column in Malaysia. The careful censorship of mail and the interception of packages to refugees at the Sungei Besi Transit Center may be illustrations of sensitivity to security needs.[6]

Its close proximity to Vietnam means that Malaysia must find ways to coexist in harmony with this communist neighbor, especially when Vietnam is considered a buffer between China and Malaysia, for eventually a weak Vietnam may imply a strong China, which would be not at all in the interests of Malaysia. Along these same lines, deputy director Som indicated that it is in Malaysia's interest to maintain open communications with Vietnam.

This somewhat conciliatory attitude is evident in the suggestions Malaysians have given for dealing with the refugee issue. The deputy director pointed out that the refugee problem must be tackled at its source, specifically that Vietnam must improve economically and solve its problem of corruption in order to curb the flow of refugees. In his research, Derani indicated that the formation of the ODP between Vietnam and the United States came about because of a suggestion by Malaysia. However, with only the limited success of the ODP to stem the refugee tide and Vietnam's economic problems, the deputy director of Task Force Seven feared the exodus might increase, especially if Vietnam expelled any remaining Chinese. This certainly proved to be the case in 1987 and 1988, when the numbers of asylum seekers grew.[7]

5. Derani, "Refugees from Indochina," 187.
6. Interview with Hamidah Yusoff, Embassy of Malaysia, Washington, D.C., February 16, 1984.
7. Interview with Tuan Haji Mohammed Som; Derani, "Refugees from Indochina," 185.

In addition to the security problem posed by the refugees, their influx triggered a political reaction related to the careful racial composition of Malaysia, where the population is 45 percent Malay, 35 percent Chinese, 10 percent Indian, and 10 percent indigenous Sabah and Sarawak, with no one group commanding a majority. In March, 1984, the governmental ban on the discussion of racial issues and advance warnings to me from American refugee personnel that I needed to be careful in interviews about refugees were evidences of racial sensitivities. Also in March, 1984, there were radio broadcasts of a government policy to encourage population growth among the Malay minority, with the expressed objective of a Malay majority after five years, a curious goal for a developing country intent on improving economic and social conditions.[8]

As early as 1978, Secretary of the National Security Council of Malaysia Abdul Malek mentioned to a U.S. congressional delegation the government's anxiety over what might happen in race relations if the refugee exodus continued. The delegation wrote the following in its report: "There is a long history of ethnic tension in Malaysia between the Malays and the Chinese and there is concern that the ethnic Chinese refugee flow could upset the delicate racial/political balance currently existing between these two groups." Historically, the Chinese in Malaysia have represented economic wealth disproportionate to their numbers. A current national economic plan calls for Chinese divestiture and increased Malay representation in the nation's corporate wealth. In 1978 and 1979, the refugees, who arrived along the eastern coast of Malaysia—the "heartland of Malay conservatism"—in the poor and underdeveloped provinces of Kelantan, Trengganu, and Pahang, enflamed existing racial tensions, with political repercussions. Perceived to be interfering with social and economic policies and development programs for Malaysian citizens, the refugees brought public resentment, unwelcome to the government. The segregation of arriving refugees from the local population by situating them on the barren island of Pulau Bidong still brought allegations that the refugees were living better than local Malaysians. Even today there is resentment because refugees are thought to receive better medical treatment than Malaysian citizens get. In 1978, National Security Council secretary Malek said that "we must be able to tell them (the local villagers)

8. Terry George (ed.), *The On-Your-Own Guide to Asia* (Stanford, 1983), 199.

that substantial numbers of Vietnamese refugees are departing for overseas resettlement."[9]

The diversion of government funds from local citizens for refugees has also been a political liability. Derani reported that refugee boats scuttled offshore by refugees who had then been rescued instead of having been denied entry posed a danger to local shipping. The taxpayers resented the expensive government salvaging operation that had to be mounted in order to clear the boats. The growth of a black market, local inflation, and finally centralized purchasing of relief supplies mostly from Chinese merchants in western Malaysia have been additional political hindrances. In Trengganu today, political issues include concerns about how much longer the island of Bidong will be used for refugees and how citizens who own sections of the island that have been damaged by refugees can get compensation.[10]

When the influx increased in 1978 and 1979, Malaysia responded with a hard-line policy, including push-offs and a purported threat to shoot refugees on sight. Political analyst Suhrke noted that although this harsh response was soon reversed, the original policy was a response to political challengers' criticisms about the government's ineffectiveness in dealing with the refugee problem. She described the inherent conflicts and threats of the refugee situation: "To accommodate refugees came increasingly to be viewed as tantamount to not protecting Malay interests in the broader relationship between Malays and non-Malays at home. . . . The refugees may threaten the framework for ethnic cooperation that so far has been the basis for economic growth and stability in Malaysia." Derani reported that the ruling government party, the United Malay National Organization (UMNO), was also responding to internal criticism from the youth faction of the party.[11]

In February, 1984, diplomatic official Yusoff echoed what Home Minister Shafie had stated in 1979: that the Malaysian government,

9. House Judiciary Committee, *Indochinese Refugees: An Update*, 32–33; Suhrke, *Indochinese Refugees: The Impact*, 19; anonymous interview, Kuala Lumpur, March 27, 1984; House Judiciary Committee, *Indochinese Refugees: An Update*, 32.

10. Derani, "Refugees from Indochina," 155–56; U.S. Department of State, *World Refugee Report*, 33.

11. Suhrke, *Indochinese Refugees: The Impact*, 20; Derani, "Refugees from Indochina," 154.

with limited resources, must first take care of its own people and that expenses related to refugees diverted funds from development programs for Malaysian citizens. An American refugee official in March, 1984, said that though the refugee problem was no longer the high-profile issue it once was in Malaysian politics, the present government was still vulnerable. For example, the government did not want the refugees to be an issue in the upcoming elections, but the opposition was casting about for points of government vulnerability, including the continuing refugee problem.[12]

Unlike Thailand, Malaysia has restricted and therefore controlled foreign involvement in its refugee problem, except for a few voluntary agencies. The UNHCR acts as the international protection agency, even though Malaysia did not sign the UN Convention and Protocol instruments. Allegations about the violations of the rights of refugees prior to July, 1979, have been ameliorated by current cooperation between the UNHCR and Malaysia. For example, the UNHCR and the Malaysian government currently cooperate in an incentive award program that encourages Malaysian fishermen to assist arriving refugee boats.

The MRCS is the operational organization in charge of overseeing the welfare of the refugees. It exercises tight control over the few voluntary agencies from abroad who assist in relief services at the two remaining refugee camps. These camps remain segregated from local populations. Pulau Bidong, located off the east coast of Malaysia, is a first asylum camp. Sungei Besi, near Kuala Lumpur, is a transit center for refugees en route to resettlement. An MRCS deputy explained that his organization is careful to encourage local Malaysian volunteers in refugee relief work and to ensure that refugees do not receive attention at the expense of local needs.[13]

As in Thailand, it is also difficult here to find verifiable information concerning economic benefits or disadvantages associated with the refugee problem. Deputy Director Som noted the continuing expense of two military battalions plus personnel that had to be diverted from other duties in order to attend to the refugee issue. Suhrke, in 1980,

12. Interview with Hamidah Yusoff; anonymous interview, Kuala Lumpur, March 27, 1984.
13. Interview with Mr. Phillips, Deputy, Malaysian Red Crescent Society, Kuala Lumpur, March 27, 1984.

found no major economic burden for Malaysia and referred to the boon for local economies on the east coast, though this seemed chiefly to benefit Chinese merchants. And Derani found that local inflation and black marketeering resulted in the centralization of purchases for refugee relief, again benefiting Chinese entrepreneurs. In March and April, 1984, refugee workers spoke of the MRCS as "not the best" but workable and deserving of praise, given the situation. Some spoke of alleged nepotism and corruption among local contractors. Most major expenses have been funded by the UNHCR. In fiscal year 1985 it had a budget of $7.6 million; however, its budget for 1988 was expected to be only $4.77 million.[14]

The issue of piracy seems to have been only a minor source of irritation for Malaysia within the context of foreign policy and security interests that preclude its cooperation in antipiracy efforts. Malaysia does not want to jeopardize its relations with Thailand for fear of harming overall ASEAN unity and losing Thai cooperation in the common threat of communist insurgency in northern Malaysia and southern Thailand.

The rate of refugee arrivals in Malaysia has been attributed to Thai piracy as well as to push-offs and humane deterrence policies in Thailand that make Malaysia a more desirable destination. In 1984, approximately 35 percent of the refugee boats arriving in Malaysia were attacked by pirates, but rarely, only 5 to 6 percent of the time, were Malaysian fishermen involved, according to a UNHCR spokesman. In fact, the Malays frequently are themselves the victims of piracy, and tension already exists between Thai and Malaysian fishing communities. Malaysian involvement in antipiracy measures would mean detaining Thai fishing boats, a step the government is unwilling to take. However, new efforts in the UNHCR-administered antipiracy program emphasize land-based policing. Thai authorities are encouraged to interview boat people who arrive in Malaysia and are victims of alleged Thai pirates. Pirate attacks continued to decline in 1986 and through most of 1987, but increased again by 1988 and 1989.[15]

14. Interview with Tuan Haji Mohammed Som; Suhrke, *Indochinese Refugees: The Impact*, 19; Office of the UNHCR, "Fact Sheet," no. 11 (January, 1985), II, no. 1 (April, 1988).
15. Anonymous interview, Kuala Lumpur, March 26, 1984; "The U.S. and Anti-

In 1984, UNHCR representative to Malaysia Darioush Bayandor saw the refugee problem winding down in Malaysia as the success of the ODP was increasing, as special and compelling reasons for departures were dropping, and as the impoverishment of the Vietnamese people was making it increasingly difficult for refugees to pay corrupt officials for permission to leave by boat. However, this optimistic outlook changed by 1987 with the increase in arrivals and a perception that world interest, particularly the interest of the resettlement countries, is fading. For Malaysia, as for Thailand, dependence on international assistance, especially resettlement offers, an awareness that liberal first asylum and resettlement are magnets attracting refugees, and sensitivity to international criticism remain notable concerns.[16]

In 1987, 8,030 Vietnamese refugees arrived in Malaysia, whereas 8,181 departed. During fiscal year 1988, 13,293 boat people arrived, so that by the end of September of that year there were 12,467 refugees at Pulau Bidong Holding Center and Sungei Besi Transit Center. The sudden increase in arrivals begun in late 1987 and continuing during 1988 resulted "in part, from the redirection of boats from Thailand and Indonesia." As many as 3,200 of the arrivals were reported to be refugees who had first attempted to reach Thailand but were forced away from the Thai coast. Threats to close the Pulau Bidong camp within a year were later softened by Malaysian authorities. The threat came in reaction to the harsh asylum policies of Thailand and Hong Kong, which were causing the refugees to seek asylum in the more hospitable Malaysia. The situation by 1988 merely underscored the fact that the refugee crisis was continuing in Malaysia.[17]

Refugees in Malaysia move on to permanent resettlement elsewhere fairly quickly, compared to refugees in Hong Kong and, in some cases, Thailand. Yet in 1987 close to 40 percent of the refugees in Malaysia had been there for more than one year.[18] Although Deputy

---

Piracy Efforts: New Results but Violence Persists," *Refugee Reports*, VII (April 18, 1986), 2; Virginia Hamilton (ed.), *World Refugee Survey: 1987*, 50.

16. Interview with Darioush Bayandor, Representative, UNHCR, Kuala Lumpur, March 26, 1984.

17. Office of the UNHCR, "Fact Sheet," II, no. 1 (April, 1988); "Indochinese Refugee Activity Since April 1975," *Refugee Reports*, IX (December 16, 1988), 7; "Asylum Crisis Widens for Refugees in Southeast Asia," *Refugee Reports*, IX (May 20, 1988), 11; Murray Hiebert, "Sink or Swim," *Far Eastern Economic Review*, February 23, 1989, p. 27.

18. Virginia Hamilton (ed.), *World Refugee Survey: 1987*, 50.

Director Som was careful to emphasize the importance of continuing the resettlement offers in order to relieve Malaysia's refugee burden, he noted problems associated with the selective criteria instituted by resettlement countries—problems that have resulted in the buildup of a residual population. He pointed out that in 1984, 3,316 refugees had been rejected for resettlement. Diplomatic official Yusoff remarked on the high rejection rate of the aged and sick.

Malaysia is cooperating with education efforts, especially in the area of economic skills, to increase the chances of admission for some of the rejected. This group is predominantly young males, aged eighteen to twenty-four. Tuan Haji Mohammed Som also observed, as did several refugee personnel, that increasingly there are economic migrants among the refugees, evidence of the pull-factor dilemma that may increase refugee numbers for Malaysia. As early as 1978, National Security Council secretary Malek remarked that "each announcement of a U.S. program encourages others to come."[19] Som discussed a refugee phenomenon known as an "anchor." A family member, usually a young male, is sent out as a refugee from Vietnam with the goal of resettlement in the West. This "anchor" sends money back to Vietnam to support other relatives, and ultimately these relatives migrate abroad through family reunification, a high-priority criteria category in refugee admissions to resettlement countries. Som also claimed that aerograms given to arriving refugees invariably are sent to Vietnam with precise directions and advice for future escapees. In this same context, Yusoff discussed the "greener pastures" motive among refugees in Malaysia.

Task Force Seven's deputy director emphasized that though Malaysia has cooperated fully with humanitarian efforts since July, 1979, this policy would change if the international community reneged on its resettlement commitment. Malaysia's concern about large numbers of Chinese refugees among the asylum seekers does not seem to lessen even though fewer than 12 percent of those arriving by 1986 were actually ethnic Chinese; from the perspective of the Malays, the Vietnamese are too culturally similar to the Chinese for there to be a distinction between the two groups. The continuous replacement of departing refugees with new arrivals and the sudden increase in the

19. House Judiciary Committee, *Indochinese Refugees: An Update*, 33.

influx by 1987, plus anxiety about resettlement, make the Indochina refugee issue a protracted problem for Malaysia. It has been actively promoting a new UNHCR international conference on the issue for 1989, similar to the one held in 1979. Important preliminary meetings for this conference were hosted in Kuala Lumpur in March, 1989.[20]

Singapore

Strategically located, densely populated, and only 227 square miles in size, the city-state of Singapore, on the southern tip of the Malay peninsula, is home to 2,400,000 people, three-fourths of whom are ethnic Chinese. For over twenty-five years, Singapore has thrived under the tight control and leadership of Prime Minister Lee Kuan Yew and the People's Action Party (PAP). The government has become identified with economic prosperity, making Singapore the world's second busiest port, and with carefully engineered and wide-reaching social programs, including housing, education, and family-planning projects.[21] Size and population density naturally influence Singapore's refusal to accept refugees for local integration and its reluctance to offer even temporary first asylum; at the same time, national interests related to foreign policy and threats to stability and domestic well-being also contribute to its reaction to the Indochina exodus.

Singapore's refugee policy can be characterized as clear, hard-line, pragmatic, and, according to some critics, ruthless. Although Singapore allowed 200 Vietnamese fishermen to remain, as a goodwill gesture during the first wave of refugees in 1975, stringent measures were quickly instituted when the exodus increased. Because Singapore is an important port of call for commercial ships, the trafficking in refugees by large freighters was alarming. Having denied refugee boats access from the start, by July, 1977, Singapore required written guarantees of resettlement abroad before refugees who had been rescued at sea by passing ships could disembark. Since October, 1978, written guarantees from third countries to resettle rescued refugees within ninety days are required before disembarkation. The maximum

20. U.S. Department of State, *World Refugee Report*, 33.
21. George (ed.), *On-Your-Own Guide*, 312–13.

number of refugees allowed asylum at any one time in Singapore is 1,000. Therefore, Singapore's refugee population of only 345 in late 1988 was in stark contrast to the thousands of refugees in camps throughout other Southeast Asian countries and in Hong Kong.[22]

Like Thailand and Malaysia, Singapore is not a signatory of UN Convention and Protocol instruments protecting refugees. It has cooperated in allowing refugees transit through it from other first asylum countries to the Refugee Processing Center at Galang, Indonesia, forty miles away. All costs related to refugees are carried by the UNHCR and the shipping industry.

Singapore's hard-line refugee policy is related to a focus on the threat the exodus from Vietnam poses to regional stability—a threat Singapore clearly attributes to Vietnam's calculated expulsion of its people, but especially its ethnic Chinese minority. Prime Minister Lee, speaking in 1979 about the struggle for power in Southeast Asia, observed that "unless we, the small nation states, can find greater stability and security by rafting with each other, then we will be the arenas in which this contest for supremacy will go on."[23]

The prime minister warned that the stakes in this power struggle are higher than the "fine sentiment" expressed in Geneva on behalf of the refugees. Foreign Minister S. Rajaratnam echoed Lee's warning in explaining that the first priority of Singapore is to protect its citizens, not the refugees from Vietnam. The foreign minister noted that the exodus is a military exercise by Vietnam, part of a larger political scheme that includes the invasion and occupation of Cambodia, especially the stationing of several thousand Vietnamese troops near the Thai border and antagonism toward China. Singapore perceives Vietnam as calculating and controlling its power to send out millions of refugees as part of Vietnam's design to destabilize and eventually dominate the entire region of Southeast Asia. Rajaratnam said, "If we keep it at the humanitarian level then the consequences will be disastrous for us and irreversible." The foreign minister continued: "Each junkload of men, women, and children sent to our shores is a bomb to

22. Wain, *The Refused*, 124, 200; Derani, "Refugees from Indochina," 161; "Indochinese Refugee Activity Since April 1975," *Refugee Reports*, IX (December 16, 1988), 7.

23. Singapore, Ministry of Foreign Affairs, "Keynote Speech by the Prime Minister, Mr. Lee Kuan Yew, on the Agenda Item 'World Political Scene' at the Commonwealth Heads of Government Meeting" (Lusaka, Zambia, August 1, 1979), 6.

destabilise, disrupt, and cause turmoil and dissension in ASEAN states. This is a preliminary invasion to pave the way for the final invasion."[24] For Singapore, the policy has been to blame Vietnam, to curb the flow at its source, to defend against the exodus' potential for destabilization, and to strictly tie temporary first asylum in Singapore to quick resettlement abroad.

Singapore was the first ASEAN state to intercept, refuel, offer provisions, and then tow out to sea refugee boats approaching its shores. Barry Wain reported that eighteen refugees drowned when the Singapore navy stood by and refused assistance to a sinking boat in May, 1980. According to a UNHCR protection officer in 1984, refugee boats were still being escorted away from Singapore, and the UNHCR rarely discovered how many actually made it to first asylum elsewhere. For example, in January, 1984, a refugee boat that had hit an oil rig was spotted by a Singapore aircraft and towed out to sea without food and water. The boat arrived in Indonesia with eighty-eight people aboard, two dead of dehydration. Very few refugee boats are able to penetrate Singapore's tight coastal security. Although the UNHCR protests, boats are often turned away without its knowledge.[25]

Behind the often quoted response of Prime Minister Lee—"You must grow callouses on your heart . . . otherwise you will bleed to death"—lie important national concerns. According to Ministry of Foreign Affairs official Michael Yeong, Singapore's response to the exodus involved looking ahead two or three steps to the possible consequences of the influx. He also mentioned that other ASEAN nations have come around to Singapore's point of view.[26]

Basically, the purging of a minority group, such as the ethnic Chinese from Vietnam, is totally unacceptable to Singapore because of the precedent it establishes in areas known to experience tensions related to minorities. If the influx of ethnic Chinese refugees into Indonesia and Malaysia ignited existing racial tensions in those countries, resulting in a general anti-Chinese movement, then Singapore, sandwiched

24. *Ibid.*; Singapore, Ministry of Culture, "Statement Delivered by the Leader of the Singapore Delegation, Mr. S. Rajaratnam, Minister for Foreign Affairs, at the Twelfth ASEAN Ministerial Meeting" (Bali, June 28, 1979).

25. Wain, *The Refused*, 198; interview with Ann-Christine Gullesjo, Protection Officer, UNHCR, Singapore, March 30, 1984.

26. Wain, *The Refused*, 200.

between Indonesia and Malaysia, would be most vulnerable to a flood of Chinese migrants. Accusing Vietnam of waging psychological warfare with the exodus, Singapore believes Vietnam could "exacerbate the simmering Chinese minority problems" in other Southeast Asian states. Derani wrote that Singapore, possibly economically attractive to ethnic Chinese refugees, has taken a hard-line approach to the exodus so as to avoid being associated with sympathy for the Chinese—sympathy that could have later repercussions in its relations with other ASEAN states.[27]

Communist agents among the refugees are also an expressed concern for Singapore, especially the communist threat via Malaysia. The following commentary appeared in Singapore's *Straits Times*, in July, 1979: "There have even been reports that many of these former Vietcong cadres are deliberately infiltrated into South-east Asia under the guise of refugees either as spies or as fifth columnists to be called on to disrupt stability in the area when the time is ripe."[28]

Foreign Ministry official Yeong acknowledged that bilateral problems occur when refugees are pushed out toward Indonesia and Malaysia by Singapore authorities. An American embassy official noted that the refugee issue is a sensitive one between Singapore and Indonesia and is avoided in bilateral talks so as not to jeopardize good relations. An ICM official concurred that Indonesia is particularly irritated when refugee boats are given food and water and a map to Indonesia by Singapore coastal authorities. However, he also indicated that the rest of ASEAN is admiring and even envious of Singapore's hard-line policy.[29]

Although of the ASEAN countries Singapore is the most unfriendly and least conciliatory toward Vietnam, Singapore's UN ambassador Mahbubani explained a weak Vietnam is not in ASEAN's interests either. Singapore supports the withdrawal of Vietnam from Cambodia, but it does not necessarily press for a settlement that ignores the interests of Vietnam. However, Singapore maintains an interest in the

27. Interview with Michael Yeong, Ministry of Foreign Affairs, Singapore, April 3, 1984; Singapore, Ministry of Foreign Affairs, *Vietnam and the Refugees* (Singapore, 1979), 9; Derani, "Refugees from Indochina," 162.

28. Singapore, Ministry of Foreign Affairs, *Vietnam and the Refugees*, 10.

29. Interviews with Michael Yeong and with Jorgen Stoen Olesen, Intergovernmental Committee for Migration, Singapore, March 30, 1984, and anonymous interview, March 30, 1984.

300,000 Cambodian refugees along the Thai-Cambodian border specifically related to its support of direct military assistance to the two noncommunist factions of the resistance CGDK. While emphasizing ASEAN unity on the Cambodian issue, Singapore has been the foremost spokesman pressuring for U.S. military aid to the noncommunist resistance.[30]

Frank about its national interests in the exodus of Indochina refugees, Singapore is also sensitive and outspoken about international criticism of its hard-line refugee policy. Refugee personnel pointed out that Singapore's willingness to accept any refugees at all came as a result of international pressure. At the ASEAN Bali conference, in late June, 1979, Foreign Minister Rajaratnam complained about the new morality that permits nations to expel unwanted segments of their populations and places guilt on those who refuse to accept the influx, not on "perpetrators of the crime." Rajaratnam warned of the dangers of emphasizing the humanitarian rather than the political aspects of the issue. Defending his country's policy, he said it is "calculated callousness" to raise the hopes of refugees and encourage the dangerous journey on the high seas when chances for permanent asylum and resettlement are minimal. Prime Minister Lee prophetically warned that once temporary first asylum was granted by ASEAN countries, resettlement countries would quickly forget their responsibilities to move the refugees. Rajaratnam, noting the pull effect of liberal refugee policies, said, "If you are honest, the flow of refugees started from a trickle to a flood when the world spoke of resettling refugees from hundreds, to thousands and now to millions." In April, 1984, refugee personnel also spoke of pull factors, pointing to the evidence of economic migrants among the refugees in Singapore.[31]

In 1984, the UNHCR publicly expressed concern about the noticeable decrease in refugee rescues at sea. Although recognizing that the overall decline in departures by boat from Vietnam was partially responsible for the decrease in rescues, the UNHCR and others feared that ships were passing or avoiding refugee boats in distress in violation of the law of the sea in order to curtail losses of time and expense

30. Mahbubani, "Kampuchean Problem," 408–409; New York *Times*, October 12, 1984, p. 11.
31. Singapore, Ministry of Culture, "Statement Delivered by Mr. S. Rajaratnam"; Wain, *The Refused*, 200.

and to avoid bureaucratic legal and political entanglements associated with disembarkation. This humanitarian concern has obvious implications for Singapore as the second busiest port in the world. At that time, a program developed by the UNHCR in 1979 with the cooperation of the United States, France, Australia, Sweden, and Switzerland was already in effect. Called the Disembarkation and Resettlement Reserve Scheme (DISERO), it provides a "resettlement pool" that can be utilized when ships rescuing refugees at sea cannot secure resettlement guarantees from their own flag countries. Another program, the Rescue at Sea Resettlement Offer (RASRO), was instituted in May, 1985. RASRO complements DISERO and expands the rescue at sea effort by facilitating resettlement of refugees who are rescued by ships flying the flag of a resettlement country.[32]

Indonesia

Indonesia is an important first asylum country for refugees from Vietnam, but it has been spared the effects of a massive influx, in contrast to Thailand and Malaysia. In 1977, 927 refugees arrived in Indonesia, followed by 3,855 in 1978. However, during the critical year 1979, which marked a substantial increase in the exodus of boat people and the adoption of hard-line measures by other ASEAN countries, including push-offs by Malaysia, 48,651 refugees reached Indonesia, a safer and more desirable destination. That year, Malaysia reportedly towed 51,632 refugees away from its shores. Like its neighbors, Indonesia was alarmed by the increasing exodus, including the trafficking in refugees by large commercial freighters in 1978 and 1979 and began turning refugees away.[33]

National interest factors are also related to Indonesia's reluctance to accept refugees, though official pronouncements of unity with ASEAN's position, which sounded the alarm and limited access to first asylum, have been tempered in practice. Indonesia did not enforce its ban on asylum and has contributed generously by relieving

32. "Rescue At Sea," *Refugees*, II (February, 1984), 21–28; U.S. Department of State, *World Refugee Report*, 41.
33. Wain, *The Refused*, 131; Derani, "Refugees from Indochina," 156.

the burden of other first asylum states, by cooperating with resettlement countries, and even by facilitating dialogue with Vietnam on the
refugee issue. Indonesia has given asylum to an estimated 100,000
refugees. In addition, until 1986 it hosted, on the island of Galang, a
refugee processing center that was an important extension of the refugee pipeline. Refugees accepted for resettlement were moved to Galang for a six-month cultural orientation and language training program to ease eventual adjustment in permanent resettlement countries. This middle step also reduced the refugee burden in other first
asylum countries.[34]

Indonesia's reaction to the refugee issue is related to domestic national interest factors, including population, unemployment, poverty,
and ethnic antagonisms involving its Chinese minority. Indonesia is a
developing country with a population of 150,000,000. It is the fifth
most populated country in the world and still growing, with the majority of Indonesians living on the crowded island of Java. Although its
Chinese minority makes up only 3 percent of the population, racial and
religious differences and ill feeling stemming from an attempted coup
in 1965 contribute to tensions. In 1966, racial violence led to the killing
of several thousands of Chinese. Relations with China have been
frozen until recently.

Potentially serious problems with the influx of refugees, including
ethnic Chinese, are offset because the asylum seekers land on remote,
underpopulated, outlying islands within the Anambas and Natunas
archipelagoes. Remaining out of sight, they pose little threat for most
Indonesians. The segregation of the refugees from local communities
and the consolidation of eleven camps into two after 1979 have allayed
fears of possible infiltration by refugees loyal to China. Although conditions in Indonesia preclude permanent resettlement possibilities for
the refugees, resettlement commitments by the West keep pace with
arrivals. Added to that factor, international funding estimated at $1.5
million for fiscal year 1988 from the UNHCR and limited adverse impact on national interests account for Indonesian cooperation and generosity. For Indonesia, it appears that the refugee influx is manageable.
As of late September, 1988, there were 2,118 first asylum refugees in
Indonesia. The decline in arrivals recently has been attributed to the

34. Office of the UNHCR, "Fact Sheet," II, no. 1 (April, 1988).

new escape route Vietnamese refugees take (to the east coast of Thailand), the closing of the coastal reception centers, and, reportedly, the redirection of approaching boats to Malaysia. However, by 1988 arrivals were increasing once again, with 2,253 asylum seekers registered that year, compared to 1,421 in 1987. Reportedly, nearly 600 boat people who had been turned away by Indonesia eventually arrived in Malaysia during the period January to September, 1988.[35]

In his research, Derani found that in 1979 Indonesia set a different policy; it privately agreed to accept refugees pushed away from Malaysia, thereby helping to diffuse the issue in Malaysia and promote ASEAN peace and stability, which had been threatened by the refugee crisis. This gesture was an effort by Indonesia to improve its international image. In addition, Suhrke wrote that Indonesia's reaction to the refugees was intended to foster its leadership role within ASEAN and is evidence of President Suharto's effort to improve and maintain good relations with the United States. Along these lines, Suharto's visit to the United States in 1982 was seen as an effort to establish Indonesia's credibility as an important Third World leader.[36]

Estranged from and viewing China as the region's long-term threat and unafraid of Vietnam, Indonesia has maintained a degree of leverage with the latter. It is able to pursue open dialogue and possibly eventual accommodation with Vietnam, while maintaining a leadership role in ASEAN and giving its ASEAN partners adequate assurances of unity. For example, though vocal in blaming Vietnam for the exodus in 1979, Indonesia is credited with influencing Vietnam to attend a regional meeting in May, 1979, to address the construction of a processing center on Galang and to participate with the international community in Geneva in July, 1979, to seek a solution to the refugee crisis. Indonesia has also taken the lead in pursuing dialogue with Vietnam on the Cambodian stalemate. Its role in the refugee issue appears to have been enhanced by the fact that the problem has had only a minor negative impact on its own national interests. This rela-

35. Suhrke, *Indochinese Refugees: The Impact*, 21; Derani, "Refugees from Indochina," 158; Virginia Hamilton (ed.), *World Refugee Survey: 1987*, 47; "Indochinese Refugee Activity Since April 1975," *Refugee Reports*, IX (December 16, 1988), 8; "Indochinese Refugee Activity," *Refugee Reports*, VIII (December 18, 1987), 8; "Update," *Refugee Reports*, IX (November 11, 1988), 8.

36. Derani, "Refugees from Indochina," 157; Suhrke, *Indochinese Refugees: The Impact*, 21.

tive detachment permits flexibility and cooperation in relations with ASEAN, the United States, and perhaps Vietnam regarding the exodus.[37]

Today, Indonesia expresses concern about the smaller yet continuing influx of Vietnamese boat refugees. Authorities worry about declining international burden sharing, evident in reduced resettlement rates. The number of long-term refugees is "gradually creeping up," and Indonesia fears it will be saddled with these refugees in the end. Officials make mention, too, of the growing numbers of economic migrants among recent arrivals.[38]

The issue of refugees arriving in Indonesia via a shuttle service, apparently "with some degree of official connivance," was raised in talks between Jakarta and Hanoi in August of 1985. Soon after, as a warning to Vietnam, Indonesia began to sink shuttle boats, after allowing the refugees to disembark safely. In 1986, 19 Vietnamese crewmen were arrested and expelled for participation in the transport for hire of refugees to Indonesia. In April, 1988, an approaching refugee boat off Natuna Island was fired upon, with a loss of a single life. This incident was but a recent indication of Indonesia's weariness and hard-line policy concerning the refugees.[39]

The Philippines

The Philippines is perhaps the ASEAN country least adversely affected by the Indochina refugees. Its distance from Vietnam makes a journey by sea risky, but over 39,000 boat refugees have reached its outlying islands or have been picked up in the South China Sea and have disembarked there. Since January, 1980, the Philippines has hosted an important processing center similar to but larger than Galang, with a capacity for 16,000 refugees, at the famous World War II site Bataan. Here, refugees who have been accepted for resettlement in the United States arrive from first asylum countries to spend six months in English

37. Derani, "Refugees from Indochina," 191.
38. Lincoln Kaye, "About Those Refugees," *Far Eastern Economic Review,* September 26, 1985, pp. 34–35.
39. New York *Times,* February 23, 1986, p. 4; "Asylum Crisis Widens," 11; *Wall Street Journal,* June 29, 1988, p. 18.

language and cultural orientation training before moving on to permanent resettlement. By the end of 1987, over 221,000 refugees had been accommodated at the Refugee Processing Center.[40]

Local resettlement is not permitted in this rapidly growing and developing country of over 55,000,000 people. However, approximately 1,800 refugees have been allowed to remain in the Philippines because of family ties between these arrivals and Filipinos who had previously worked in Indochina during the Vietnam War years. As of May, 1988, 3,250 boat people were at the first asylum camp on Palawan Island, and 13,892 refugees were at the Refugee Processing Center at Bataan.[41]

The political, social, and economic impact of the refugees on the Philippines seems minimal. In 1979, in a display of ASEAN unity, the Philippines decried the destabilizing effects of the exodus on regional unity, warned it would not accept refugees, kept the *Tung An*, a refugee-carrying freighter, in Manila Bay for seven months before permitting disembarkation, and questioned at times whether the Vietnamese were truly refugees. In practice, however, it has accepted refugees and has cooperated with ASEAN, the United States, and the UNHCR in efforts to relieve the burden elsewhere. For the Philippines, the refugee issue has remained manageable. With the change in government in February, 1986, came assurances that it would continue to cooperate in efforts to assist the Indochinese refugees. In 1987, close to 2,700 arrivals were registered, apart from those refugees going to Bataan. This number included 905 refugees who arrived aboard a single "mercy ship." During fiscal year 1988, arrivals increased to 3,878. As the crisis heightened during 1988, the Philippines was reportedly reassessing its response to asylum seekers.[42]

The symbolic location of the refugee processing center at Bataan points to the special relationship and consequent leverage the United States has with the Philippines, a former colony and its oldest Asian ally, which contribute to overall cooperation. The offer by the Philip-

40. Office of the UNHCR, "Fact Sheet," II, no. 1 (April, 1988).
41. U.S. Department of State, *Country Reports*, 45–46; "Indochinese Refugee Activity," *Refugee Reports*, IX (August 12, 1988), 16.
42. U.S. Department of State, *Country Reports*, 46, and *World Refugee Report*, 35; Wain, *The Refused*, 111, 134; "Asylum Crisis Widens," 12; Office of the UNHCR, "Fact Sheet," II, no. 1 (April, 1988).

pines to host a refugee processing center was made in Geneva in July, 1979, and was deemed "a timely and useful gesture." An American refugee official noted that prestige is associated with the Philippines' involvement in the refugee issue. Another official alluded to benefits when he remarked frankly that "the Filipinos make out like bandits." The assistance of the Philippines also contributed to international recognition for the government of Ferdinand Marcos. For example, the reception center at Bataan included an extensive photographic display that especially highlighted the contributions of the Marcos government.[43]

The government has provided land and a road for the Bataan center, and the UNHCR and about twenty voluntary agencies have met other costs, including payment for extensive Filipino administrative and training staffs. In 1987, the UNHCR expected to contribute $5.8 million to the refugee program in the Philippines.[44]

Even though the processing center is deliberately located away from densely populated areas, the presence of refugees did, at first, cause local resentment among villagers in Morong. The foraging habits of some refugees especially irritated residents, and conditions in the camps were perceived to be better than conditions locally. As a result, "Task Force Morong" was formed to provide social and economic services to area residents. Morong inhabitants have access to camp medical facilities, which include the best hospital within one hundred miles. Buying goods and services for the camp locally, with priority given to local purchasing and employment, is a stimulus to the local economy. For example, a busy and lively Filipino market is the focal point in the camp. A visiting California legislative delegation reported in 1983, however, that "the only difference between the American RPC and the Filipino village is that the Filipinos speak better English and live poorer."[45]

Over 700 Filipinos are employed as teachers in the English lan-

43. House Foreign Affairs Committee, *Reports on Refugee Aid*, 89; anonymous interviews, Bangkok, March 13, 1984, and Manila, April 6, 1984.
44. Interview with Loring A. Waggoner, Deputy Coordinator for Refugee Programs, U.S. Embassy, Manila, April 6, 1984; U.S. Department of State, *World Refugee Report*, 36.
45. House Foreign Affairs Committee, *Reports on Refugee Aid*, 92; California Legislature, Joint Committee on Refugee Resettlement and Immigration, *Report of the Fact-Finding Mission to Refugee Camps in Southeast Asia, October 24 to November 16, 1983* (Sacramento, 1983), 79.

guage and cultural orientation program at Bataan, where they receive wages three times the going national rate for educators. A Filipino sociologist at the camp commented that the local villagers think "the refugees are lucky." Yet a refugee worker said local people "get the jitters thinking about the RPC ending." Although refugee operations run relatively smoothly, serious tensions have at times existed between the UNHCR in charge of oversight for the camp and the Philippines' government authority, whose priorities are based on national sovereignty rights. In 1985, the Refugee Processing Center at Bataan was upgraded, followed by the expansion of its educational facilities.[46]

Hong Kong

An Asian crossroads, an important shipping, manufacturing, and trade center, the British colony of Hong Kong, situated on the end of China's southeast coast, has a long history of immigration. Hong Kong's current population of 5,500,000 grew from 1,500,000 in 1946 because of a high birthrate but also because of periodic influxes from China. The post-1949 years brought a large migration, repeated in 1962, as a result of economic and other hardships in China. Another wave of legal and illegal migrants from China commenced in 1978, related to China's liberalization of exit visas. This event coincided with the massive exodus of refugees from Vietnam. Today, 27,000 people from China are allowed to enter Hong Kong legally each year.[47]

In 1975, a Danish container ship brought 3,740 refugees from Vietnam to asylum in Hong Kong, which was followed by 191 refugees arriving in 1976, 1,001 in 1977, and 6,609 in 1978. During 1979, 68,748 refugees reached Hong Kong. Comprised of only 404 square miles of territory that is three-quarters barren islands and steep hillsides, Hong Kong has taken 14,500 refugees for permanent resettlement and as of mid-1989 has received nearly 150,000 refugees. Neither was Hong Kong spared large freighters carrying refugees, including the *Huey*

46. Anonymous interviews, Bataan Refugee Processing Center, April 9, 1984; House Foreign Affairs Committee, *Reports on Refugee Aid*, 91; U.S. Department of State, *World Refugee Report*, 36.

47. Kosol Vongsrisart (ed.), *Indochinese Refugees, Thailand*, 70–71; U.S. Department of State, *World Refugee Report*, 34.

Fong and the *Sky Luck* in 1979. However, it was foremost in cracking down on large-scale racketeering in refugees through successful prosecution, its adoption of harsh penalties, and the monitoring and surveillance activities of its Refugee Ship Unit (RSU).[48]

Through most of the refugee crisis, Hong Kong could pride itself on being the most generous first asylum country for Indochina refugees. At the Geneva conference in July, 1979, the governor of Hong Kong reported, "I can claim with pride that we have carried out our obligations to the full."[49] However, humanitarianism gave way to resentment and disillusionment when liberal asylum policies became a pull factor attracting thousands, when the ASEAN countries made asylum unattractive and even denied asylum, prompting refugees to seek out Hong Kong, and when permanent resettlement from Hong Kong became increasingly difficult. In addition, the close proximity of Hong Kong naturally influenced refugees from northern Vietnam to seek refuge there.

Refugees arriving prior to 1982 were housed in crowded, urban, but open camps. Many became gainfully employed, albeit at low wages, within the Hong Kong economy. This freedom of movement and employment possibilities contrasted sharply with the inhospitable treatment refugees received in the ASEAN countries. Barry Wain wrote that in 1979 "the formal denial of asylum by ASEAN left Hong Kong as the only publicly proclaimed haven for the boat people." Hong Kong eventually felt penalized for its generosity when resettlement countries increasingly ignored the crisis in Hong Kong and awarded larger resettlement quotas for ASEAN countries who were "screaming the loudest." Wain summarized Hong Kong's position: "Hong Kong . . . paid a price for its humanity in terms both of refugees attracted by its attitude and of resettlement nations rushing off to assist countries threatening mass murder."[50]

By mid-1982, Hong Kong thought it was necessary to take a drastic step in addressing the growing refugee problem, so it instituted a deterrence policy of closed, austere, camp asylum to all refugees arriving after July 2, 1982. Although Hong Kong continues to offer asylum,

48. Hong Kong Government Secretariat, "Fact Sheet," No. SRD 703/5/RII (May, 1988); Washington *Post*, June 18, 1989, p. 27; Wain, *The Refused*, 110–17.
49. Kosol Vongsrisart (ed.), *Indochinese Refugees, Thailand*, 78.
50. *Ibid.*; Wain, *The Refused*, 210.

all arrivals are now deemed illegal immigrants initially. Approaching refugee boats are met before disembarkation, and refugees are offered a choice: either submitting to a screening process to determine refugee status and probable indefinite confinement in detention centers with remote chances of future resettlement or moving on. A dramatic increase in 1985 in the number of refugee boats bypassing Hong Kong raised serious human rights concerns. For example, the UNHCR reported that 1,782 Vietnamese refugees approaching Hong Kong chose to sail on, after receiving fuel and provisions, rather than face incarceration in the crowded closed camps. "Little is known about their fate though some are thought to have headed for the Philippines." That year, 1,050 refugees arrived in Hong Kong.[51]

Important national interest factors contribute to Hong Kong's present harsh, deterrent refugee policy, a departure from earlier practices. Domestically, the influx of refugees, coupled with a low resettlement rate, raised serious concerns. Hong Kong was in the midst of implementing major social and economic programs when the refugees started to arrive. The influx was perceived as possibly undermining recent achievements and threatening future progress. For example, officials considered a ten-year housing project plan, begun in 1973, to be in jeopardy because it depended on reliable population projections, which the refugee influx made impossible. Although some benefits from paying low wages to refugees may have accrued to manufacturers, the general economy began to experience a slowdown, which put many jobs in jeopardy. A refugee official mentioned the overt tension between Hong Kong residents and the refugees from the Jubilee camp concerning employment competition.[52]

In 1979, the refugees cost Hong Kong taxpayers $14 million. The refugees were highly visible, as arriving boats "moored not at some discreetly distant beach but in the heart of the city." And they were housed in full view in camps in densely crowded areas. A delegation of legislators from California in late 1983 reported that health care for the refugees might be "somewhat better than what is available to a low

51. Rob Burrows, "Not Enough Hope To Go Around," *Refugees*, XXXIII (September, 1986), 31–33; Allen K. Jones, *Living in Limbo: The Boat Refugees of Hong Kong and Macao*, U.S. Committee for Refugees (Washington, D.C., 1986), 8.

52. Kosol Vongsrisart (ed.), *Indochinese Refugees, Thailand*, 70–72; anonymous interview, Hong Kong, April 12, 1984.

income Hong Kong citizen." To this day, then, the refugees are considered to be a strain on Hong Kong's resources. Hong Kong authorities report that from 1979 to 1987, $100 million was spent on the refugee problem by the government.[53]

Hong Kong's refugee problem conflicts with another issue, the influx of immigrants from China. Between 1978 and 1988, an estimated 630,000 entered from China, legally and illegally, a 12 percent increase in the population. In one month, May of 1979, an average of 465 Chinese per day were caught trying to enter Hong Kong. By 1981, the government of Hong Kong had enacted employer sanctions to curb the flow. Presently, with the cooperation of China, Hong Kong automatically returns all illegal entrants. In April, 1984, for example, a group of illegal Chinese entrants was imprisoned at the Argyle Street Detention Center. The camp's director noted they would be returning to China shortly. In 1988, 79 persons per day, on the average, were caught trying to enter Hong Kong illegally and were returned.[54]

It is estimated that thousands of the 265,000 ethnic Chinese who fled to China from Vietnam in 1978 and 1979 tried to enter Hong Kong, some successfully. Resettled on over two hundred state farms, many refugees have found life in China dissatisfying. A Chinese refugee official, Ji Hua, observed that "some refugees refuse to do manual work or to do farming work, and an estimated 20 percent of the population are reluctant to settle down in China." An estimated 30,000 refugees in China have applied for resettlement elsewhere, but they have little chance of acceptance by another country. Hong Kong authorities screen refugees for any evidence that they may have spent time in China and return to China any that are caught. Over 12,000 persons were returned, from 1979 to 1986.[55]

The rejection of illegal migrants from China and the acceptance of refugees from Vietnam are a source of tension in Hong Kong. Al-

53. Wain, *The Refused*, 138; Kosol Vongsrisart (ed.), *Indochinese Refugees, Thailand*, 74; California Legislature, *Report of the Fact-Finding Mission*, 36; Hong Kong Government Secretariat, "Fact Sheet."

54. Hong Kong Government Secretariat, "Fact Sheet"; Kosol Vongsrisart (ed.), *Indochinese Refugees, Thailand*, 74; U.S. House of Representatives, Committee on the Judiciary, *Refugee Issues in Southeast Asia and Europe*, 97th Cong., 2nd Sess., No. 90-514 0, p. 8; interview with Tom Wu, Superintendent, Argyle Street Detention Center, Hong Kong, April 13, 1984.

55. "Rural Integration," *Refugees*, XIII (January, 1985), 22; Virginia Hamilton (ed.), *World Refugee Survey: 1987*, 47.

though earlier refugee arrivals were estimated to be 70 percent ethnic Chinese, since 1980 the arrivals have been 98 percent ethnic Vietnamese. The popular perception is that many of these refugees are economic adventurers. The high birthrate among refugees, 3.1 percent, is also an expressed concern and is attributed to their ignorance, "since most arrivals now are poorly educated farmers and fishermen." A Hong Kong editorial written in June, 1984, discussed the existence of "California dreamers" among the asylum seekers, implying that many were not bona fide refugees but rather adventurers seeking to make their fortunes in the United States. Also, it questioned government policy that accepted Vietnamese refugees but rejected illegal immigrants from China, "our own kith and kin."[56]

Hong Kong continues to have the highest population of Vietnamese boat refugees, many of them staying a long time, and the lowest resettlement rate of the first asylum countries. Although arrival rates decreased in each of the years after 1979, the rate was again increasing by 1986. By late 1987, Hong Kong began expressing alarm at this increase. For example, in one month alone, April, 1988, 1,381 refugees arrived. By the end of fiscal year 1988, the total refugee population in Hong Kong exceeded 25,000, of which 18,702 had arrived that year. By mid-1989, there were more than 38,000 Vietnamese refugees in Hong Kong.[57]

Several factors contribute to low resettlement rates. "Hong Kong does not have the political stick that ASEAN holds" and is politically powerless, according to UNHCR representative Dolores B. Lasan. In some countries, but not in Hong Kong, refugees serve a political purpose. The United States, having resettled more than 60,000 of Hong Kong's refugees, does not have compelling foreign policy reasons to assist Hong Kong further, as it does to assist the ASEAN countries, whose peace and stability are related to American objectives. An American refugee official in Hong Kong explained that overall American foreign policy objectives require compatible refugee policies that

56. Hong Kong Government Secretariat, "Fact Sheet"; U.S. Department of State, *World Refugee Report*, 34; "Viet Refugees Problem Refuses to Leave," *Asian Bulletin*, VII (July, 1984), 86.

57. "Indochinese Refugee Activity," *Refugee Reports*, IX (August 12, 1988), 16; Hong Kong Government Secretariat, "Fact Sheet"; *Wall Street Journal*, June 29, 1988, p. 18; "Indochinese Refugee Activity Since April 1975," *Refugee Reports*, IX (December 16, 1988), 7; Washington *Post*, June 18, 1989, p. 27.

ask, "How does it play in Kuala Lumpur; in Jakarta?" American refugee policies need to be sensitive, for example, to "keeping the Thais
happy." This is not the case for Hong Kong, where the refugee problem
is judged to be only a minor irritant for the American consulate general. A U.S. foreign service officer pointedly explained that Hong Kong
is not strategically important to the United States, that Hong Kong has
no political clout. Therefore, it remains handicapped in its competition
with ASEAN for resettlement numbers. There may actually be some
U.S. interest in keeping a certain number of refugees coming from
Vietnam to Hong Kong so as to serve Sino-U.S. interests by fostering
the poor international image and isolation of Vietnam. However,
UNHCR's Lasan did think that an increase in resettlement offers resulted from the harder line Hong Kong has taken since 1982.[58]

Another American refugee official said that in Hong Kong "you
dance to Britain." Britain's conservative government, led by Prime
Minister Margaret Thatcher, has maintained a strong reluctance to
assume Hong Kong's refugee burden, despite continued pressure
from Hong Kong and the United States. In 1979, it was Thatcher who
called for a conference in Geneva to promote the concept of international burden sharing, though Britain was apparently irked at being
pressured to take 10,000 refugees as a result of that meeting. Some
commend Britain for taking the 10,000 without discrimination, unlike
other resettlement countries. Refugee personnel in Hong Kong say the
major resettlement nations point to Hong Kong's refugee problem as a
British responsibility, whereas Britain considers it to be a French and
American issue. These days, political attention on the uncertain future
of Hong Kong when it reverts to Chinese control in 1997 eclipses
concern about real and immediate problems such as the refugee issue.
The bloody turmoil in China, June, 1989, only exacerbated anxiety
about the refugee issue in Hong Kong.[59]

The frustration in Hong Kong over increasing numbers of residual
refugees is also caused both by characteristics of the refugee case load

58. Interviews with Dolores B. Lasan, Chargé de Mission, UNHCR, Hong Kong,
and Hal Meinheit, U.S. Consulate General, Hong Kong, both April 12, 1984, and anonymous interviews.

59. Interviews with Dan Larsen, Joint Voluntary Agency, U.S. Consulate General,
Hong Kong, April 12, 1984, and with Duncan Pescod, Assistant Secretary, Security
Branch, Hong Kong Government Secretariat, Hong Kong, April 13, 1984, and anony-
mous interviews.

unique to Hong Kong and by high rates of rejections for admission to the United States by the INS. A refugee official in 1984 noted that close to 1,000 of Hong Kong's 12,258 refugees were residual and that for Hong Kong, resettlement was a "dead issue." These refugees are mostly from northern Vietnam and do not fall within U.S. admissions priority criteria. Refugees must demonstrate that they have close relatives in the United States, are former U.S. government employees, were closely associated with the United States in some way, or were former military or civil servant personnel in the South Vietnamese government. Few refugees from northern Vietnam meet these criteria.[60]

Compounding the resettlement problem in Hong Kong by the early 1980s was a broader tension between the State Department and the INS. This discord basically reflected the State Department's interest in generous refugee resettlement for foreign policy objectives and the INS's intent to screen refugees more stringently for admission to the United States. The State Department's perspective was dictated by efforts to maintain good relations with the first asylum countries, whereas the INS wanted to control the borders of the United States. At that time, the INS, on a case-by-case basis, began to defer decisions on and deny admissions to many Indochinese refugees throughout Southeast Asia. The INS maintained that according to the U.S. Refugee Act of 1980, many were not bona fide refugees but rather economic migrants who had not fled Indochina because of persecution. At issue was the control of refugee admissions, with the INS charging that the State Department was making undue use of foreign policy objectives in refugee policies for the Indochinese.[61] Mandated to protect the borders of the United States, the INS felt its authority was being usurped by the State Department.

This sharp, sometimes acrimonious, debate had serious implications in Hong Kong, where a powerful and uncompromising "old guard" stood its ground. In 1984, Jack Fortner, the INS officer in Hong Kong, explained his view that the economic failures of communist governments in Indochina motivating people to leave do not make them refugees. The State Department, acting according to foreign pol-

60. Anonymous interview, Hong Kong, April 12, 1984.
61. California Legislature, *Report of the Fact-Finding Mission*, 40–41.

icy interests, has been inclined to assign refugee status to those who are persecuted economically because of past political associations or views. Fortner made a distinction between "persecution," which implies refugee status, and "prosecution," which does not. Those who leave for economic or other nonpolitical reasons but fear prosecution if they return are not refugees, said Fortner. A congressional judiciary committee report agreed with the INS and noted the State Department's contrasting position: "Officials in the State Department maintain that it is not necessary to demonstrate past persecution or a well grounded fear of persecution which forces one to leave the homeland. In this view all that is required is a showing that one cannot return to the homeland because of a fear of future persecution."[62]

Although opinions differ, some officials estimate that as many as 50 percent of the Vietnamese refugees, north and south, now arriving in Hong Kong and elsewhere may be economically motivated. However, many also leave because of political and religious persecution, forced labor, conscription, and discriminatory taxation. Nonetheless, "there is wide agreement that once people leave Vietnam, they cannot return."[63]

The adamant position of the INS in Hong Kong did not bode well for refugees seeking resettlement. A congressional fact-finding delegation to Hong Kong in March of 1982 reported that "the majority of refugees did not allege that specific acts of persecution or deprivation were directed at them." By way of answering this charge, refugee officials in Hong Kong replied that uneducated fishermen and farmers, intimidated by the admissions process, find it hard to articulate their experiences, especially in a brief INS interview. One refugee official claimed that criteria that are applied inordinately and stringently to refugees in Hong Kong are not used in other first asylum countries and thus that "Hong Kong refugees in any other place would be accepted for resettlement in the United States." After 1984, references to this discord between the INS and the State Department lessened. However, the low acceptance rates for resettlement for refugees from Hong Kong by the United States and other nations point to the relative lack of foreign policy interests in Hong Kong for the resettlement

62. Interview with Jack Fortner, Officer, INS, Hong Kong, April 13, 1984; House Judiciary Committee, *Refugee Issues in Southeast Asia and Europe*, 15.
63. Jones, *Living in Limbo*, 6.

countries. In 1987, only 2,212 refugees were resettled, and in the first eight months of 1988, a mere 1,768 asylum seekers were approved, despite growing alarm about human rights violations, including serious overcrowding.[64]

For Hong Kong, national interest factors contribute to a reaction to the refugees that includes the hard-line deterrence measures of screening, detention centers, and closed camps. Although Hong Kong, to its credit, has not refused asylum to refugees, its policies raise important questions about human rights. Conditions in both open and closed camps are crowded and deplorable, some of the worst in Southeast Asia. For example, the open Jubilee camp, a pre–World War II British army housing unit with a capacity for 500 people, sheltered 1,864 refugees in 1987. Conditions in the closed camps are even worse. At the Chi Ma Wan Camp, a refugee family of five or six persons is assigned a six-by-four-foot space for sleeping. What happens in places like this is that "as time passes, social problems, including poor mental health, drug abuse, and diminished readjustment capacities, increase." One refugee officer expressed his frustration by asking, "Where does national interest end and humanitarianism begin?" A journalist wrote, "All the refugees I met in Hong Kong gave me the feeling that their situation is irreparable." A recent OXFAM report indicated that nearly 5,000 refugees have been in Hong Kong camps for more than five years. By late 1988, these already deplorable conditions worsened with the arrival of thousands more refugees. For example, the eleven-story, former San Yick factory building was turned into a refugee detention center. Lacking a sufficient water supply, the facility housed "650 people crowded together on each floor."[65]

The sudden increase in arrivals to Hong Kong in 1988 prompted a policy change that became effective June 15, 1988. Legislative Council member Rita Fan remarked that "we in Hong Kong are faced with an impossible situation." When more than 1,000 refugees arrived during the first week in June, Hong Kong decided to institute a screening

64. House Judiciary Committee, *Refugee Issues in Southeast Asia and Europe*, 9; anonymous interview, Hong Kong, April 12, 1984; "Conditions Worsen for Refugees in Hong Kong as Vietnamese Arrivals Continue," *Refugee Reports*, IX (September 9, 1988), 10.

65. Jones, *Living in Limbo*, 1, 11–13; "Journalist's Seminar in China," *Refugees*, XIII (January, 1985), 31; "Indochinese Camp Populations," *Refugee Reports*, VIII (March 20, 1987), 20; "Asylum Crisis Widens," 12; "Conditions Worsen for Refugees in Hong Kong," 8.

program. After being given the option to turn their boats away from Hong Kong, those asylum seekers electing to disembark are detained as illegal immigrants at Hei Ling Chau Camp, located on a "rocky outer island." With the expectation that as many as 90 percent of refugees now arriving will be screened out as illegal immigrants, officials in Hong Kong indicate that those screened out will remain in detention until they are taken back by Vietnam. Talks among Hong Kong authorities have led to meetings with Vietnam about the repatriation of those not assigned refugee status after the screening process. However, observers who have already expressed concern about the violation of the human rights of refugees in Hong Kong warn that repatriation must be voluntary, not forced. Five refugees were the first to return voluntarily to Vietnam in August, 1988, followed by 149 more in March and May, 1989. Despite the new, stringent screening program, however, 4,500 asylum seekers came to Hong Kong in July, 1988. By May, 1989, the screening process was having no effect in curtailing arrivals, with as many as 2,000 refugees per week coming to Hong Kong. A sign of improvement came with Hong Kong's reversal in late 1988 of the closed camp policy. The UNHCR now has permission to build a new facility for as many as 16,000 refugees. A U.S. refugee official explained the reasoning behind the policy reversal: "In effect, they want to move the closed camp people into open camps. The closed camps, in turn, are now detention centers. The government is trying to house everyone. The problem is that everything is full." The detention centers will house those the screening process has determined not to be bona fide refugees.[66]

Thirteen years after the exodus from Indochina began, the continuing and worsening of the refugee problem in 1988 resulted in an emergency conference in Cha-Am, Thailand, attended by delegates from all the temporary first asylum countries. In a summary statement, the representatives declared that "immediate action is required by the international community to respond with a greater sense of urgency to what amounts to the gravest Indochinese refugee crisis since 1979." Calling for a comprehensive and coordinated response to the current situation, the conference report suggested that a regional screening

66. *Refugee Reports*, IX (June 24, 1988), 7–8, X (January 27, 1989), 14–15, IX (September 9, 1988), 8–10, IX (August 12, 1988), 8, and X (May 19, 1989), 10–11.

program be established, along with a regional UNHCR holding center for all persons screened out. The report also called for Vietnam to curtail once again large-scale, organized departures, to accept repatriation, and to expand the ODP. In addition, the delegates called for a renewed commitment to resettlement from the international community that would include "more predictable and multi-year resettlement guarantees with priority given to those refugees who have been in the camps for more than two years." By early 1989, plans were underway for a major conference on the Indochina refugee crisis, to be held in Geneva under UNHCR auspices in June, 1989. However, anticipation of a restrictive regional screening program as a result of the Geneva conference may actually have caused the exodus to increase, as asylum seekers may be attempting to flee before implementation of the screening plan.[67]

Other nations not discussed also contribute to asylum as refugee-carrying boats from Vietnam travel as far as Macao, Taiwan, South Korea, Japan, and Australia. As of September, 1988, there were 465 refugees in Macao, 188 in Taiwan, 123 in South Korea, and 496 in Japan.[68] The relatively small numbers of refugees who come to these countries have not had a major effect on national policy.

67. *Refugee Reports*, IX (June 24, 1988), 8.
68. "Indochinese Refugee Activity," *Refugee Reports*, IX (December 16, 1988), 6.

V

The United States
and Resettlement

The solution to the plight of over 1,600,000 refugees from Indochina has been permanent resettlement in countries far from original homelands and from places of temporary first asylum. This final step in the refugees' journey involves admission to the United States, Canada, Australia, or one of several European nations. In addition, by 1979, nearly 263,000 ethnic Chinese refugees from Vietnam had found resettlement in the People's Republic of China. At the end of September, 1988, over 884,000 of the resettled refugees had been admitted to the United States.[1]

As was the case with the countries of first asylum, for the United States the impact of and its reaction to the Indochina refugee exodus are related to national interests. The invitation to a young Vietnamese refugee, who was then a West Point cadet, to be an honored guest at President Reagan's 1985 State of the Union address perhaps best symbolized the continuing foreign policy objectives associated with the refugee issue. The image of the young cadet was a poignant reminder to many Americans of the thousands of Indochinese refugees who have fled and continue to flee their homelands to escape persecution and who ultimately find freedom in the United States. In addition to highlighting the shortcomings of the Indochinese governments and the leadership of the United States in the noncommunist world by "voting with their feet," the refugees figure in other American foreign

1. *Refugee Reports*, IX (December 16, 1988), 7.

policy goals. These goals include the international isolation of Vietnam, the stability of and good relations with the noncommunist countries of Southeast Asia, and good relations with China. Besides foreign policy interests, the American response to the refugees also reflects a sense of responsibility, feelings of guilt, and a genuine humanitarianism, as the memory of its past experiences in Indochina merges with its democratic ideals in the American consciousness. However, the American reaction to the crisis—its resettlement of refugees—has not been without domestic social, economic, and political components supporting the contention that "global flows may have unanticipated longer-term consequences."[2]

The reaction of the United States is a large, complex story that warrants the attention of a separate research effort. This investigation, therefore, highlights for discussion three of several important aspects of the American response. First, the exodus from Indochina prompted the enactment of revised refugee legislation, namely, the Refugee Act of 1980, a significant departure from the traditional ad hoc treatment of refugee crises. Second, the influx of refugees has seen the emergence of a debate between the INS and the State Department regarding political power and the adjudication of refugee admissions, similar to the debate between the Eisenhower administration and immigration restrictionists in Congress in 1957 concerning Hungarian refugee admissions. Third, liberal admission of refugees from Indochina and elsewhere, which coincides with increasing concern over illegal entrants into the United States, has brought the refugee issue into the larger context of a major immigration problem. The subject of immigration also includes an ethical component that raises questions about infinite moral responsibilities for refugees existing within the framework of finite national capacities.[3]

The United States has resettled more Indochinese refugees than any other country, continues to pledge large quotas for resettlement (for example, 46,500 for fiscal year 1989), and funds all refugee programs in the amount of over $794 million annually in federal monies,

2. Kevin F. McCarthy and David F. Ronfeldt, "Immigration as an Intrusive Global Flow," in Kritz (ed.), *U.S. Immigration and Refugee Policy*, 391–92.
3. U.S. Coordinator for Refugee Affairs, "An Edited Transcript of a Conference on Ethical Issues and Moral Principles in U.S. Refugee Policy, March 24 and 25, 1983" (Washington, D.C.), 16–17.

plus millions more at the state and local levels.[4] Although the consensus is that the United States has been generous, the American response to the exodus has not been without its critics.

The bungling of the evacuation from Saigon in 1975, which brought 130,000 refugees to the United States but left many of those clearly associated with the United States behind, is described by Frank Snepp. At the time, President Ford apparently felt strongly about American responsibility and insisted that the "United States could not desert the Vietnamese." Many in Congress wanted to limit the numbers of Vietnamese brought out, fearing the rumor that Ford wanted to evacuate a million refugees. Barry Wain wrote that this later exodus has been, in part, a result of the failure of the United States to evacuate enough people in 1975. He criticized the United States for failing to exert leadership during the crisis as it was building in 1976 and 1977, attributing American reluctance to the American people's desire to withdraw from the trauma of the war experience. Wain judged the situation thus: "Measured against the task at hand, the contribution of the United States was puny." This poor showing was especially hypocritical in view of the Carter administration's human rights policy, Wain claimed.[5]

By 1979, when the exodus reached crisis proportions in terms of both humanitarian aspects and foreign policy factors, culminating in an international Geneva conference in July, the United States was finally more forthcoming in pledging generous resettlement quotas. At that time, it assumed an important leadership role and sought to deflect the issue by calling for increased funding and quotas from other countries, emphasizing the concept of international responsibility and burden sharing. The American response in 1979 may be attributable to increased pressure by interest groups for humanitarian purposes but also to the political motivations of a variety of individuals and committees in Congress "jockeying for position in the boat people campaign which has become a popular issue." The New York *Times* reported that "President Carter, mindful of Senator Kennedy's activities on behalf of the refugees, is expected to take a more active role, pressing European and Asian nations to accept more refugees."[6]

4. *Refugee Reports,* X (January 27, 1989), 16, and IX (October 14, 1988), 4.
5. Snepp, *Decent Interval,* 412–13; Haley, *Congress and the Fall,* 103; Wain, *The Refused,* 37, 174, 176.
6. Washington *Post,* July 26, 1979, p. 2; New York *Times,* July 2, 1979, p. 9.

Leo Cherne of the International Rescue Committee, who played a principal role in that organization's efforts on behalf of the Hungarian refugees, tempered his praise for the American response to the Indochinese refugees, perhaps influenced by his experiences in 1956 and 1957. He pointed out, for example, that though the United States has taken in more refugees than has any other nation, Canada and Australia outperform it on a per capita basis. Sylvano Tomasi, migrations specialist, emphasized the influence of national interests and warned against placing too much credence in motivations based on guilt and responsibility. Shifting the emphasis in precisely that direction, Senator Mark Hatfield, while recognizing the importance of national interest factors, especially foreign policy objectives in Thailand, pointed to the influence of American humanitarianism, responsibility, and even guilt vis-à-vis the refugees. Making a case for continued American commitment, the senator wrote in 1984 that "America's willingness to assist in dealing with the Vietnamese, Lao, and Cambodian refugees stems in part from its role in exacerbating the problems in that region years ago." Finally, Roger Winter in 1985 noted, "Our nation's resettlement of over 725,000 Vietnamese, Lao and Cambodians ranks as one of the largest, most dramatic humanitarian efforts in history."[7]

The slow response at first of the United States to the Indochina refugee crisis reflected, in part, inadequate provisions for the admission of refugees under existing immigration law. As evidenced in the Hungarian situation, but also in regard to the refugees from Cuba in 1960, from Czechoslovakia in 1968, and from Vietnam in 1975, refugee measures in the post–World War II era were a patchwork of programs stitched together by crisis situations. These programs relied on the parole authority of the U.S. attorney general. Then attorney general Griffin Bell mentioned that he felt uncomfortable with the parole authority required of him in order to admit large numbers of Indochinese refugees, whereas the Congress was concerned about the apparent "unlimited authority" of the attorney general. The pressures of the Indochina refugee emergency prompted congressional action on a more equitable and regulated refugee program, which resulted in the

7. U.S. Coordinator for Refugee Affairs, "Transcript of Conference on Ethical Issues," 34–35, 37; Mark O. Hatfield, "U.S. Refugee Policy and Southeast Asia, Time for a Renewed Commitment," in Tripp (ed.), *World Refugee Survey: 1984*, 28–29; New York *Times*, March 3, 1985, p. 3.

Refugee Act of 1980. The new law conformed with UN Convention and Protocol definitions of a refugee, removed prior discriminatory restrictions that had provided for the admission of refugees only from communist and Middle Eastern countries, regularized consultations between Congress and the executive branch, created an office of coordinator for refugee affairs to oversee domestic and international refugee policies and programs, set a ceiling of 50,000 refugees for annual admissions, which could be revised pending need, and provided for federal assistance in refugee resettlement.[8]

The initial success of the Refugee Act when it was applied to the Indochina refugees was checked almost immediately, however, on two different, but related, fronts. First, the arrival of Haitian refugees and of Cuban refugees from the port of Mariel pointed to a serious flaw in the new law. That is, the act did not anticipate the United States being a first asylum country.[9] Second, the Refugee Act as interpreted by the State Department appeared to some to emphasize foreign policy goals unduly.

Indochinese refugees selected and resettled after temporary first asylum in Southeast Asian states contrasted with those refugees arriving unexpectedly on American shores directly from Haiti and Cuba. The influx of Cuban refugees, including criminals and other undesirables, was interpreted as a flagrant act of aggression, an invasion by Cuba.[10] The arrivals from Haiti raised several questions, including the conflict between refugee policy goals and foreign policy goals as they concerned noncommunist Haiti. In essence, when it was faced with political realities, the Refugee Act fell short of its objective, which was, in theory, to balance foreign policy goals and humanitarian concerns via the American penchant for legalism.

The growing perception that American refugee policy was responding to the Indochina refugee crisis primarily for foreign policy reasons forced a confrontation between the INS and the State Department concerning authority over refugee admissions. Then U.S. coordi-

---

8. Victor H. Palmieri, "Foreword," in Kritz (ed.), *U.S. Immigration and Refugee Policy,* xvii; Senate Judiciary Committee, *U.S. Immigration Law and Policy,* 77, 101.

9. Charles B. Keely, "Current Status of U.S. Immigration and Refugee Policy," in Kritz (ed.), *U.S. Immigration and Refugee Policy,* 350.

10. H. Eugene Douglas, "The Problem of Refugees in a Strategic Perspective," *Strategic Review* (Fall, 1982), 12.

nator for refugee affairs H. Eugene Douglas wrote that American refugee policy needed to be flexible if it was to serve "as an effective component of foreign policy." A great deal of that flexibility could be found in the language of the Refugee Act, which provided that asylum could be granted those refugees who were of "special humanitarian concern" to the United States. In the opinion of the INS and its supporters, this flexible, and perhaps ambiguous, phrase in the law was liberally interpreted by the State Department so as to foster its foreign policy goals in Southeast Asia. Severer critics thought that the State Department had breached the intent of the Refugee Act. Asserting its own authority in late 1980, the INS began to apply admissions criteria more stringently, on a case-by-case basis, and to defer decisions on the admission of many refugees. By April, 1981, 7,000 cases had been deferred, including 5,000 in Thailand.[11] This change in American policy caused alarm in the first asylum countries and influenced, in part, the adoption of a humane deterrence policy in Thailand and eventually a closed camp policy in Hong Kong.

The debate saw a temporary reprieve when Attorney General William French Smith agreed that the liberal guidelines for admissions in use before the INS stepped in would again be applied until September, 1981, and a commissioned, blue-ribbon committee, led by Marshall Green, reported in favor of giving the State Department the lead in Indochina refugee matters. But the controversy continued over the adjudication of refugee admissions. For example, a congressional judiciary committee report in 1982 stated a different opinion on the merits of various factors: "Political and foreign policy considerations— while important—are not the controlling factors in deciding which refugees are to be admitted to the United States. The controlling factors are domestic policy considerations, the particular plight of the individual refugee, and the refugee's tie to the United States."[12]

The debate illustrated the "diversity of interests and policy areas" affected by immigration and refugee issues. Kennedy aide Jerry Tinker criticized the "petty squabbling in the field" between the State Depart-

11. *Ibid.*, 16; House Judiciary Committee, *Refugee Issues in Southeast Asia and Europe*, 17.

12. U.S. Department of State, *The Indochinese Refugee Situation: Report to the Secretary of State by the Special Refugee Advisory Panel* (August 12, 1981), 11; House Judiciary Committee, *Refugee Issues in Southeast Asia and Europe*, 17.

ment and the INS, who "act as if they were not working for the same government." He went on to berate the INS: "INS officers on temporary duty from U.S. border inspection posts are not qualified to make a determination of an Indochinese refugee's eligibility—even if their interviews were expanded to one hour instead of 6 minutes." Opponents, however, advocated the strict application of the definition of a refugee and reaffirmed that "Congress intended, in the 1980 Act, that INS officers continue to exercise exclusive responsibility for determining eligibility of refugee status."[13]

Population expert Michael S. Teitelbaum wrote that the INS and its border patrol have been "the whipping boys and the laughing stocks of the executive branch." He clarified the situation, however, by detailing the reasons for their tarnished image: "It is notorious that they are—simultaneously—underfunded, mismanaged, undermanned, inadequately supplied, riven by internal dissension, and politically manipulated, yet they are also routinely pilloried for failures to fulfill assigned missions under such impossible circumstances." Indeed, by their own account, INS officers are professional law enforcement agents, unjustly maligned in the Indochina refugee debate. Others feel differently. A refugee official in Singapore called INS officers "a bunch of ex-border patrols." Another in Hong Kong said, "The INS thinks the whole refugee program is a political tumor on immigration law." A UNHCR representative believed the problem is that the INS has no foreign policy or moral concerns regarding refugees. A State Department officer in Manila thought the INS had too much discretion and was too subjective in admissions interviews.[14]

According to INS officer Jack Fortner, the State Department's conduct in the Indochina refugee issue made the INS's job of controlling the borders of the United States more difficult. Fortner expressed the opinion that the State Department had usurped power from the INS in order to foster its foreign policy goals and that it resented the INS's

13. McCarthy and Ronfeldt, "Immigration as an Intrusive Global Flow," in Kritz (ed.), *U.S. Immigration and Refugee Policy,* 393; Senate Judiciary Committee, *Refugee Problems: 1981,* 35–41; House Judiciary Committee, *Refugee Issues in Southeast Asia and Europe,* 19.

14. Michael S. Teitelbaum, "Right Versus Right: Immigration and Refugee Policy in the United States," *Foreign Affairs,* LIX (Fall, 1980), 54–55; interviews with Jack Fortner and with Dolores B. Lasan; anonymous interviews, Singapore, Hong Kong, and Manila, March 30–April 12, 1984.

screening of refugees as an intrusion in the pursuit of those goals. He believed the INS acted as a necessary brake on the admissions of refugees to the United States, for if the State Department was "given the reins, there would be no stopping the refugee flow." Fortner went on to say that the entire Indochina refugee program at the State Department had grown too large. He compared the current situation to the time prior to 1975 when the INS controlled the entire American refugee program, which was "run out of a single desk drawer" at the INS. Fortner explained that State Department officials and others who supported the resettlement of large numbers of refugees were wrong about the nature of the Indochina exodus but that they were reluctant to admit their mistake. He went on to point out that it is difficult to change or stop the American government's complex and bureaucratic refugee program, which now "feeds a huge conveyor belt" of voluntary agencies that assist the refugees.

Reflecting on internal problems at his agency, Fortner explained that the "INS has become a political pawn . . . headed by political appointees off the street." He bemoaned the fact that it reflects badly on an agency when middle- and upper-echelon department heads are "all chiefs from the outside." In fact, some observers noted a "new breed" of INS field officers being assigned throughout the ASEAN countries—officers who are cooperating in attempts to facilitate admissions. Hong Kong was cited as the last bastion of the "old guard" INS. Fortner observed that the INS has a job to do, to see that only bona fide refugees are admitted to the United States, and no directive has ever come from the White House to do it any differently, according to him. Funding, however, has never been commensurate with the task. Fortner felt strongly that public opinion regarding refugee admissions was on the side of the INS. He recalled that California, the state most heavily impacted by Indochinese refugees, was complaining about its refugee burden.

In October, 1986, Congressman Romano L. Mazzoli, chairman of the Subcommittee on Immigration, Refugees, and International Law, again called attention to the influence of foreign policy objectives on refugee admissions. Mazzoli noted that refugee admissions for fiscal year 1987, as proposed by the State Department, were "again weighted heavily in favor of the Indo-Chinese refugees." With the allocations for admissions from East Asia as high as 60 percent of total admissions, the congressman urged that the much smaller ceilings recommended by the State Department for Africa and Latin America be monitored. Mazzoli mentioned that many deserving asylum seekers from countries other than Indochina are denied refugee status and admission to the United States because of foreign policy considerations.[15]

In March, 1987, Senator Hatfield reiterated the continuing differences between foreign policy goals and the INS. In legislation calling for renewed commitment to the Indochinese refugees, Hatfield was critical of high rejection rates by INS in the screening of Indochinese refugees for admission to the United States. The senator commented that the "persistent INS screening problem . . . is directly causing a major diplomatic problem for the United States" in the region of Southeast Asia. Hatfield went on to propose a solution: "I believe that Congress can best implement its . . . foreign policy objectives by removing INS from the process of determining whether to admit refugees into the United States." It is interesting to note that the INS would have lost authority over admissions only in East Asia, not in other parts of the world, according to the proposed legislation.[16]

In addition to the question of authority in the debate between the INS and the State Department, the controversy has brought to the fore changes in the refugee flow and the influence of pull factors. The supporters of the INS emphasized that many of those leaving Indochina are not refugees but economic migrants, lured by the possibility of opportunities in the West and supporting the contention that "once started, migration flows become largely self-perpetuating and difficult to stop or control." The State Department, on the other hand, often took the position that the flow of refugees, though perhaps economically motivated of late, has been the result of persecution and that many of those leaving Indochina have suffered economic disadvantages that constitute persecution.[17]

Several sources cited the Voice of America as a pull factor early in the exodus, one remarking that broadcasts "deal with life in the West,

15. U.S. Congress, *Congressional Record*, 99th Cong., 2nd Sess., H11623.

16. "Senator Hatfield Introduces Indochinese Bill," *Refugee Reports*, VIII (April 17, 1987), 6.

17. McCarthy and Ronfeldt, "Immigration as an Intrusive Global Flow," in Kritz (ed.), *U.S. Immigration and Refugee Policy*, 388; House Judiciary Committee, *Refugee Issues in Southeast Asia and Europe*, 15.

especially the United States, in glowing terms." Refugees arriving in first asylum countries are said to have extensive knowledge of the latest American refugee policies and programs, probably gleaned from these broadcasts. William Shawcross saw as a cruel hoax, however, the encouragement given Cambodian refugees in 1979 to come to the Thai border for food and sanctuary, only for them to be denied entry into Thailand and resettlement abroad. Leo Cherne warned that the "noble image" of itself the United States projects abroad is costly in terms of the "generation of expectations" the United States cannot and will not fulfill. The presence of the U.S. Seventh Fleet in the South China Sea was mentioned as another pull factor, as the fleet was thought to deter pirates and to decrease loss of life at sea.[18] As the exodus continues, however, fewer and fewer Indochinese can claim they had close associations with the United States, a high-priority criterion for refugee admissions.

The question of security in the screening of Cambodian refugees was raised in early 1985. A Senate Foreign Relations Committee aide said that stringent screening was necessary to prevent the admission of communist Khmer Rouge to the United States. INS official Jack Fortner also mentioned the security issue in Thailand, pointing out that many young, male, Vietnamese refugees are former Vietcong. Fortner mentioned in particular that a former deputy mayor of Ho Chi Minh City survived the admissions screening process.[19]

As the screening of Cambodians still in Thailand was winding down during 1985 and 1986, it became apparent that nearly 15,000 refugees at Khao-I-Dang had been rejected for admission. Many of those denied admission allegedly were affiliated with the Khmer Rouge. Critics, including Senator John Glenn, questioned the accuracy of the processing, which seemed to reject refugees based on circumstantial evidence. In a highly critical report, "Looking for Phantoms," Stephen Golub took issue with the INS's "fundamentally flawed assumption that most or all of the 14,500 rejected applicants could well be Khmer Rouge." In describing the "arbitrary and capricious" screening

18. House Judiciary Committee, *Refugee Issues in Southeast Asia and Europe*, 14, 49, 53; U.S. Department of State, *Indochinese Refugee Situation*, 14; Shawcross, *Quality of Mercy*, 405; U.S. Coordinator for Refugee Affairs, "Transcript of Conference on Ethical Issues," 34.
19. New York *Times*, January 21, 1985, p. 3.

by INS officials with dubious credentials and according to ambiguous guidelines, Golub perceived ethical dilemmas on two points. First, he asked, is it not preferable to allow a few Khmer Rouge to be admitted, if indeed they do exist, rather than to screen out "thousands of innocent persons"? Second, he pointed out that the irony of the issue is underscored by the American support of the CGDK (which includes the Khmer Rouge faction) as the legitimate government of Cambodia.[20]

Many of the displaced Cambodians near the Thai-Cambodian border reportedly want to return home. Both Thai and American policies support this goal. For the United States, this position would appear to reflect not only foreign policy concerns but also domestic ones, for resettlement, with its magnet effect, would simply bring untold thousands more to the border area and compound the problems. More to the point, according to a 1985 congressional report, "large scale third country resettlement runs counter to remarkable efforts of those working and fighting for an independent and democratic Cambodia." And experience has shown that any resettlement processing for the Cambodians would be difficult to limit; "tremendous pressures . . . to continue such processing until the entire population is processed for resettlement" would result in large numbers of refugees coming to the United States. The report recommended against military funding for the noncommunist resistance forces near the border for a rather interesting reason: "Direct military assistance would be most inadvisable and would probably only serve to insure that all of those receiving the benefit of such aid would then have a claim to refugee status in the United States based upon their military association with us."[21] In the case of the border Cambodians, then, it appears that foreign policy objectives and domestic interests in favor of limiting admissions are in agreement.

In March, 1985, Jerry Tinker wrote that the refugee exodus in fact had shifted toward being a migration of economic migrants and those seeking family reunifications, a claim borne out by my interviews in Southeast Asia in 1984. He warned that unless the United States separated the bona fide refugees from the rest, a growing backlash in this

20. Washington *Post*, June 14, 1986, p. 10; Stephen Golub, *Looking for Phantoms: Flaws in the Khmer Rouge Screening Process*, U.S. Committee for Refugees (Washington, D.C., 1986), 1–36.
21. Senate Judiciary Committee, *U.S. Refugee Program: 1985*, 11.

country would undermine efforts to assist those who had truly been persecuted. In April, 1984, a refugee official in Manila expressed the opinion that there were still many refugees, especially those in the reeducation camps, who needed asylum, in contrast to "the corrupt generals who got away in 1975."[22]

Tinker urged that attention be given to the option of voluntary repatriation, long an anathema to the United States and therefore ignored. The option of repatriation has also been emphasized by others. Frank Johnston of the Australian High Commission in Malaysia said that what is needed is a creativity involving "a mix of programs," not only resettlement. Yet the United States has been against exploring other possibilities. An American refugee official thought, however, that "repatriation is down the road," given the current situation. Ernest Allen, with the Canadian High Commission in Singapore, also noted that up to 1984 the United States had been unwilling to discuss repatriation.[23]

By 1988, however, a change was apparent. In a tour of Southeast Asia in July of 1988, Secretary of State Shultz, in response to growing concern about the refugee situation, said that voluntary repatriation should be considered as an alternative to resettlement. A short time later, Vietnam indicated to a UN official that repatriation without recriminations would now be possible. This change, in talk if not yet in practice, would appear to reflect both the crisis associated with the sudden increases in refugees from Vietnam as well as the recent, if slight, thaw in U.S.-Vietnam relations.[24]

Along the same lines, Tinker and others cited development aid to Indochina as a possible contribution to solving the refugee problem at its source, though this would conflict with American foreign policy objectives to internationally isolate Vietnam. INS officer Fortner concurred: "Just open a consulate in Vietnam. . . . If Vietnam got $50 billion in aid it would be cheaper than resettlement." Ruth Cadwallader, of the American Friends Service Committee, found the entire

22. Jerry M. Tinker, "U.S. Refugee Policy: Coping with Migration," *Indochina Issues,* LV (March, 1985), 1–2; anonymous interview, Manila, April 6, 1984.
23. Tinker, "U.S. Refugee Policy," 3–4; interviews with Frank Johnston, Australian High Commission, Kuala Lumpur, March 27, 1984, and with Ernest Allen, Canadian High Commission, Singapore, April 3, 1984, and anonymous interview, Kuala Lumpur, March 27, 1984.
24. *Refugee Reports,* IX (July 15, 1988), 8, and IX (August 12, 1988), 7.

resettlement program illustrative of American vindictiveness and not the best or only answer to the refugee problem. Finally, Tinker encapsulated the problem in this way: "Yet we seem frozen . . . into sustaining an on-going third country resettlement program, even though the character of the outflow has changed."[25] By 1987 and 1988, private aid, albeit on a small scale, was resuming and reflected a modification in American foreign policy concerning Vietnam.

Heeding the call for fresh approaches to the Indochina refugee issue, a special Indochinese Refugee Panel was appointed by Secretary Shultz in September of 1985. The panel was headed by former Iowa governor Robert D. Ray. The report of the so-called Ray Panel was issued in April, 1986, and it recognized the changed nature of the exodus. Those who now flee are "no longer predominantly persons who were associated with the United States, nor does it appear that the majority have been singled out for harsher treatment than that generally suffered by the rest of the population." The report indicated that those who now leave search for "economic and political freedom or to be reunited with family members"; in any case, no matter what their motives for leaving, "once having left, few can now return."[26]

The panel's recommendation reflected the desire both to reform the American resettlement program and to tighten up the application of the Refugee Act of 1980. Yet the report also expressed a commitment to continued preservation of first asylum for bona fide refugees. The report suggested a two-track program to be phased in over a two-year transition period. One track would continue the resettlement of refugees; the second track would utilize normal immigration channels for family reunification cases. The two-track program ostensibly would assure the first asylum countries that they "will not be left with a residual refugee population." In addition, a new approach, called "sharing-out," would, with international cooperation, involve the resettlement of residual refugees now in the camps. Selection would be based on length of stay in the camps.[27]

Generally well received, some of the report's recommendations

25. Interviews with Jack Fortner and with Ruth Cadwallader; Senate Judiciary Committee, *U.S. Refugee Program: 1985*, 40.
26. "Panel on Indochinese Refugees Recommends Continued Refugee Program and New Emphasis on Immigration," *Refugee Reports*, VII (May 16, 1986), 1–4.
27. *Ibid.*

have been difficult to implement. The bureaucratic backlog of visas has called for expediting resettlement by way of humanitarian parole. In addition, petition for family reunification using immigration channels requires citizenship for the already resettled refugees who may want to file on behalf of relatives. At the end of 1986, only 46,073 of the more than 800,000 resettled Indochinese refugees had become naturalized citizens. More problematic, however, is the need for those filing for relatives to be able to demonstrate an ability to sponsor their family members economically. Although many refugees have already become financially self-sufficient, others remain in poverty. Over half of the refugees who have been in the United States for three years or less "are on public assistance," according to former director of the Office of Refugee Resettlement Phillip N. Hawkes.[28]

To temper a more restrictive application of the Refugee Act, the Ray Panel also recommended that provisions be made for special humanitarian cases by using the parole authority of the attorney general. The parole authority allows persons to be admitted to the United States at the discretion of the attorney general without prior congressional approval. The panel urged that humanitarian parole be "used generously and for especially compelling cases." In raising the issue of immigrant visa backlogs, Senator Edward Kennedy advised that those who have been waiting in the refugee camps for two, three, and even four years until their visas become current be paroled to the United States right away.[29]

However, Senator Alan Simpson, chairman of the Subcommittee on Immigration and Refugee Policy, cautioned that the Refugee Act of 1980 was intended to correct the abuses of humanitarian parole. The senator's words express the concern some felt about the parole authority, especially its potential to admit large numbers of refugees: "[I want to know] how many will come in under humanitarian parole. I would like to have someone give me a figure. No one does. . . . It was because of the parole policy of the United States that we had to come to the Refugee Act. Parole was abused and misused." Senator Simpson may have been referring to the Hungarians who were paroled into the

28. Washington *Post*, April 18, 1985, p. 1; *Senate Documents*, 99th Cong., 2nd Sess., No. J-99-129, p. 23, No. J-99-113, pp. 94, 39.
29. "Panel on Indochinese Refugees Recommends," 1–4; *Senate Documents*, 99th Cong., 2nd Sess., No. J-99-113, pp. 51–52.

United States in 1956 and 1957. Then, as now, some thought parole was not being used liberally enough, whereas others believed it allowed too many refugees to enter the United States. A refugee advocacy group, concerned especially about the compelling Cambodian cases at the border that seemingly have been forgotten, has called for "clear criteria" for humanitarian parole. The group recommended that parole authority be used without "preference and prejudice," to avoid the compromise of human rights by foreign policy and other interests. By the end of 1988, only 1,000 Cambodians had been approved for resettlement under the new immigration visa and humanitarian parole programs, which began in 1985. Thailand's restrictions on access to the refugees at the border are the major problem, but complicated regulations and narrow interpretations of guidelines are also obstacles.[30]

Sociologist Peter Rose explained that the symbolic and heart-rending image of refugees as victims of persecution is tempered by the reality that they are also dependents. According to Bruce Grant, refugees make costly claims on others. The first waves of refugees entering the United States were families headed by urban, educated, elite professionals, for the most part. They quickly demonstrated their ability and willingness to work hard, to help themselves, and to avoid the welfare rolls. However, by 1979, the later waves of less educated and unskilled refugees from rural areas coincided with economic problems in the United States, including high inflation and unemployment, and fed fears of uncontrollable numbers entering in the near future.[31]

According to opinion polls, the American public has never been enamored of the idea of resettling large numbers of Indochinese refugees. In 1980, only 19 percent of the population sampled supported President Carter's plan to admit 168,000 refugees for that year; 46 percent wanted a reduction in admissions. Michael Teitelbaum noted that there is "no economic justification for admitting large numbers of unskilled and ill-educated immigrant workers and their dependents." He also said that though racial prejudice is far less than what it has been historically in immigration issues, it still exists. Senator Simpson, long an advocate of immigration reform and restriction, commented

30. *Senate Documents*, 99th Cong., 2nd Sess., No. J-99-113, pp. 90–91, 65; *Refugee Reports*, IX (October 14, 1988), 13.

31. U.S. Coordinator for Refugee Affairs. "Transcript of Conference on Ethical Issues," 23–24.

that constituents complain when more is given to refugees while government programs, including food stamps and welfare benefits, are being cut for American citizens. At a congressional hearing in late 1981, a county official from Iowa spoke of the adverse impact federal cuts in domestic programs have on local refugee resettlement. Another remarked that if American Blacks and other minorities had the assistance refugees receive, they too could find employment and be taken off welfare.[32]

The California delegation report, which came out two years later, in late 1983, indicated that "U.S. resettlement was subordinate to many other American foreign policy objectives." The report was highly critical of the refugees' dependence on public assistance and of inadequate programs abroad, especially the English language training and cultural orientation program at Bataan, which ill prepared refugees for life in the United States. In 1985 and 1986, educational facilities at Bataan were expanded and new programs for children and adolescents were developed in order to ease their adjustment to American life.[33] However, the dilemma over conflicting agendas was perhaps best summarized by Paul J. Strand and Woodrow Jones, Jr., whose study of refugee adaptation reminds us that the Indochinese refugees are different from immigrants who come to the United States: "Employment and self-sufficiency are particularly troublesome issues for the Indochinese refugees . . . as they do not come to the U.S. to market skills that are supported by the U.S. economy. They came to escape persecution."[34]

Researcher Charles B. Keely found that the Refugee Act's provision for the federal government, instead of the private sector, to be the responsible agent for refugee resettlement has relegated voluntary agencies to the position of referral services that steer refugees toward public assistance. The California report recognized the "unshakeable moral obligation" of the United States to the Indochinese but asked

32. Teitelbaum, "Right Versus Right," 21, 35; U.S. Coordinator for Refugee Affairs, "Transcript of Conference on Ethical Issues," 47; *Senate Documents*, 97th Cong., 1st Sess., No. J-97-68, pp. 94–95.

33. California Legislature, *Report of the Fact-Finding Mission*, 72–80; U.S. Department of State, *World Refugee Report*, 36.

34. "Southeast Asian Refugees' Resettlement Problems Analyzed in San Diego Study," *Refugee Reports*, VII (April 18, 1986), 15. The article refers to a study by Paul J. Strand and Woodrow Jones, Jr., *Indochinese Refugees in America: Problems of Adaptation and Assimilation* (Durham, 1986).

how long this obligation was to last. Early in 1985, a State Department spokesman said the government anticipated increased lobbying by heavily impacted states to curb the refugee flow.[35]

A report by the Washington-based Refugee Policy Group found that for fiscal year 1984, Indochinese refugees had a higher welfare utilization rate than did other refugee groups. In addition, public assistance rates vary among the states. For example, in California, 85 percent of the refugees in the country for three years or less used some form of public assistance; in Texas, only 20 percent used that assistance. However, as the study pointed out, there was a dramatic decrease in welfare assistance for those households in the country for more than three years. For this group the rate was 39 percent.[36]

Like other federally funded programs, the American resettlement program has been affected by efforts to reduce the budget deficit. For example, for fiscal year 1986, the Gramm-Rudman-Hollings legislation resulted in the overall reduction of refugee admissions to the United States from an expected 67,000 to 61,000 refugees. For the Indochinese refugees specifically, the revised level of admissions was 43,500, down from the proposed ceiling of 45,500. In addition, the Office of Refugee Resettlement experienced a budget cut of 4.3 percent.[37]

By 1988, refugee advocates had become more critical of the gap between admissions ceilings and actual resettlement. For example, though the overall admissions ceiling for fiscal year 1988 had been set at 68,500 refugees, as requested by the State Department, the Office of Refugee Resettlement was working with a budget only large enough to resettle 52,000. A similar discrepancy was expected for 1989. According to U.S. Coordinator for Refugee Affairs Jonathan Moore, speaking in June, 1988, out of a ceiling of 28,500 allocated for Indochinese refugees apart from the ODP, 27,000 were expected to be resettled. And a shortfall of 1,000 was expected in the ODP category. Appearing before a congressional subcommittee, Roger Winter commented, "We believe the U.S. resettlement process has been deliberately managed so as to

35. Keely, "Current Status of U.S. Immigration," in Kritz (ed.), *U.S. Immigration and Refugee Policy,* 351; California Legislature, *Report of the Fact-Finding Mission,* 87; New York *Times,* March 3, 1985, p. 3.

36. Susan S. Forbes, *Adaptation and Integration of Recent Refugees to the United States,* Refugee Policy Group (Washington, D.C., 1985), 15.

37. *Senate Documents,* 99th Cong., 2nd Sess., No. J-99-113, pp. 18, 42.

significantly fall short of FY 88 ceilings for Southeast Asia." In addition, a 38 percent reduction in federal funding for refugee programs administered at the state level was expected to result in the curtailment, and in some cases the elimination, of important social services. Some believed that the reduction in funding would contribute to an increase in welfare dependency rates and possibly influence negative public attitudes regarding refugee resettlement. In a surprise move, congressional appropriations for fiscal year 1989 included over $794 million for refugee programs. This amount was $175 million more than was requested, though a congressional report chided the administration for not requesting enough money to meet refugee needs.[38]

Another refugee issue emerging in 1987 and continuing into 1989 prompted concern about the resettlement of Indochinese refugees. With the increase in the numbers of asylum seekers from the Soviet Union, especially Armenians, came speculation that admissions numbers already allocated to other refugee groups would be reassigned to these newest refugees. Although an emergency request eventually adjusted the admissions ceiling for fiscal year 1988 by 15,000 in order to accommodate the Soviet asylum seekers, the problem continued. By midyear, admissions processing for the Armenians and others from the Soviet Union was suspended, ostensibly for budgetary reasons but also amid growing concern about the Armenians' claims for refugee status and continuing criticism of State Department and INS screening procedures. As the number of asylum seekers from the Soviet Union continued to climb, creating a backlog of cases, the Reagan Administration announced in December, 1988, that 6,500 admissions places would be transferred from the Southeast Asian admissions allotment to the Soviet Union allotment. Specifically, the action cut 5,500 from the ODP and 1,000 from the first asylum countries. In defense of the decision, U.S. Coordinator for Refugee Affairs Jonathan Moore pointed out that the transfer of numbers, especially from the ODP category, was justified because Vietnam had all but suspended the agreement to allow reeducation camp prisoners and their families to emigrate. Therefore, according to Moore, the original ODP numbers

38. "End of Year 'Bulge' Predicted on Refugee Admissions," *Refugee Reports*, IX (June 24, 1988), 1–4; "States Protest Deep Cuts in Administrative Budgets, Say Welfare Costs Will Increase," *Refugee Reports*, IX (April 15, 1988), 1–6; "Refugee Appropriations for FY 89," *Refugee Reports*, IX (October 14, 1988), 4.

would probably not be utilized. Refugee advocates, however, disagreed. Le Xuan Khoa, director of the Indochinese Resource Action Center, spoke of the implications of this change in policy: "The transfer of numbers sends a negative signal indeed. Such a precipitous transfer hints that Indochinese refugees—especially those seeking to leave Vietnam in a safe and orderly fashion—are not of priority concern to the United States."[39]

The shortfalls in refugee resettlement (though not large), the debate over resettlement funding, and now the competition for admissions between Soviet refugees and other refugee groups, especially the Indochinese, coincided with and were no doubt related to the hard-line policies and harsh reactions provoked in the first asylum countries in Southeast Asia, particularly in Thailand and Hong Kong, by the sudden upsurge in refugee arrivals from Vietnam by 1988. The perception of dwindling assistance from the United States no doubt contributed in part to this latest response to the exodus.

A survey of public attitudes about refugees commissioned by the U.S. Committee for Refugees in 1984 found that people's opinions about refugees changed for the better as their knowledge of who the refugees were and why they had come to the United States increased. According to the survey, few people, politicians included, make a distinction between refugees and other immigrants; to most, they are all foreigners. Therein lies the connection between refugees and an overall immigration problem.[40]

Kevin F. McCarthy and David F. Ronfeldt observed that refugee flows underscore "the contradiction of a global superpower unable to exercise control over its own borders." Other factors that have combined to substantiate this view and to fuel an apocalyptic perception of refugee exoduses are explained by Michael Teitelbaum: the importance attached to nation-states, advances in communication and transportation that highlight attractive images of life in the West and images of suffering in the Third World, and population increases and their potential for mass migrations. In addition to the influx from Indochina, arrivals from Haiti and Cuba and increasing unrest in Central America

---

39. *Refugee Reports,* IX (March 18, 1988), 6–9, IX (June 24, 1988), 10–13, IX (July 15, 1988), 9–11, IX (August 12, 1988), 11–12, and X (January 27, 1989), 6–10.
40. Tripp (ed.), *World Refugee Survey: 1984,* 31.

and elsewhere, which carries with it refugee components, compound the negative assessment of the crisis.[41]

Overall increases in immigration, brought about by liberalized reforms in immigration law in 1965, and the growing problem with illegal immigrants, estimated to have been between 4,000,000 and 6,000,000 in the late 1970s, bodes ill for the Indochinese refugees. By 1985, concern about illegal immigration heightened with the INS's estimation of and apprehension of over 1,300,000 illegal aliens that year. By 1989, there were no firm estimates of the numbers of Central American aliens living in the United States, though the Salvadoran population alone was thought to be at least 1,000,000 and Nicaraguans were estimated to be 400,000, with thousands more expected shortly. These arrivals raise concerns about the control of borders as well as cultural and political unity and stability. For example, recent efforts to make English the official language in some states is a reaction to anxieties about growing pluralism.[42]

Although there is broad consensus that immigration should be curbed, any limits on legal immigration would be a political liability, if not an impossibility, given the activities of powerful ethnic interest groups. Thus, politicians look for the weak spot in the immigration population. James Towey, aide to Senator Hatfield, and Roger Winter share the view that politicians single out refugees in their attempt to control legal immigration. Illegal immigrants pose a problem that is without a comprehensive solution. Loring Waggoner, a refugee official in Manila, saw some of the repercussions and remarked, "Our own illegal immigration problem is a problem for the refugees." However, recent immigration legislation involving amnesty and employer sanctions reflects a real effort to check illegal entry. The adoption of hard-line policies regarding asylum seekers is another example of growing restrictiveness. In 1983, then attorney general William French Smith summarized the situation when he said, "Simply put we have lost control of our borders."[43]

---

41. McCarthy and Ronfeldt, "Immigration as an Intrusive Global Flow," in Kritz (ed.), *U.S. Immigration and Refugee Policy*, 391; Teitelbaum, "Right Versus Right," 22–23.

42. Teitelbaum, "Right Versus Right," 23; Lawrence H. Fuchs, "Immigration, Pluralism, and Public Policy: The Challenge of the Pluribus to the Unum," in Kritz (ed.), *U.S. Immigration and Refugee Policy*, 290–92; James Silk, *Despite a Generous Spirit: Denying Asylum in the United States*, U.S. Committee for Refugees (Washington, D.C., December, 1986), 11; Washington *Post*, January 15, 1989, pp. 1, 22.

43. Interviews with James Towey, Office of Sen. Mark O. Hatfield, Washington,

Although refugees constitute only 5 percent of the total annual immigration to the United States, legal and illegal, the public does not distinguish between them and other immigrants. They, however, are the ones in the public eye as refugee policy and quotas are reviewed each year, allowing politicians to give their constituents the perception that they are doing something about the immigration problem by attempting to reduce the admissions of refugees. According to Towey, refugees have become the "ugly stepchild" in the move for immigration reform.

Along the same lines, the assertiveness of the INS toward the Indochinese refugees may reflect that agency's attempt to compensate for its poor performance in controlling illegal entry, especially along the Mexican border. The recent efforts to pursue Nazi war criminals resettled in the United States after World War II are also examples of the INS's attempt to change its image. Related to the deportation of alleged Nazis may be the vigilance with which INS screens Cambodian refugees; its rejection of Khmer Rouge elements among the refugee population could preclude later embarrassment for immigration authorities.

Increasingly, others raise the question, as the delegation from California did, about the United States paying off its debt to the Indochinese in the form of refugee resettlement. Fewer and fewer of the refugees can now claim any association with the American experience in Vietnam. A recent New York *Times* article reported that a State Department official "believed the United States has now paid its moral debt for its involvement on the losing side in Indochina." The dilemma that yet remains is well expressed by Senator Simpson: "There has got to be some kind of finality to the program which does not in any way reduce our commitment to the world's refugees."[44]

Others speak of the finite ability of the United States to absorb more refugees. John Silber, a philosopher and the president of Boston University, said that the "sin of pride" is evident in the assumption by any nation of moral responsibility in excess of its capacities. Nonetheless, the United States continues to admit large numbers of Indochinese refugees. A quota of 46,500 refugees from Indochina approved for

D.C., February 7, 1984, with Roger Winter, Director, U.S. Committee for Refugees, Washington, D.C., February 8, 1984, and with Loring Waggoner; Silk, *Despite a Generous Spirit*, 10.

44. New York *Times*, March 3, 1985, p. 3; *Senate Documents*, 99th Cong., 2nd Sess., No. J-99-113, p. 102.

fiscal year 1989 reflects a continuing and clear commitment by the United States for both foreign policy and humanitarian reasons. The U.S. commitment to Indochinese refugees was also apparent in late 1987, when a "sense of the Congress" resolution, sponsored by refugee advocate Senator Hatfield, passed by a two-thirds majority vote. The resolution called for a three-year commitment to a resettlement rate of at least 28,000 persons per year, apart from the ODP. U.S. Committee for Refugees' spokesman Court Robinson believed the resolution was having an impact on the overall resettlement process. In addition, the Amerasian Homecoming Act, enacted in late 1987, was expected to bring many Amerasians and their relatives, estimated to be as high as 30,000 persons, to the United States by 1990. However, the departure rate has been disappointingly slow. During the period 1982–1987, approximately 9,500 Amerasians and their family members left Vietnam. During the first half of 1988, after expectations had risen with the passage of the Homecoming Act, a mere 1,660 persons arrived, though there was a backlog of nearly 5,000 others who had been approved for departure and who were still waiting to leave.[45]

Former U.S. refugee coordinator Victor Palmieri indicated that in regard to immigration and refugee matters, a dilemma still exists between American laws and issues of national sovereignty on the one hand and respect for human rights and democratic ideals on the other. The depiction of some important aspects of the resettlement of Indochinese refugees in the United States supports Palmieri's thinking. As the resettlement program has evolved, unforeseen results have raised thorny questions involving the competition among national interests and between interests and humanitarian concerns.[46]

45. U.S. Coordinator for Refugee Affairs, "Transcript of Conference on Ethical Issues," 16–17; U.S. Department of State, *Proposed Refugee Admissions for 1988*, 2; telephone interview with Court Robinson, U.S. Committee for Refugees, Washington, D.C., September 21, 1988; Stephen D. Goose and R. Kyle Horst, "Amerasians in Vietnam: Still Waiting," *Indochina Issues*, LXXXIII (August, 1988), 1–7.

46. Palmieri, "Foreword," in Kritz (ed.), *U.S. Immigration and Refugee Policy*, xx.

VI

Humanitarian

Concerns

The chaotic, conflict-ridden world that generates refugee problems but also renders assistance to the victimized is evidence of man's dual nature, his capacity for both good and evil. The aid given to Indochina refugees, in the forms of direct relief, temporary asylum, and permanent resettlement, by a host of international organizations, governments, voluntary agencies, and individuals, though perhaps imperfect, constitutes an extraordinary humanitarian effort and is testimony to man's potential for magnanimity.

Since 1975, almost 2,000,000 refugees have received temporary first asylum, with Thailand alone providing sanctuary to nearly 1,000,000 displaced people from Indochina. Over thirty countries have permanently resettled more than 1,600,000 refugees, with the United States, Canada, Australia, France, and the People's Republic of China taking sizable numbers.[1]

Commenting on the American response to the Indochinese refugees, Roger Winter remarked, "I don't know of another situation in history where a nation has taken in such a large number of people from a distant culture for whom it felt a dramatic responsibility." The United States has resettled more than 884,000 refugees from Vietnam, Laos, and Cambodia and has given them an estimated $1 billion in federal assistance annually.[2]

1. U.S. Department of State, *Proposed Refugee Admissions for 1988*, 8; *Refugee Reports*, VIII (December 18, 1987), 8.
2. Washington *Post*, April 18, 1985, p. 8.

A critical component of refugee problems, these humanitarian concerns as rooted in standards of morality are the subject of this chapter. In particular, the investigation focuses on the role of the UNHCR, the leading international coordinating agency mandated to protect and assist refugees. In theory, this demanding task means that "on every continent the UNHCR stands as the first line of defense for refugees: it speaks out for their protection; it provides for their care and maintenance; it seeks humane alternative solutions to their plight."[3] The effectiveness of the UNHCR is thus very important and needs to be examined in the context of the Indochina refugee problem. In addition to drawing on the political theory of realism, this discussion is informed by the theory of natural law as related to human rights, by the interpretations of eminent legal scholar, Paul Freund, and by the theory of the "moral constitution" according to the late moral philosopher Edmond Cahn. The study also highlights and incorporates some of the important ethical aspects and dilemmas posed by the Indochina refugee issue, including the role of international law and its definition of refugees, the dichotomy of push and pull motivating factors in the exodus, the seemingly infinite ramifications of human rights in an imperfect and finite world, and problems of moralism versus the more profound concept of morality. Finally, the context of the discussion is the continuing collusion and collision of national interests and humanitarian concerns in the ongoing story of the Indochina refugees.

The UNHCR, twice the recipient of the Nobel Peace Prize, in 1954 and 1981, has aided more than 25,000,000 refugees since it was founded in 1951 with the mandate to protect the rights of and provide assistance to the world's refugees. Created in response to the refugee situation in Europe after World War II, the UNHCR program and office have grown and expanded fivefold as the global refugee problem has increased in complexity, size, and scope. With its headquarters in Geneva and over eighty field offices all over the world, the UNHCR's annual budget exceeded $500 million by 1981. Although a variety of organizations, large and small, including other UN affiliates, have been involved with the refugees in Southeast Asia since 1975, the UNHCR is often considered the leading agency in the region. Having

3. U.S. Department of State, *Proposed Refugee Admissions for FY 1987*, No. 866 (September 16, 1986), 2.

spent over $300 million in Thailand alone since the exodus began, it estimated its expenditures for the Indochina refugees for fiscal year 1989 to be over $60 million.[4]

The performance of the UNHCR in the Indochina refugee issue, however, has met with serious criticism on several fronts. Some of the complaints concerning its effectiveness have to do with the internal organizational behavior of the UNHCR.[5] More important, many criticisms are related to external factors, for the UNHCR, a humanitarian agency, seeks to protect and assist refugees within a politically charged context. National interests involving power politics and issues of sovereignty compete and conflict with the UNHCR's efforts to carry out its humanitarian mandate.

Part of the disappointment with the UNHCR is due to our general perceptions of transnational organizations—perceptions that influence, if not determine, our expectations of what these organizations can accomplish. Transnational organizations like the UNHCR can be viewed in one of at least three ways. First, they are sometimes viewed idealistically as rising above politics and the interests of nations in pursuit of a cooperative, utopian, global community where the world's problems are solved peacefully and rationally. Second, these agencies are more commonly viewed with skepticism and even pessimism, particularly when empirical evidence points to a wide gap between optimistic, naïve expectations and real results. Critics of international agencies frequently point to the UN citing unrealistic goals, charter limitations, marginal involvement in truly significant world issues, failures to produce solutions to problems, and financial and bureaucratic difficulties to justify their cynicism.[6] Third, the perspective of realism enables us to look at transnational organizations, specifically the UN and its affiliates, with an honest and frank appraisal of what is possible within recognized limits. By considering a multitude of factors, including the power of national interests and the capacity for

4. *Ibid.*; United Nations, Office of the United Nations High Commissioner for Refugees, *UNHCR* (Geneva, 1982), 10; Leon Gordenker, "Organizational Expansion and Limits in International Services for Refugees" (Typescript, Princeton, 1984), 3; Office of the UNHCR, "Fact Sheet," II, no. 1 (April, 1988).

5. William H. Lewis, "The Operations of the United Nations High Commissioner for Refugees: An Indepth Evaluation of Performance" (Typescript, George Washington University, n.d.), 35–42.

6. *Ibid.*, 3–7.

politics not only to generate problems but also to solve them, the realistic point of view avoids polarization and the inflexibility of either optimistic or pessimistic positions.

The UNHCR and the charges leveled against it, then, are discussed here from the premise that this organization must operate not with the authority that characterizes sovereign nations but with limits imposed on it by the nations that created it and on which it must rely for funds. The successes and failures of the UNHCR in protecting and assisting refugees in large part reflect the successes and failures of those national governments associated with refugee problems. William H. Lewis perceived the real nature of the transnational organization: "[It] can never evolve into anything more than 'a mirror of the world as it is.' . . . it is as good or as bad as the nations which compose it."[7]

That the UNHCR is slow and reluctant to act in refugee emergencies was a criticism I frequently heard in interviews throughout the ASEAN states and in Hong Kong. A partial explanation often given was that UNHCR policy is set in Geneva and field personnel in Southeast Asia do not have enough discretionary authority to adapt the policy to their areas. An Australian diplomat thought the UNHCR needed revamping, that it was too "Eurocentric" in dealing with refugee problems in Southeast Asia and elsewhere in the Third World. INS officer Jack Fortner said that the UNHCR was a "bunch of overpaid bureaucrats" with "too many philosophers." In 1982, several African nations publicly protested the reappointment of Poul Hartling, a former Danish diplomat, to head the UNHCR. They recommended that the agency be led by someone from a country experiencing a refugee problem. They also complained that Hartling recruited top aides from only Western countries.[8]

The successor to Hartling as head of the UNHCR, Jean-Pierre Hocke, assumed his duties in January, 1986. A Swiss citizen, Hocke was a former director of operational activities of the International Committee of the Red Cross. Commenting in a recent interview about the new directorship and the UNHCR's future, Kazuo Chiba of Japan, chairman of the executive committee of the UNHCR, echoed earlier criticisms: "UNHCR cannot operate in a European-oriented or a Euro-

7. *Ibid.*, 5.
8. Anonymous interviews, March 13–April 12, 1984; Washington *Post*, December 12, 1982, p. 30.

centrist mental and physical set-up. We must, all of us, try to help UNHCR [become] more global-oriented."[9]

There are early indications that High Commissioner Hocke may attempt to bring about changes in the UNHCR. One of Hocke's first actions was an administrative reform, undertaken in March, 1986. This fundamental restructuring was apparently a reaction to anticipated criticisms of the agency's cost effectiveness. In 1986, the United States reduced its contribution to the UN by more than half of the $206 million assessment made by UN Charter. Although the UNHCR budget was not "directly threatened . . . administrative 'housecleaning' . . . [was] an effort to avoid criticism." Yet two years later, in 1988, an internal UN panel investigating the UNHCR still found poor management and a "general climate of helplessness." With a total staff of 2,300 officers around the world, the UNHCR appears administratively top-heavy, for 800 work at the Geneva headquarters.[10]

In addition to reforms that address fiscal responsibility and performance in field operations, Dale de Haan, former deputy UN high commissioner for refugees and now director of the Immigration and Refugee Program of Church World Service, was impressed in 1986 with what he saw as the UNHCR's broader interpretation of its mandate. The then-new director appeared to de Haan to be willing to protect and assist refugees who "do not fall within the classical refugee definition of the UNHCR statute." However, a more cautious observer perceived problems in the new emphasis to "get in and out of situations quickly" and a possible consequent reduction in the effort to protect refugees. By 1988, refugees' advocate Roger Winter observed that the UNHCR was in "retreat . . . from its only statutory duty, that of protecting refugees in the fullest legal and moral sense."[11]

In his analysis of the UNHCR, William Lewis found fault with an "encrusted senior bureaucracy" that generated a gap between head-quarters and junior officers in the field, thus contributing to resentment and malaise. He also mentioned that field personnel often do not have enough cultural background to make them effective in develop-

9. Michael S. Barton, "Interview," *Refugees,* XXVI (February, 1986), 42.
10. "Shake-Up at UNHCR Avoids Major U.N. Cuts," *Refugee Reports,* VII (November 14, 1986), 13–15; Washington *Post,* September 13, 1988, p. 22.
11. "Shake-Up at UNHCR Avoids Cuts," 13–15; Washington *Post,* September 13, 1988, p. 22.

ing countries. Lewis also discussed problems associated with recruiting in order to achieve geographical balance and representation, which results in what he sees as the application of lower recruitment standards.[12]

Although portrayed today as a universal agency, the UNHCR is philosophically and politically rooted in the European experience with refugees in the aftermath of World War II. Its Western origins exert much influence on it and are at times the source of complaints as the UNHCR grows and evolves in response to the changing refugee situation worldwide. It is the latest transnational refugee organization, succeeding the High Commissioner for Refugees of the League of Nations, the UN Relief and Rehabilitation Administration, and the International Refugee Organization.[13]

Philosophically, the present concern for refugees can be traced in part to the idea of human rights as it is rooted in the theory of natural law. The founding of the UNHCR and the development of the UN Convention legal standard that defines a refugee and serves to guide the UNHCR came three years after the UN Declaration of Human Rights in 1948. These international legal instruments recognize the natural rights of refugees that, though abrogated by governments, actually transcend nation-states. Although the devastation of war and of the Jewish Holocaust in Europe gave evidence to support the existential idea of the world as an absurdity, these same experiences somehow also generated for some a recognizable remnant of man's faith and hope in himself and in the future. In the postwar period, the attention to human rights, brought to the fore by the abuses of power by a number of states, constituted a revival in natural law theory.

John George Stoessinger pointed out the existence, in classical Greek thought, of an equalitarian philosophy in the ideas of the Stoics, in marked contrast to the Platonic idea of human inequality. The law of nature as the Stoics envisioned it advocates equal political, economic, and legal rights for all and provides for the capacity to reason as universal and just, binding on all human beings, regardless of their station in

12. Lewis, "Operations of the UNHCR," 36–37.
13. *Ibid.*, 13–15. A critical analysis of the problems faced by these earlier refugee agencies can be found in Stoessinger, *Refugee and the World Community.* The story of the growth of the UNHCR from its work in Europe to the present level of assistance it offers throughout the world is carefully chronicled in Holborn, *Refugees.*

life. Judeo-Christian thought, expanding the closed law of nature, developed the idea of transcendent destiny. Relying on the premise that man is both human and divine, it conceived of the individual as being able to rise above the power of the temporal state. Prominent scholar of morality and politics, J. Bryan Hehir used that conception as the basis for his conclusion about human rights: "Because of that destiny, no civil power, political cause or ideological vision can claim the right to subordinate the person to its ends." This explanation of human rights corresponds with the UNHCR definition of a refugee, which says that a person's fear of such subordination makes that individual flee his country and its protection.[14]

Enlightenment thinkers endowed the law of nature with intellectual integrity and romantic spirit as they codified it into the natural rights of man. Stoessinger pointed to the sacred and religious characteristics attributed to these inalienable rights in such documents as the American Declaration of Independence. However, in the use of individual rights as protest ideology or as "defensive instruments to protect individual freedom from encroachment by the state," thinkers like Thomas Paine saw an inherent conflict, because the protection of those individual rights is dependent on the will of the sovereign state. Ideally, man is born free; realistically, he is destined as a social being to live within the context and confines of a society. Hehir noted that there is a difference between liberal-secular thinking and Christian thought regarding the protection of individual rights. John Locke, representing the liberal-secular view, thought states would protect rights out of necessity, because it would be in their interests to do so. Christian thought declared states would safeguard rights out of a moral sense of responsibility.[15]

The rights of refugees—the right to flee persecution and the right to seek and enjoy nationality and asylum—can be viewed as recent interpretations of human rights, based on natural law. The relationship of these rights to the state is obvious, as the role of national interests in the Indochina refugee issue has demonstrated. Whether these rights

14. Stoessinger, *Refugee and the World Community,* 4; J. Bryan Hehir, "Human Rights from a Theological and Ethical Perspective," in Thompson (ed.), *Moral Imperatives of Human Rights,* 7.

15. Stoessinger, *Refugee and the World Community,* 5; Hehir, "Human Rights," in Thompson (ed.), *Moral Imperatives of Human Rights,* 7–9.

are upheld by nations out of a necessity associated with self-interest or out of ethical responsibility, the role of the state is essential. The UNHCR's former director Hartling remarked that "it is ultimately in the power of governments, not UNHCR, to create the fundamental conditions in which existing problems can be solved and fresh problems avoided."[16]

The UNHCR mandate, then, to protect the rights of refugees, is rooted in Western thought. The nature of the Indochina refugee issue gives evidence of complications in this regard, for the rights of refugees within the context of human rights may be bound by culture and influenced by circumstance. Kenneth Thompson concurred that "not only the concept of 'rights,' but also the concept of law embodied in modern constitutionalism and international treaties, can be seen as typically Western, not universal." Adda Bozeman warned that not all societies subscribe to the same idea of what constitutes the correct relationship between the individual and the state. For example, the Indochina states regard the refugees as disloyal citizens who are unwilling or unable to conform to the goals of the state at the expense of individual liberties. Marxist thought criticizes liberal Western ideas, which give inordinate attention to civil and political rights and freedoms while they ignore gross social and economic inequalities. Marx saw human rights as radically egoistic: "Thus none of the so-called rights of men goes beyond the egoistic man, the man withdrawn into himself, his private interest and his private choice and separated from the community as a member of civil society."[17]

The ASEAN states do not share the view of the United States and other Western nations that Indochina refugees are entitled to an alternative to life under communism. Although important national interests influence this perspective, cultural factors may also play a role. Sadruddin Aga Khan commented that the UN Declaration of Human Rights is far from universally applied and remains "unheeded by many states in practically every continent."[18]

The UNHCR is guided by two legal instruments regarding refugees: the 1951 Convention and the 1967 Protocol. Although more than

16. D'Souza, *Refugee Dilemma*, 14.
17. Kenneth W. Thompson, "Implications for American Foreign Policy," Bozeman, "Human Rights in Western Thought," and Hehir, "Human Rights," all in Thompson (ed.), *Moral Imperatives of Human Rights*, 240, 25–38, and 9, respectively.
18. Suhrke, *Indochinese Refugees: The Impact*, 3; Aga Khan, *Study on Human Rights*, 9.

one hundred nations have acceded to these international standards, including China, Japan, and the Philippines, many Asian nations are not signatories. In the Indochina refugee issue, then, the UNHCR must seek to carry out its mandate with the cooperation of governments not bound by international legal codes. Regarding the Declaration of Human Rights, Thompson indicated why such examples of international law have always been at best only partially successful: "[It is] a device through which satisfied powers legitimate the power that supports their concepts of justice and seek to protect it against the revisionist demands of the dissatisfied. This quality of international law, plus its obvious Western origins, gives it standing with non-Western states only when that is convenient."[19]

Politically, the UNHCR is rooted in the European experience, created as a temporary and special agency to deal with the refugee problem in Europe, which was interfering with postwar economic, social, and psychological reconstruction. Spared the vicissitudes of the UN General Assembly, the UNHCR is overseen by an executive committee, which was expanded from its original twenty-five members to forty-three members in order to include Third World nations who are experiencing refugee problems. Conspicuous by their absence on the committee are East European bloc countries, with the exception of Yugoslavia.[20]

From the beginning, the creators of the UNHCR have imposed limitations on it that are a source of criticisms of its effectiveness today in the Indochina refugee problem. Foremost among those arguing for a restricted role for the UNHCR was the United States, represented by Eleanor Roosevelt. Among the more serious restrictions imposed on the UNHCR, as delineated by William Lewis in his analytical study, are five major limitations. First, the UNHCR must have the approval of the host government before it can protect and assist refugees in any country. Second, the UNHCR must be nonpolitical. Third, it is to be nonoperational, contracting with and coordinating the efforts of agencies that provide direct material assistance and services to refugees. Fourth, it is a temporary agency. And fifth, the UNHCR is to "stimulate action by governments to achieve more favorable treatment" for refugees,

---

19. Virginia Hamilton (ed.), *World Refugee Survey: 1987*, 4; Thompson, "Implications for American Foreign Policy," in Thompson (ed.), *Moral Imperatives of Human Rights*, 240.
20. House Foreign Affairs Committee, *Reports on Refugee Aid*, 26.

instead of directly rendering protective services. These limitations clearly indicate that the authority of the agency can never supersede the power of sovereign states.[21]

With these limitations it is not surprising that the UNHCR has maintained a "modest role in Southeast Asia," bringing into question whether it can truly be called a leading agency in the Indochina refugee issue. A congressional study in 1981 summarized the UNHCR's position: "Governments are the HC's ultimate source of authority, the primary source of funds." Nonpolitical and dependent on the approval of host governments, it is like the guest whose invitation and length of stay is contingent on acceptable behavior. Caught in the tension between its humanitarian mandate to individuals and the interests of nations, it proceeds warily in the ASEAN states whose responsibility to the refugees is already curtailed by their not having acceded to the Convention or Protocol documents. Human rights advocates find the UNHCR does not protect refugees enough whereas host governments complain that it emphasizes the humanitarian aspects of the refugee situation at the expense of important political factors. The result, then, is dissatisfaction with the agency and confusion regarding its legitimate role.[22]

The UNHCR's nonpolitical stance means it has no leverage in a highly politically charged event, for any "disclaimers of politics" merely "mask a political reality." One refugee official remarked that the UNHCR is "no match" for the immigration laws of nations. The ambiguity of its position precludes establishing a place for the UNHCR at the center of the Indochina crisis. In his analysis, Lewis commented that the UNHCR is "trapped between general responsibility and limited authority, between rising demand and limited capacity." With regard to the Indochinese refugees, he wrote: "The UNHCR had little opportunity (or capacity) to address the legal issue of recognition of refugee status, of protection of rights, or the return under appropriate safeguards of the Kampucheans and Vietnamese to their homelands. As a result, the UNHCR was not at the center of the decision making or operational processes involved in the 1979 refugee crisis."[23]

21. Lewis, "Operations of the UNHCR," 17, 19.

22. *Ibid.*, 13; House Foreign Affairs Committee, *Reports on Refugee Aid*, 26; Wain, *The Refused*, 202; Lewis, "Operations of the UNHCR," 27.

23. Gordenker, "Organizational Expansion and Limits," 6; Lewis, "Operations of the UNHCR," 27–28.

The ASEAN countries were highly critical of the UNHCR's non-political position in late 1978 and 1979 when the refugee exodus reached crisis proportions. The agency offended first asylum countries by criticizing their negative responses to the influx but not leveling any corresponding blame on Hanoi, the source of the problem, or on resettlement countries, who were not doing their fair share. Its bias toward humanitarian aspects was clearly perceived to be insensitivity to the plight of those countries receiving refugees. The UNHCR was reluctant even to call an international conference to discuss the situation. At the two conferences eventually held in Geneva, in December, 1978, and July, 1979, it tried to limit discussion of the political factors in the event, ostensibly to prevent the meetings from degenerating into polemical exchanges that might jeopardize any efforts to render humanitarian assistance to the refugees. In his account of the conferences, Abdul Hadi Derani assessed the agency's position: "The UNHCR had set views on the refugee problem. To the agency the whole of the Indochinese refugee problem was essentially a human tragedy which had to be approached purely from a humanitarian consideration."[24]

William Shawcross wrote about the overly cautious UNHCR office in Thailand, where the refugee problem has always been severe, that was reluctant to increase its role and hesitant to protect the refugees. It was UNHCR policy not to protest Thai actions lest the organization anger the government, in effect making Thailand less tolerant of the refugees than they already were. The Thais did not like "external pressure." In one incident, the Thais complained about a junior UNHCR field officer who "infringed on Thai authority" when he tried to prevent the repatriation of some Cambodian refugees to the border region. According to Shawcross, many small groups were forced back to Cambodia without "effective protests by UNHCR."[25]

An American official also said the UNHCR had performed badly; he was appalled that it "did not utter a peep" when 42,000 Cambodians were forcibly repatriated in mid-1979. Voluntary agency co–field director Ruth Cadwallader noted that when Thailand announced it would close and consolidate camps in 1983 and 1984, the UNHCR had no choice but "to cave in" to the new government policy.[26]

24. Derani, "Refugees from Indochina," 207, 241.
25. Shawcross, Quality of Mercy, 83–84.
26. Anonymous interview, Bangkok, March 13, 1984; interview with Ruth Cadwallader, March 20, 1984.

The limits of the UNHCR's authority and its reluctance to act can be seen in the case of a recent refugee camp closing in Thailand. Secretary General Prasong, in announcing the phasing out of Khao-I-Dang, the major Cambodian holding center, in late December, 1986, and expressing his country's weariness regarding the refugee problem, remarked, "There will be no UNHCR camps."[27] Conspicuously absent was any strong protest by the UNHCR, which had been charged with the protection of the nearly 25,000 refugees at Khao-I-Dang. With the refugees' return to evacuation sites near the border, where they joined 300,000 fellow Cambodians, they lost international protection.

In 1986, advocacy groups again called upon the UNHCR, among others, to address various issues concerning Lao refugees in Thailand, including poor camp conditions, forced pushbacks, and involuntary repatriation by Thai authorities. In July, 1985, Thailand began a screening process for asylum seekers from Laos, using UNHCR observers, yet pushbacks occurred as late as March, 1987. In addition, those Laotians screened but denied asylum "continue to remain in the limbo of border detention centers." The UNHCR cannot facilitate and monitor their return to Laos until Laos reaches "an agreement with Thailand on an orderly and appropriate process."[28]

In Malaysia, a refugee worker at the Sungei Besi refugee camp said that though there are known instances of the violation of the refugees' rights, the UNHCR keeps a low profile to avoid offending the Malaysian government. We might conclude that though the UNHCR is restricted in its ability to influence refugee policy and to solve refugee problems, perhaps it should condemn the violation of human rights by nation-states. The UNHCR's representative in Malaysia, Darioush Bayandor, replied that "it is easy to sit in London and criticize UNHCR." The UNHCR, he explained, is not solely a human rights advocacy agency; it is responsible for assistance to refugees that requires the cooperation of host governments. Bayandor spoke of the organization's "exemplary relationship with the Malaysian government," pointing to the cooperative effort of the UNHCR and Malaysia to encourage Malaysian fishermen to rescue and assist approaching refugee boats.[29]

27. New York *Times*, December 30, 1986, p. 1.
28. Cerquone, *Refugees from Laos*, 19–21.
29. Anonymous interview, Kuala Lumpur, March 28, 1984; interview with Darioush Bayandor.

Malaysia has limited the involvement of outside international voluntary agencies in the refugee camps, preferring to rely almost exclusively on the MRCS. The UNHCR, mandated to contract with other agencies to provide for assistance to refugees, would appear to be limited in the sources it can draw on to provide relief services. In Singapore, a UNHCR protection officer spoke of frustration concerning the agency's inability to do anything about refugee boats allegedly towed out to sea by Singapore authorities. Some of these incidents apparently occurred without the UNHCR detecting them. In all these cases in first asylum countries, though its protection of refugees is far from perfect, the UNHCR appears to have been grateful for permission to assist the refugees at all.

By contrast, the agency is also criticized for being too aggressive and undiplomatic. For example, in a refugee boat push-off incident in early 1984 in southern Thailand, the UNHCR issued an official public protest. An American refugee official said the organization would never have done that without sufficient proof in the case. However, another official said the UNHCR had been "undiplomatic," setting back efforts to aid refugees. In his mind, the incident "should have been handled differently," in order to avoid the public national humiliation of Thailand. The UNHCR's public relations officer in Bangkok admitted that its relations with the Thai government had suffered. Push-offs and piracy may actually have increased. A congressional report noted the problems in the Philippines between the UNHCR and the government regarding authority at the Bataan processing center. An American refugee official said the UNHCR officials in the Philippines were abrasive at times and tended to confront the government in ways that ultimately limited effectiveness.[30]

A UNHCR protection officer in Thailand observed that the agency is sometimes caught in the middle, between refugees and host governments, and is often a scapegoat, the victim of the frustrations brought about by the refugee problem. Ruth Cadwallader said, "I feel sorry for UNHCR." In several instances, refugee personnel reported a change in their assessment of the UNHCR, brought about by a more realistic appraisal of what it could be expected to accomplish under the circumstances but also by improvements in its performance in the last couple

30. Anonymous interviews, Bangkok, March 13–15, 1984, Manila, April 6, 1984; House Foreign Affairs Committee, *Reports on Refugee Aid*, 91.

of years. For example, an American consulate political officer in Hong Kong said that the UNHCR had been "totally inept" in the early years of the crisis but "has become reasonably successful" lately. Another official in Bangkok saw changes in it for the better, probably the result of experience in Southeast Asia during the past decade.[31]

The ability of the UNHCR to carry out its mandate is also hampered because it is a temporary, nonoperational agency. Even though the urgency of the global refugee situation makes it easy to renew the UNHCR's charter repeatedly, a built-in sense of impermanence about the organization seems to preclude long-range planning. As a non-operational agency, it contracts and cooperates with other organizations, which then actually deliver services to refugees. It responds to refugee crises on an ad hoc, emergency basis and is unable to stockpile relief goods or to maintain a permanent field staff.[32]

Its annual budget from the UN covers only administrative costs, meaning that the UNHCR itself must also function as a fund-raising organization for each new refugee problem. Because it is responsible to refugees all over the world, it is sensitive to the problem of limited resources and to the criticisms of inequities in the distribution of funds and services. For example, African nations, where the bulk of the world's refugees are, have questioned the inordinate attention given to the Indochinese refugees. In Southeast Asia, there has been a reliance on the more costly solution of resettlement for the refugees instead of on local integration or repatriation, as usually practiced in Africa. Some are critical of the UNHCR's lack of initiative in pursuing alternatives to resettlement. In addition, nations tend to earmark contributions to the UNHCR to reflect their own national interests. For example, Japan, a major contributor, stipulates that all its donations go to the Indochinese refugees. These limitations inevitably affect the UNHCR's performance in Southeast Asia. A refugee official in Manila said the agency has "so few top notch people" that it sends them to the most immediate trouble spots, "but other places suffer." Another official said the UNHCR "plays down the Indochinese problem" in order to give attention to Africa.[33]

31. Interviews with Joan Edwards and with Ruth Cadwallader, March 20, 1984, and anonymous interviews.
32. Gordenker, "Organizational Expansion and Limits," 11.
33. *Ibid.*, 19; interview with Lois McHugh, Congressional Research Service, Library

In an assessment of the world refugee situation in 1984, Roger Winter wrote that decent treatment of refugees has seriously eroded recently, despite international attention and aid. Winter specifically cited push-offs and piracy in Thailand and harsh closed camps in Hong Kong. An American refugee official noted that people often erroneously assume refugees are being protected if they are under the care of a UN agency. But the UNHCR, instead of directly protecting refugees, can only encourage governments to treat refugees favorably. The UNHCR's representative in Hong Kong said that the agency "can only act as a moral force."[34]

A congressional study in 1981 found that though the UNHCR has assisted "in developing international refugee law," it has been "less than successful in promoting acceptance of refugee principles among Asian states." My own tour of Southeast Asia turned up many examples of this failure. A voluntary agency worker and several others in Thailand spoke of the hardships endured by refugees assigned to humane deterrence camps. In the Ubon Repatriation Center for Lao refugees, medical care and food appeared to be inadequate. Adolescent boys received a two days' food ration in their hands—two bony fish, small pieces of chicken, old and broken rice, and some vegetables. The voluntary agency's request to increase the numbers of refugees receiving supplementary feedings was denied. An infant with a high fever was in need of immediate medical attention but stood little chance of receiving it. At the same time, a UNHCR protection officer who had been in Thailand for three years stood outside the camp, denied admission because he lacked proper authorization. In Hong Kong, at the Kai Tak open camp, hundreds of Vietnamese lived crowded together inside corrugated metal dormitories, whole families sharing a section of a tiered bunk as their only living space. At the Argyle Street Detention Center, refugees were incarcerated in similar conditions, this time locked behind barbed wire fences.[35]

---

of Congress, Washington, D.C., October, 1982; anonymous interviews, Manila, April 6, 1984.

34. Tripp (ed.), *World Refugee Survey: 1984*, 3; interview with Dolores B. Lasan; anonymous interview, Hong Kong, April 12, 1984.

35. House Foreign Affairs Committee, *Reports on Refugee Aid*, 1, 10; observations made during visits to Ubon Repatriation Center, March 21, 1984, Kai Tak camp, April 13, 1984, and the Argyle Street Detention Center, April 14, 1984.

Rob Burrows, the UNHCR's public information officer in Bangkok, pointed out that refugees are brutalized everywhere, not just in Southeast Asia where criticism of UNHCR is usually focused. Burrows, along with Roger Winter, mentioned in particular the abuses suffered by refugees seeking asylum in the United States. Although the American Refugee Act of 1980 was modeled after UN Convention and Protocol documents, the UNHCR has met with difficulty in trying to protect Salvadoran refugees in the United States from long-term detention and deportation, according to one of its officials. The United States, for a variety of domestic and foreign policy reasons, has tended to view Salvadorans as illegal immigrants, not refugees. The UNHCR does not have permission to render assistance. Letters from the UNHCR protesting alleged abuses have been dismissed by American authorities as "conclusive without evidence."[36]

In spite of complaints regarding the agency's performance in protecting refugees, it is in the area of moral force that the UNHCR has pursued international consciousness raising about the global refugee problem in general and the Indochina refugee issue in particular. The UNHCR's numerous publications, posters, films, seminars, and workshops capitalize on the power of the media and attest to efforts to inform the world community of its responsibility in this area. For example, the agency recently focused its energies on the problem of violations of the law of the sea, involving the reluctance of passing ships to rescue refugee boats in distress in the South China Sea. Broadcasts and printed materials describing rescue obligations and procedures to facilitate disembarkation at nearby ports were repeatedly and widely disseminated. The UNHCR's annual Nansen Medal, given for assistance to refugees, was presented to a ship captain and crew members who had rendered assistance to Vietnamese boat people in 1984. Despite the moral persuasion efforts of the UNHCR, the rescue of refugees in distress at sea yet remains a serious problem. In 1988, a particularly grim account of cannibalism aboard a Vietnamese refugee boat brought accusations against a U.S. Navy ship commander who reportedly had not rendered adequate assistance when his vessel passed the refugee boat in the South China Sea in June.[37]

36. Interview with Rob Burrows; Tripp (ed.), *World Refugee Survey: 1984*, 3; anonymous interview with UNHCR representative, Washington, D.C., October, 1982.

37. "Nansen Laureates: Reagan Tribute," *Refugees*, XIII (January, 1985), 7; "Dossier:

In 1986, the Nansen Medal was given to the "people of Canada in recognition of the major and sustained contribution made to the cause of refugees." Canada has been an important resettlement country for refugees from Indochina. The UNHCR's effort to highlight Canada as a model in the international community, however, was soon followed by a more stringent Canadian refugee policy.[38]

Although we tend to view the refugee crises as contemporary phenomena, some scholars indicate that the refugee problem is not unique to today, that refugees have always existed in large numbers throughout history. What is different, however, is that technological advances in transportation and communication make the plight of the refugees better known, especially to the developed world. In his organizational study of the UNHCR, Leon Gordenker wrote that from its early days, the agency consciously developed its public image and "an ability directly to approach publics which would offer it support." High Commissioner "Van Heuven Goedhart had managed almost at once to dramatize his new agency and then to win the Nobel Prize for it."[39]

An understanding of the UNHCR's function as a social conscience may be found in the idea of the "moral constitution" as expressed by the late eminent scholar of morality Edmond Cahn. Cahn theorized that we possess a tacit, intrinsic moral sense of right and wrong. People are instinctively repulsed by wrong and not only want but need to demonstrate the ability to do right. We dramatically exhibit this capacity for doing right by projecting onto others what we care about most in the name of self-preservation. Along these lines, then, what we see reflected in the refugees is the fragility of our own humanity, our own naked vulnerability. Cahn declared that principles are real not in the universal abstract but only if they can be found in concrete examples.[40] As a social conscience, the UNHCR projects the image of a refugee as a member of the universal brotherhood of which we are all a part. Recognizing that man's evil nature may generate refugee problems, the

---

Rescue at Sea," *Refugees*, II (February, 1984), 21–28; Washington *Post*, August 10, 1988, p. 15.

38. "Nansen Medal to the People of Canada," *Refugees*, XXXV (November, 1986), 7.

39. Teitelbaum, "Right Versus Right," 22; Gordenker, "Organizational Expansion and Limits," 11.

40. Edmond Cahn, *The Moral Decision: Right and Wrong in the Light of American Law* (Bloomington, Ind., 1956), 16–19.

UNHCR focuses on our human capacity for good, which persuades us to reach out and assist those who flee.

However, the complex moral dilemmas posed by the Indochina refugee issue are not the result of clear distinctions between right and wrong. Rather, the issue elicits a number of thorny questions that reflect tensions among a plurality of competing interests and principles and that demand the art of moral reasoning, even blind groping. The refugee problem brings to mind Herbert Butterfield's admonition that some situations are irreducible dilemmas beyond "the ingenuity of man to untie." Law scholar Paul Freund noted in his profound study of constitutional law that serious issues are rarely clear, single-minded cases of right versus wrong. Usually they are complicated because they are cases of right versus right, where competing principles reflect the validity of opposing sides. Freund advised that attention be given to insights found at the "crosslights" of competing principles.[41]

In one sense, the UNHCR may be viewed as an alter ego of nations or perhaps as an arena where a balance in the tension between competing principles, namely, the individual rights of refugees and the rights of sovereign states, is sought out. If at their best nations are capable of acting out of enlightened self-interest, they need to realize the value of deflecting refugee concerns onto the international arena, where the conflict between states' goals and individual rights can be diffused and can ultimately be made to serve the interests of both. For example, in 1977, the refugee problem in Somalia was part of a larger political conflict involving itself, supported by the United States, and Ethiopia, aided by the Soviet Union and Cuba. For several reasons, the United States decided that checking its escalating involvement by deflecting the Somalian refugee issue onto the broader world community through the UNHCR was in its best interests. A congressional study advised the following policy be adopted: "The United States should avoid becoming embedded in a bilateral aid relationship on refugees in Somalia which could lead to a perception of an indefinite U.S. commitment to continue carrying the bulk of the refugee burden. It is in the U.S. interest to push for stronger leadership and coordination by UNHCR and WFP."[42]

41. Thompson, *Political Realism*, 53; Paul A. Freund, *On Law and Justice* (Cambridge, Mass., 1968), 21–37; Thompson, *Morality and Foreign Policy*, 136–37.
42. House Foreign Affairs Committee, *Reports on Refugee Aid*, 68.

Along similar lines, the United States emphasizes repeatedly the concept of burden sharing on behalf of the Indochina refugees, in order to play down the American role in Southeast Asia by increasing the involvement of the international community. In the Thai piracy situation, a UNHCR official said the United States wanted to internationalize the antipiracy program, with the UNHCR assuming a lead role, so as to avoid jeopardizing bilateral U.S.-Thai relations. Other examples of UNHCR oversight include the ODP and the two rescue-at-sea programs, RASRO and DISERO.[43]

However, since the UNHCR is the creation of nation-states, solutions to refugee problems are often partial, uneasy compromises that reflect concessions to national interests as much as, if not more than, they provide full protection for the refugees. In the Indochina refugee issue, this fact is illustrated in the curb on the exodus by Hanoi and the establishment of the ODP, both results of the UNHCR-sponsored Geneva conference in July, 1979, that were heralded as progress on behalf of the refugees. Certainly, both measures helped to decrease the loss of lives at sea, but they also reflected the interests of those nations adversely affected by the influx. The curb on the exodus represented, in effect, the world community's sanctioning of Hanoi's abuse of the right to leave the country to escape persecution. The ODP today, though certainly a safer mode of exit, probably does not attract many bona fide refugees, those who are too impatient and desperate to flee through this program or who may be intimidated by the prospect of coming forth and cooperating with a government that constitutes their reason for leaving.[44]

The UN Declaration of Human Rights, and subsequently the Convention and Protocol documents that define a refugee and serve to guide the activities of the UNHCR, is a moral standard of the ideal rather than a depiction of reality. Warning against looking for absolutes in law, Paul Freund saw law as resembling art "in its capacity to respond through interpretation to changing needs, concerns, and aspirations." He also indicated law's flexibility: "New vistas open in art as in law." Long ago, Erasmus warned that "all definitions are dangerous." U.S. Catholic Bishop Anthony J. Bevilacqua remarked, "I

43. U.S. Department of State, *World Refugee Report*, 23, 37; interview with Rob Burrows.
44. Wain, *The Refused*, 229; *Washington Post*, September 7, 1984, p. 22.

would rather help a refugee than know how to define one." The UNHCR's interpretation of its mandate and guidelines reflects, with what Freund would call "creative ambiguity," both a strict adherence, which limits its effectiveness, and a liberal application, which widens the scope of its protection.[45]

The reluctance at times of the UNHCR to interpret its mandate liberally has resulted in serious breaches in protection. William Shawcross is highly critical of the agency's reticence and cites at least two instances. First, it decided in 1979 not to pursue protection and assistance for refugees at the ill-defined Thai-Cambodian border region. By accepting Thailand's interpretation that the border camps were located in Cambodian territory, the UNHCR could not help the camps' inhabitants because it had to adhere to the guideline that it could only aid refugees *outside* their homeland. By definition, a refugee is someone who has crossed his national boundary. To this day, refugees at the Thai-Cambodian border receive help from other organizations, including UN affiliates, but not from the UNHCR. In a second instance, the UNHCR declined to help Vietnamese land refugees who had arrived in Thailand via Cambodia, on the grounds that Cambodia was their country of first asylum, something of an absurdity considering the state of affairs in Cambodia. In another strict UNHCR interpretation, Vietnamese refugees of Chinese origin who fled to China, some of whom are unhappy with life on state farms—farms perhaps similar to ones they might have been assigned to had they remained in Vietnam—have no recourse because China is their country of first asylum. In each of these instances, the UNHCR presumably chose to adhere to a conservative interpretation of its mandate, at the expense of the refugees, in order to avoid confrontation with Thailand and China.[46]

On occasion, more liberal and creative interpretations have led to increased UNHCR protection. For example, the Hungarian refugee exodus in 1956 required that the agency "assume operational responsibility which set a precedent for future involvement in emergency situations," proving that the clause requiring it to be nonoperational was

45. Aga Khan, *Study on Human Rights*, 8, 12; Freund, *On Law and Justice*, 22; U.S. Coordinator for Refugee Affairs, "Transcript of Conference on Ethical Issues," 19; Thompson, *Morality and Foreign Policy*, 181.
46. Shawcross, *Quality of Mercy*, 248, 409–10.

indeed negotiable. Leon Gordenker wrote that the Hungarian exodus taught the UNHCR that "it could hardly limit itself to modest legal protection and minimal support."[47]

The flexibility of the UNHCR's mandate was tested almost at the start, when refugees in Hong Kong who had fled China after the revolution of 1949 were formally ineligible for UNHCR protection. Nonetheless, the UNHCR was able to render assistance under its "good offices" clause. The "good offices" concept gives the UNHCR the flexible authority to meet emergency refugee situations. For example, the UNHCR has sometimes exceeded strict interpretation of its mandate by offering aid to those not assigned formal and legal refugee status. According to William Lewis, "This represents an accommodation to existing realities."[48]

In the case of the Indochina refugees, the UNHCR has to work with refugees in first asylum states that have not signed the UN Convention or Protocol documents and that refer to the refugees as illegal entrants or displaced persons. In the case of the Vietnamese who left their homeland aboard freighters in 1978 and 1979, it was questionable whether they qualified as "genuine refugees," since they had made financial arrangements to leave with alleged government complicity. The UNHCR's regional representative said, "We consider them refugees."[49] In a similar case, the agency avoided strict legalities when it decided to assist refugees leaving Vietnam under the ODP.

In many respects, the UNHCR's work is still in transition. Some criticisms of this organization are related to new demands that arise as the UNHCR evolves in response to the increased size, scope, and complexity of the global refugee problem, especially in the developing world. In addition, limitations on its authority in favor of the power of sovereign nations lead to confusion regarding its legitimate function and actual capabilities.[50] Created and funded by nations, this agency, ostensibly nonpolitical, nevertheless must operate within the international political arena, attentive to the power of national interests; it

47. Gordenker, "Organizational Expansion and Limits," 8–9.
48. *Ibid.*; Lewis, "Operations of the UNHCR," 8.
49. Wain, *The Refused,* 33.
50. Lewis, "Operations of the UNHCR," 24; Sheila Avrin McLean, "International Institutional Mechanisms for Refugees," in Kritz (ed.), *U.S. Immigration and Refugee Policy,* 176.

cannot solely consider the humanitarian aspects of refugee issues. Realistically, it must seek to fulfill its mandate in the "moral margins," where national interests and ethical concerns intersect.

Human rights advocates criticize the UNHCR for not protecting refugees enough and for being a tool of national interests. Nations complain that the agency emphasizes humanitarian aspects of refugee problems while ignoring important political factors. When asked how the UNHCR is able to accomplish anything at all, one analyst replied tersely, "It punts." In a discussion of the failure of nations to provide for territorial asylum for refugees in international law, Sadruddin Aga Khan, former director of the UNHCR, tempered hope for durable solutions to refugee problems with realism: "Politics would have to take second place and governments might have to accept a more flexible interpretation of national sovereignty. Such conditions are not about to be established. We live in an imperfect world."[51]

The UNHCR's accomplishments, then, on behalf of the Indochina refugees may be credited to those instances in which the UNHCR's humanitarian efforts coincide with the interests of nations. Its failures, in large part, have come when national interests take precedence over humanitarian concerns, something that happens frequently in the real world. Given such constraints, an overview of the agency's performance vis-à-vis the exodus from Indochina raises questions about whether the UNHCR actually did and continues to do all it possibly can within the moral margins where interests and human rights overlap. As with nations, it would appear that if the organization were enriched with more of the art and skills of diplomacy, more initiatives regarding the protection of refugees and the search for durable solutions might be forthcoming. The limits imposed on the UNHCR should be acknowledged as real but never offered as excuses for its not having pursued the execution of its mandate as far as possible.

The continuing Indochina refugee problem, now well into its second decade, engenders the discussion of a host of other dilemmas associated with humanitarian concerns, in addition to those related to the UNHCR. The ongoing exodus forces serious consideration of at least three interrelated issues: the influence of moralism, especially as it is reflected in American thinking about Indochina refugees; the com-

51. Interview with Lois McHugh; Aga Khan, *Study on Human Rights*, 17.

plexity of motives, evident in people's decisions to flee Indochina, including both push and pull influences; and the question of apparent infinite responsibility for endless streams of refugees in a world of finite resources and capabilities.

In his writings, Kenneth Thompson described a strain of moralism that appears to be deeply ingrained in the character of the United States: "National self-righteousness has run like a red skein through much of American diplomatic history . . . a rather extravagant estimate of the American national character and American foreign policy." However, moralism, as the focusing on an espousal of a single moral precept without any anticipation of the ramifications of the precept's application in real events or as the covering of national interests with moral principles, is to be distinguished from the more complex concept of morality. Morality and the process of moral reasoning involve the dynamics of a plurality of competing interests and principles in search of a tenuous balance that requires prudence and perhaps a sense of humility.[52] The American penchant for moralism's self-righteousness and its aftereffects were apparent in the American response to the Hungarian refugees. In that case, the refugees were extolled as freedom fighters and became an important part of foreign policy. Even today, the influence of moralism's self-righteousness can be found in attitudes about refugees. Accepting his first nomination for the American presidency, Ronald Reagan, bringing to mind the astute observations on America by Alexis de Tocqueville, asked, "Can we doubt that only a divine providence placed this land, this island of freedom, here as a refuge for all those people in the world who yearn to breathe freely?"[53]

However, such pronouncements are challenged by refugee policies that seem to offer asylum selectively, only to those who flee persecution in nations considered to be American adversaries. Michael Teitelbaum, of the Carnegie Endowment for International Peace, warned that the use of refugee admissions "as hostile acts aimed at foreign adversaries, as the United States has done, makes it more difficult to admit bona fide refugees from friendly nations." The exclusion of Haitians and Salvadorans and the admission of large numbers of Indochina

52. Thompson, *Morality and Foreign Policy*, xi, 21–28.
53. U.S. Coordinator for Refugee Affairs, "Transcript of Conference on Ethical Issues," 37.

refugees illustrate the point. A refugee official at the State Department who agreed with this assessment pointedly asked the rhetorical question, "Is the life of an Indochinese refugee worth more than the life of an Ethiopian?" Teitelbaum questioned, in addition, whether liberal refugee admissions will continue to be supported by a broad base of American citizens. Ceilings on refugee admissions, generous though they are, may indicate that the American commitment to the freedom to flee is "valid only up to an arbitrary point." Recent discussion of the duration of American responsibility to the Indochina refugees illustrates this concern.[54]

Contrary to Skinnerian behaviorism's single-cause-and-effect explanations, the human condition is a vast repertoire of behaviors that are responses to a myriad of stimuli at work simultaneously. Motivations influencing refugees to flee their homelands are a combination of push and pull factors. In the case of the Hungarian exodus it was certainly true that though they fled persecution or the fear of persecution by "voting with their feet," the refugees were also influenced by a suddenly opened border, the opportunity to pursue a better life elsewhere, an enticing image of the noncommunist world as portrayed by Radio Free Europe and letters from abroad, weariness with lives that were dull and drab, plus a host of reasons unique to each individual. It was with disillusionment, then, that the public and some elected officials reacted to the knowledge that the Hungarians did not all measure up to the ideal image of the refugee who was fighting for freedom.

Today, the shift in the locale of refugee migrations from Europe to the developing world interpolates the North-South dichotomy into an issue traditionally associated with East-West relations. A U.S. State Department official nostalgically noted the end of "the good old days" when "in a world of Manichean simplicity, the notion that persecution could have economic roots and manifestations was not entertained."[55]

In the course of the Indochina exodus the existence of pull, as well as push, factors has come to be acknowledged. Push factors include

---

54. *Ibid.*, 22; interview with Frank Sieverts; U.S. Coordinator for Refugee Affairs, "Transcript of Conference on Ethical Issues," 22; Ronald S. Scheinman, "Refugees: Goodby to the Good Old Days," in Gilburt D. Loescher and John A. Scanlan (eds.), *The Global Refugee Problem: U.S. and World Response*, Vol. CDLXVII of *Annals* (May, 1983), 78–88.

55. Scheinman, "Refugees: Goodby," 79.

repression and persecution, the expulsion of Chinese minorities, unpopular social and economic policies, population increases, the devastation of war, accompanied by continued international isolation that severely limits reconstruction aid, and the poor state of the economy, which only perpetuates poverty conditions. According to Sadruddin Aga Khan, refugees are also pulled from their homelands by knowledge of the West's commitment to human rights and its condemnation of totalitarian regimes and by the perception that they will be welcomed. In addition, he cites the refugees' knowledge of liberal immigration policies, the institutionalization of refugee relief aid, temporary asylum camps, and resettlement prospects as magnets that attract refugees.[56]

Throughout Southeast Asia and in Hong Kong, various officials mentioned increasing numbers of suspected economic migrants among the refugees, an issue that has been at the heart of the INS–State Department debate over Indochina refugee admissions. Several sources also referred to the possible influences of Voice of America broadcasts, the presence of the U.S. Seventh Fleet, and letters from abroad as pull factors inducing the refugees' decisions to flee.[57]

One suggestion for beginning to deal realistically with the refugee situation has been to broaden the definition of refugee beyond its narrow political bias to include the economic realities of the Third World. Yet, as Teitelbaum pointed out, if the definition is expanded, it will everywhere raise hopes for asylum in the West that can never be fulfilled. Kennedy aide Jerry Tinker warned that unless the bona fide refugees are separated from economic migrants and those seeking family reunification with refugees already resettled, the protection of those truly in need will be eroded by a public backlash demanding a reduction in overall refugee admissions. The dilemma is compounded by the difficulty in delineating between economic and political persecution, a distinction that is "very muddied and blurry." President of Refugees International Shepard C. Lowman best summarized the problem when he noted that "political persecution often wears an economic face in a Marxist/Leninist society, especially one such as

---

56. Aga Khan, *Study on Human Rights,* 38–43.
57. For example, see U.S. Department of State, *Indochinese Refugee Situation,* 14, and House Judiciary Committee, *Refugee Issues in Southeast Asia and Europe,* 14, 49, 53.

Vietnam still in the process of political consolidation of the regime's power."[58]

Interest in the approach Tinker advocated was sparked again by a recommendation of the Indochinese Refugee Panel Report of April, 1986. The independent panel, led by Robert Ray, had been called together by Secretary Shultz "to recommend changes in U.S. Refugee policy," based on a review of the Indochina refugee situation. The Ray Panel found that fewer Indochinese now qualify for refugee status, whereas growing numbers "seek political and economic freedom or family reunification." The panel urged adoption of a two-track system in admissions that would include both refugees and immigrants. However, in a statement in response to the panel's report, the advocacy group Refugees International raised important concerns underlining the problems of such a proposal. The already "fragile existence" of the Indochinese refugees is made more tenuous by the prospect of normal visa processing that clearly takes too long; for a two-track program, "they simply cannot wait in first asylum camps for the one or two or ten years it will take for their visa numbers to become current."[59]

The suddenness and size of recent refugee exoduses have clearly been perceived as challenging national sovereignty, security, and welfare and as fueling an increasingly apocalyptic view of the global refugee situation. For the United States, the Indochina exodus, combined with the influx of refugees and illegal immigrants from elsewhere, forces a rethinking of the infinite ramifications of America as the promised land for the world's oppressed. John Silber depicted the alternatives of this dilemma when he asked, "Do we as a nation, and do we as American people, have finite responsibilities or do we share the divine obligations of the Almighty?" For Michael Teitelbaum, the "tragic choice" is how to allocate a limited number of asylum spaces among more than fourteen million refugees worldwide. One desperate solution proffered was for the United States to deny any admissions since it could help so few.[60]

58. U.S. Coordinator for Refugee Affairs, "Transcript of Conference on Ethical Issues," 19–20; Tinker, "U.S. Refugee Policy," 1–2; Shepard C. Lowman, "A Crisis in First Asylum for Indochinese Refugees: Creating Alternatives to Flight by Boat" (Typescript, Refugees International, Washington, D.C., November, 1988), 5.

59. U.S. Department of State, *World Refugee Report*, 23; *Senate Documents*, 99th Cong., 2nd Sess., No. J-99-113, p. 62.

60. Scheinman, "Refugees: Goodby," 80–82; U.S. Coordinator for Refugee Affairs, "Transcript of Conference on Ethical Issues," 16–17.

Another response, a phenomenon known as "compassion fatigue" has come to be associated with the Indochina refugee issue, and it complicates Cahn's theory of the moral constitution. Although the international community was overwhelmed by the human tragedy at first, interest in the Indochinese refugees has waned, perhaps influenced by growing familiarity with the problem, frustration over its resolution, and the attraction of events elsewhere.[61] One refugee official speculated that incidents like the Indochina migration have a public attention span of about eighteen months. After more than ten years, some are asking how much longer the American responsibility to the Indochinese is to last.[62]

Despite considerable achievements, disturbing humanitarian concerns persist, indicating that there is still much to be done for the Indochina refugees. Long-term camp residents, or residual refugees, are a serious concern. This issue raises the problems of the psychological effects of hopelessness and desperation on the refugees and of the growing impatience of temporary first asylum countries. Refugees continue to leave Vietnam and Laos without those countries launching serious efforts to address the root causes and remedy them. Many who leave risk pirate attacks, pushbacks, involuntary repatriation, and ships' refusals to rescue them at sea. Arrivals in Thailand and Hong Kong are held in camps with such harsh conditions they may aptly be called prisons. By 1988, this dismal situation was compounded by a dramatic increase in refugee arrivals from Vietnam.

Dwindling international concern has seen burden sharing shrink to the involvement of only a few nations in resettlement, namely, the United States, Canada, and Australia. The ODP from Vietnam is just beginning to facilitate migration once again. No such regularized programs even exist for those wanting to exit safely from Laos and Cambodia. Laotian refugees suffer amid the Thai-Laotian border hostilities and tensions, and a virtual deadlock continues regarding the return of those screened out of the refugee programs. The plight of over a quarter of a million Cambodians, many of them born at the border camps and not even officially designated as refugees or afforded the protection that designation implies, remains intractable.

As the exodus from Vietnam increased and first asylum deterio-

61. For a discussion of compassion fatigue, see Shawcross, *Quality of Mercy,* 11–14.
62. New York *Times,* March 3, 1985, p. 3.

rated in 1988, the need for another international conference under UNHCR auspices became apparent, and the conference was called for. Following his visit to Southeast Asia in July, 1988, Secretary of State Shultz endorsed the idea for a conference at the same time that ASEAN ministers were issuing a call for a "comprehensive program of action" as the refugee problem continued to worsen.[63]

Addressing the world's refugee crisis, the UNHCR's Jean-Pierre Hocke admonished the developed nations for having "reacted with refugee policies which are of a defensive or even a repressive nature." In the same vein, Philip Rudge, secretary of the European Consultation on Refugees and Exiles wrote of the developed nations' penchant to see refugees as a threat or problem rather than as people who need assistance.[64] In essence, national interests and humanitarian concerns compete, conflict, and only at times cooperate in an imperfect world. The focus has been on managing the refugee problem rather than on a search for possible solutions at the source. It is clear that the world's refugee problems, including the Indochina refugee dilemma, need a fresh approach, magnanimous initiatives, a renewed commitment to help those in need, and the use of moral principles as guidelines rather than as bold determinants. The thorny ethical dilemmas inherent in the Indochina issue can only be addressed with courage, patience, artful diplomacy, and even risk, in the political arena where root causes are found.

63. "Seminar on First Asylum for Vietnamese Boat People," *Refugee Reports*, IX (June 24, 1988), 9; *Refugee Reports*, IX (July 15, 1988), 8.
64. Virginia Hamilton (ed.), *World Refugee Survey: 1986*, 5.

Conclusion

For more than a decade, refugees have been leaving the countries of Indochina. Beginning with the first Indochinese asylum seekers who made their way abroad as the United States withdrew from the region and North Vietnamese forces entered Saigon and began the process of national reunification in 1975, nearly two million people have exited their homelands. Whether the migration is viewed as an epilogue to the Vietnam War, an auxiliary to newer tensions and conflicts in the region, or both, the ongoing exodus continues to have repercussions in several nations in Southeast Asia and around the world.

The British historian and major contributor to international relations theory Herbert Butterfield indicated the great value of hindsight to an understanding of historical events: "Behind the great conflicts of mankind is a terrible human predicament which lies at the heart of the story. . . . Contemporaries fail to see the predicament or refuse to recognize its genuineness so that our knowledge comes from later analysis."[1] In some respects, our historical distance from the Indochina refugee issue may be too short for us to discern its fundamental predicament, for the value of hindsight is precluded in this case by the persistence of the exodus. Yet the lack of an understanding of the Vietnam War era by American school children queried today about an event that brought frustration, divisiveness, and soul-searching to an entire nation illustrates that significant occurrences are relegated to the

1. Thompson, *Political Realism*, 53.

back pages of history very quickly in these fast-paced, event-laden times. Future analyses of the Indochina problem will surely yield the fruits of detached, objective observation, as salient factors become more identifiable with time. This study, however, has capitalized on the important dynamic elements still at work in an event that remains protracted and is managed and tolerated rather than solved.

Employing a normative-political perspective, this investigation has sought out the predicament at the heart of the Indochina refugee story by focusing on the following questions: What are the important national interests that contribute to the Indochina refugee issue? Why do they exist? How do these interests relate to humanitarian concerns? Based on the knowledge that refugee crises constitute human tragedies and the assumption that the interests of sovereign nations are primary in international political events, this study concludes that, in essence, the predicament in the Indochina refugee case exists in the tensions among competing national interests and between those interests and humanitarian concerns.

The research contributes to an understanding of the Indochina refugee issue in particular and of the global refugee problem in general in at least three ways. First, its examination of the interests of the major participants, including nations that are the sources of the migration, countries of first asylum and resettlement that experience the impact of the outflow, and nations whose interests reflect larger regional and international balance-of-power politics, reveals the extraordinary plurality of interests at work in this refugee problem. Second, the theory of political realism as developed by major thinkers in international relations provides a valuable conceptual framework that uncovers not only the power and legitimacy of national interests but also complexities in the Indochina refugee problem—complexities that call for the art of moral reasoning, which goes beyond simply assigning responsibility and liability. Third, this study compares the Indochina refugee issue with the Hungarian exodus in 1956 and demonstrates striking similarities to support the contention that refugee migrations are not isolated, unique, nonrecurring events. However, the size and duration of the exodus from Indochina, its implications for North-South relations, its more complicated regional and superpower relations, and its serious human rights dilemmas make the Indochina refugee problem far more complex and perplexing.

The roots of the migrations from both Hungary and Indochina are found in the national interests embedded in the political struggle for power that characterized each region for years and left large segments of the populations unsettled and uncertain and fearful about the future. Aristide Zolberg pointed out that exoduses have occurred throughout history and have been associated with fervent nation building. For example, an estimated one million refugees were generated between the fifteenth and seventeenth centuries alone, in the forging of Europe's national boundaries. Religious, ethnic, political, and economic attributes were important factors in the quest for national homogeneity. Migrations of dissenting oppositions occurred following wars for independence, including the French and American revolutions.[2] In the cases of both Hungary and Indochina, the people already understood dislocation brought about by war. In Europe, Hungarians and other Europeans had been uprooted in the chaos wrought by World War II, and at the time of the Hungarian exodus a steady stream of refugees was also making its way from behind the iron curtain to asylum. In Indochina, the Vietnam War brought the experience of internal displacement to untold thousands. In both cases, then, the precedent of escaping conflict and the consequences of totalitarian rule by moving elsewhere had been established.

In both migrations, fear of persecution influenced people's decisions to flee, whereas such refugees were perceived to be potentially disloyal citizens by new governments. The Hungarians had already come to know the iron grip of Stalinism firsthand. The quick suppression of the uprising and the reassertion of Soviet hegemony brought fear of execution and forced exile for some and fear of the continuation of life under Soviet domination for many. For the Indochinese, fear of the unknown led many to flee, and others soon were influenced to leave by new government policies of reeducation camps and drastic social and economic programs that specifically affected the ethnic Chinese and others. In both events, the new regimes seemed to sanction the flight of those they feared might undermine their efforts to establish new political authority. However, the Kadar regime in Hungary,

2. Aristide R. Zolberg, "Contemporary Transnational Migrations in Historical Perspective: Patterns and Dilemmas," in Kritz (ed.), *U.S. Immigration and Refugee Policy*, 21; Zolberg, "International Migrations," in Kritz, Keely, and Tomasi (eds.), *Global Trends in Migration*, 22–23.

perhaps cognizant of the loss of its educated elite, soon offered amnesty to those who wanted to return, and it sealed the border and ended the flow within a few months. By contrast, though Vietnam made attempts to curb the flow after July, 1979, in response to international pressure, it was implicated in the actual expulsion of its ethnic Chinese minority, which figured in larger Sino-Vietnamese relations, and made no mention of the loss of its talented citizenry. In the case of Indochina, the devastation of war, plus population pressures and chronic economic woes associated with developing countries, created an exodus more complicated than the outflow from Hungary.

Both exoduses were caught up in larger, balance-of-power tensions, reflecting the interests of opposing sides. In the case of Hungary, the uprising and exodus highlighted the Cold War's ideological division of the world into free and communist camps. The tenor of the times precluded a more comprehensive understanding of national interests in terms of both the Soviet Union's historically based interest in preserving its sphere of influence in eastern Europe and the limitations placed on the United States in confronting the Soviet Union in this region. When it could no longer tolerate liberalization efforts and what those might mean for other nations on its borders, the Soviet Union intervened in Hungary and generated an exodus. The United States compensated for its inability to intervene directly in the uprising by focusing on the refugees, a limited action in stark contrast to the Eisenhower administration's Cold War pronouncements promising the liberation of eastern Europe and a "roll back of the Iron Curtain." Although it could do nothing in Hungary, it could assist the refugees and thereby alleviate the exodus' destabilizing potential in Austria and elsewhere in Europe. In place of military action, the United States exploited the moral aspects of the exodus by idealizing the refugees as freedom fighters whose flight vividly demonstrated that life under communism was intolerable. Influenced by guilt and responsibility, frustrated by the inability to do anything else, the Eisenhower administration launched an effort to bring as many refugees as possible to the United States.

The Indochina case is more complicated. The interests of several nations are evident in regional and superpower balance-of-power tensions that go beyond simple delineations of communist and noncommunist. Similar to its role in the Hungarian case, the United States assumed a leadership role on behalf of refugees, but now it cautiously avoids any direct intervention in Southeast Asian affairs. Profound guilt and responsibility for the refugees stemming from the Vietnam War in combination with the foreign policy goal of protecting American interests in the region, are manifested in a strategy to maintain a low American profile in the region and to rely on ASEAN and China to offset Soviet and Vietnamese influence.

The refugees figure in American objectives to protect its interests in ASEAN, for by alleviating the strain on first asylum countries caused by the influx, the United States gains some leverage and some gratitude. In addition, refugees reflect negatively on the Indochina countries by highlighting human rights violations, thereby fostering the international isolation of Vietnam, a foreign policy goal shared by China. However, this American strategy causes uneasiness as it is not the only, or even the most important, influence having an impact on the refugees. For example, the ASEAN countries are not all wedded to the idea of a prominent role for China in the region. Longstanding wariness of China, exacerbated by concern about large numbers of ethnic Chinese among the refugees, tempers their interest in a strategy that seeks to weaken Vietnam and implies a strong China. In the Cambodian stalemate, refugees on the Thai-Cambodian border figure in the U.S.-Sino-ASEAN attempt to undermine Vietnam's legitimacy in Cambodia, yet they also reflect the tensions among the communist and noncommunist factions of the coalition forces and their supporters.

Tensions among competing national interests often complicate refugee problems. Foreign policy goals with attendant refugee policies invariably have repercussions in other areas of a nation's political agenda. Specifically, foreign policy interests in admitting large numbers of refugees conflict with the ultimate sovereign right to control borders, making it difficult, then, to distinguish refugee admissions clearly from overall immigration.

In the Hungarian refugee case, the Eisenhower administration met strong opposition from immigration restrictionists when it tried to resettle large numbers of refugees. At the time, immigration law regulated access not only for economic and social reasons; it also was deemed an important defense to protect the country from communist infiltrators. The inability of the Eisenhower administration to counter the opposition reflected the strength of American commitment to border control at the time but also the administration's failure to garner enough support for its foreign policy goals. Cloaked in moralistic garb, the American refugee program brought allegations of hypocrisy, as Austria and others complained about selective screening procedures and the gap between lofty promises and actual admissions. The use of the Hungarian refugees as a tool of foreign policy was therefore only partially successful.

In the Indochina refugee case, competing national interests are also evident. Resettlement statistics—more than 884,000 Indochinese refugees resettled and 46,500 more admitted to the United States in fiscal year 1989—demonstrate the depth of American guilt and feelings of responsibility, but also magnanimity and support for foreign policy goals, which may reflect public appreciation for American interests abroad in an increasingly interdependent world. However, these objectives vis-à-vis the refugees have not been without criticism. The policy debate between the State Department and the Justice Department over the admission of Indochinese refugees reflects the tension between foreign policy and the control of borders. Critics mention Vietcong and Khmer Rouge infiltrators, social and economic costs, resentment on the part of minorities, and the larger problem of economic migrants among the refugees at a time when the issue of illegal immigration is high on the political agenda.

The Hungarian exodus numbered approximately 200,000 refugees, of which 38,000 came to the United States and were quickly resettled. Urban, educated, and middle-class, for the most part, they came at a time of economic prosperity. Even so, they fueled an apocalyptic view of the refugee situation when they were put in conjunction with American feelings of responsibility for other refugees in Europe and the growing problem in the Middle East at the time. However, the migration from Hungary pales by comparison with the Indochina exodus. Its size, duration, and the nature of the flow are catastrophic. Its implications for North-South relations are still evolving. Unforeseen and unpredictable developments force any new thinking about refugees to break out of the traditional mold of East-West experiences in Europe. For example, the sheer number of poor refugees from the developing countries of Indochina, which have been ravaged by war and denied international development aid and trade opportunities, highlights the difficulty of using traditional political criteria, isolated from economic motivations, to establish refugee status.

Each first asylum state—Thailand, Malaysia, Singapore, Indonesia, the Philippines, and Hong Kong—clearly illustrates how easily a country can be inundated by an influx of refugees. Each country's response to the Indochina refugee problem reflects its own, unique national interests, but each response also has repercussions elsewhere in an interdependent world. For example, when Thailand turned away boat people as the exodus increased in 1987 and 1988, Malaysia and other nearby countries experienced increases in arrivals. Especially striking are the effects of the influx on Third World countries. There, emerging political and economic infrastructures are taxed by a refugee burden that is perceived to threaten national security, political and social stability, and important economic development.

The inability and unwillingness of the first asylum countries to give permanent accommodation to the refugees necessitate international assistance from the developed world in order to alleviate the strains of the refugee burden. But the assistance also has a magnet effect, as institutionalized refugee aid and resettlement opportunities attract even more refugees. Pull factors seem to increase the difficulty in stemming a flow, once it is underway. In addition, the aid rendered by the international community becomes a sensitive issue when local populations perceive that refugees are better off than they are and when outside interference conflicts with the host government's authority and national pride.

Thus, a profound tension exists between national interests and humanitarian concerns for the refugees, with these interests invariably taking precedence over human rights and often forcing compromises that limit ideal protection for and assistance to the Indochina refugees. It is only in the narrow margins where interests and ethical considerations intersect, then, that refugees can be aided. Obviously, the performances of international organizations like the UNHCR are affected by the deference they must pay to national sovereignty. International law and codes of ethical standards that are specifically related to the refugees, such as the UN Protocol and Convention documents, are guides rooted in the European experience and may possibly be culturebound, but more important, they are adhered to only when circumstances permit.

A single-minded emphasis on human rights without regard to national interests poses problems in practice and at times results in allegations of hypocrisy. In the Hungarian case, moral precepts regarding the individual rights of refugees were exploited for propaganda purposes but resulted in some embarrassment when refugees were subjected to screening procedures and when liberal admissions to the United States were not forthcoming. In the Indochina case, in all fairness, the blatant moralism that characterized the response to the Hungarian refugees is substantially muted. Nonetheless, the first asylum countries complain about the attention given to the humanitarian aspects of the refugee problem at the expense of an appreciation for the serious political implications the influx poses for these nations. Thailand's Prasong Soonsiri observed that there is a noticeable gap between Western humanitarianism and the application of immigration laws when it comes time for the Western countries to resettle refugees from first asylum countries whom they have encouraged to take in all asylum seekers, carte blanche.

In terms of human rights, the Indochina refugee issue is far more perplexing than the Hungarian case because of continued violations there. The Indochina states stand accused of gross violations that have generated the migration. Many refugees also suffer abuses at the hands of those expected to assist them in their pursuit of asylum. In regard to the sources of the exodus, the outflow itself actually represents a less reprehensible human rights violation than what might have occurred had the refugees remained. North Vietnam's victory invited fears of a bloodbath and incarceration that new evidence indicates actually did happen. The fanatical Khmer Rouge rule in Cambodia, from 1975 until the Vietnamese invasion in late 1978, resulted in a genocide that echoes the Jewish Holocaust. The evil would have been lesser had those persecuted during the reign of Pol Pot exited from Cambodia. An ironic twist, as events proceed rather than progress, finds remnants of the Khmer Rouge among the refugees at the Thai-Cambodian border; they are part of the coalition government of Cambodia that is seated at the United Nations.

The national interests of several states have resulted in efforts to curb the flow of refugees that involve human rights dilemmas. In effect, pressures put on Hanoi by a number of nations to prevent refugees from leaving sanction that country's abrogation of the right to exit. This phenomenon is in curious juxtaposition to the advocacy of the right of Jews to leave the Soviet Union, which has figured prominently in U.S.-Soviet relations.[3] The preponderance of human rights violations are now associated with countries that attempt to discourage the influx. Piracy, push-offs, failure to rescue boats at sea, humane deterrence camps, closed camps, long-term incarceration, forced repatriation, and rejections for resettlement are evidence of the erosion of refugee protection. In essence, it appears to be easier to flee persecution, as traumatic as that flight is, than to find permanent asylum. Noting the tendency to blame rather than to assist the refugees, Roger Winter commented ironically, "Somehow they didn't suffer enough."[4]

Although national interests compromise human rights, these interests are also responsible for the, albeit imperfect, assistance rendered. It has been the recognition of each other's interests among various participants that has worked out arrangements to manage, if not solve, the refugee problem in Southeast Asia. The "daisy chain effect," which finds the ASEAN countries and the resettlement nations working together, has also involved an appreciation of these interests.[5] By contrast, one of the saddest aspects of the Indochina issue is the situation in Hong Kong: because that nation does not figure in the national interests of the resettlement countries, its 38,000 refugees are denied offers of resettlement.

The grim realities of the global refugee situation that raise thorny ethical questions and force difficult policy decisions are obviously evident in the Indochina refugee case. However, the theory of political realism tempers the natural tendency to cynicism over this matter without yielding to idealism. Time and patience may someday ameliorate the tensions among the major participants that are at the root of the issue, but realism should never be interpreted as an excuse to do nothing.

An appreciation of national interests on all sides, cautiously guided rather than driven by principles, might point to opportunities for quiet diplomacy, marginal experiments, and small, magnanimous gestures

3. Benoit, "Vietnam's Boat People," 161.
4. Comment by Roger Winter, Director, U.S. Committee for Refugees, at the "First Asylum Conference," Indochinese Resource Action Center, Washington, D.C., June 7, 1988.
5. Interview with William G. Applegate, Joint Voluntary Agency, U.S. Embassy, Manila, April 6, 1984.

to alleviate the refugee problem, as the masters of international thought have suggested. Although politics is the source of the Indochina refugee problem, it is in the political arena, where, according to Reinhold Niebuhr, "conscience and power meet," that the issue must be continually addressed.

It might be asked: What were the choices available to the participants along the way? What are the choices now? Either rehearsing of what might have been or grandiose plans for present solutions imply both an extraordinary prescience and inordinate power on the part of governments, expectations which are unrealistic. What is important for a realistic approach to the Indochina refugee problem is an appreciation for the contextual complexity of dramatic human events. At times, there are only small opportunities to move toward solving problems, as Herbert Butterfield suggested, which means that those who see the complexity have a better chance to utilize those opportunities.

Regrettably, this investigation concludes without insight into a magic formula for resolving this most perplexing refugee dilemma. In fact, the potential for increases in the tragic elements of this ongoing saga appear all too evident in the precarious Cambodian situation and in the continuing isolation of Indochina, which keeps those states chronically underdeveloped. There have been increases in the exodus, a deterioration of first asylum, proclivity toward abusing refugees who seek asylum, and a decline in resettlement opportunities. Perhaps of the greatest concern now are complacency regarding the status quo and a waning of interest in the Indochina refugee issue altogether. For example, Roger Winter argued that the United States has stepped back from its leadership role as evidenced recently by shortfalls in admissions for resettlement and overall budget cuts for refugee programs.[6] This state of affairs may be attributed to compassion fatigue, attention to events elsewhere, and frustration over the problem's protractedness.

This study can point to some areas where marginal experiments and small, magnanimous gestures might be possible if they are coupled with sensible, but sensitive, diplomacy that is open to fresh ideas and committed to efforts to see them work. One such small gesture could be the sharing-out idea, which received some attention during

6. Winter, "First Asylum Conference."

1986.[7] This concept would address the plight of long-term camp residents, or residuals. There is the possibility that resettlement nations could and would consider, as a humanitarian gesture, resettling those previously ineligible or rejected under regular admissions criteria. In addition to rectifying a human rights scandal and bringing new hope to those now languishing in the refugee camps, sharing-out could serve national interests. The effort could restore the resettlement countries' credibility with temporary first asylum countries weary of the refugee burden and critical of the resettlement countries' selectivity. This show of support, in the long run, might encourage ASEAN and Hong Kong to continue to offer temporary first asylum.[8]

More flexibility and less vindictiveness by nations on all sides of the third Indochina conflict might weaken the tendency to look to a military solution for Cambodia, with attendant repercussions for the Indochina refugees. Important signs that this shift may be happening include the changes in Vietnamese leadership, the announced withdrawal of Vietnamese military forces from Cambodia, initiatives for improving Sino-Soviet relations, with possible ramifications for Indochina, and the beginnings of a thaw in U.S.-Vietnam relations. Along these lines, William Duiker, in assessing Sino-Vietnamese tensions, drew on history to explain the long-term, periodic Chinese quest to dominate Southeast Asia that clashes with Vietnam's attempt to forge an Indochina federation for defense, a scenario being played out in Cambodia today. On a more optimistic note, however, Duiker speculated about the future, based on past occurrences: "But history teaches that China and Vietnam have, at times, succeeded in reconciling their national objectives to fashion a relationship beneficial to both."[9] Any shift would no doubt require risks and magnanimous gestures not only by Vietnam and China but by other nations in varying degrees.

Related to the Cambodian stalemate, too, are the policies of several nations regarding the Cambodian resistance. The continued rigidity of their positions has resulted in the aiding of the Khmer Rouge faction of the CGDK and the conferring of legitimacy on Pol Pot, which action

7. Cerquone, *Refugees from Laos*, 17.
8. Golub, *Looking for Phantoms*, 31–32.
9. Paribatra, "Can ASEAN Break the Stalemate?," 85–106; Duiker, "Applying the Lessons of Vietnam," 1–7.

many find "morally reprehensible."[10] This issue calls for new insights that draw on moral principles for guidance, especially as the possibility of a Vietnamese military withdrawal increases and as the prospects of chaos in the aftermath heighten interest in the pursuit of a politically negotiated settlement. There are grave implications here for the border refugee population.

Another area where reduced rigidity might affect the refugee problem is U.S.-Vietnamese relations. Although the debate continues about the feasibility and possibility of normalized relations and about whether such an event would have any effect on the overall reduction of tensions in the region, Anthony Lake saw benefits in pursuing cooperation on some bilateral issues even without normalization. Since the Vessey mission in 1987, several tenuous but important steps have been taken. The impasse over the ODP has been resolved, and overtures have been made regarding several humanitarian issues, from dialogue on the MIA issue to the release of reeducation camp prisoners. Some progress has also been made on the migration of Amerasians. The thaw in U.S.-Vietnamese relations would seem to bode well for the refugee situation.

The issue of development assistance is another area worth pursuing. Internationally isolated, some say punished, and virtually totally dependent on Soviet aid, Vietnam remains chronically poor. Its economic woes, though attributed in large part to Vietnamese policies, are thought to contribute to the flow of refugees. Anthony Lake gave this judgment of American policy toward Vietnam: "For our government to uselessly punish the people of Indochina for the sins of their governments is to perpetuate in one more way the saddest story of our generation." He suggested that at minimum and for a start, "the restrictions placed on the efforts of private, voluntary organizations to provide small-scale help . . . be relaxed."[11] Recent official American approval of just such humanitarian assistance to Vietnam is yet another sign of change.

Any realistic study of the UNHCR vis-à-vis the Indochina refugees must conclude that that organization lacks the political power to protect and assist refugees except when humanitarian concerns coincide

10. Paribatra, "Can ASEAN Break the Stalemate?," 10.
11. Lake, "Normalization: Only Cautious Steps Now," 37.

with the interests of nations. Nonetheless, the UNHCR often demon-strates a reluctance to take risks and to speak out on behalf of refugees. Its hesitancy to insist on an active role for itself at the Thai-Cambodian border and, recently, its lack of protest over the announced closing of Khao-I-Dang illustrate this reluctance. The difficulty of the problems associated with international organizations continues to command re-spect, but the prodding of the UNHCR by nations that fund it and remain responsible for its actions, coupled with an infusion of dynamic leadership, could and should improve its performance. The UNHCR needs to play a more active role in seeking creative durable solu-tions now.

If the Indochina refugee issue is at a crossroads, it is not because of a winding down of the problem but rather because the situation has worsened. Robert DeVecchi of the IRC warned that the problem is in immediate need of a "very deep re-commitment of energy, will, pas-sion and caring." Speaking for the UNHCR, Sascha Casella noted the great difficulties involved, for "few refugee crises are as complex as the Indochina crisis." First U.S. coordinator for refugee affairs Dick Clark asked, "Can we sustain the reasonably successful efforts of the past thirteen years?"[12]

Momentum may be building for a renewed commitment to the issue, as reflected in the call for another international conference. Fresh approaches will require yet more creative thinking, the continuation of marginal experiments and more of those small magnanimous gestures from several nations and organizations. Needed, too, will be the deter-mination and diplomatic skill to grapple with several difficult ques-tions, all the while retaining respect for both national interests and humanitarian concerns. For example, Thai scholar Vitit Muntarbhorn spoke of the necessity of appreciating the interdependence of several factors in devising a strategy to deal with both the short- and long-range aspects of the problem. He emphasized the need for the kind of open dialogue, regionally and globally, in which these issues can be aired and addressed.[13]

Existing political and moral dilemmas will only be compounded if

12. Comments by Robert P. DeVecchi, International Rescue Committee, Sascha Casella, UNHCR, and Dick Clark, Aspen Institute, at the "First Asylum Conference."
13. Comments by Vitit Muntarbhorn, Chulalongkorn University, at the "First Asylum Conference."

the problems resulting from reduced resettlement, especially increased arrivals joining the already long-term refugees, remain unsolved. Some anticipate such a dire situation will then eliminate pull factors that encourage refugees to seek asylum in the first place, but the Indochina refugee story thus far indicates this scenario is improbable. Despite harsh deterrents, including piracy, push-offs, and detention-type camps, refugees keep coming. Although alternatives to resettlement, including immigration through normal channels, must be pursued vigorously, resettlement should never be eliminated, as it will still remain the only viable answer for many who are persecuted. Resettlement opportunities are especially significant, since local integration and voluntary repatriation are not real possibilities at the present time. The essential protection of temporary first asylum throughout Southeast Asia hinges directly on the resettlement component.

An impetus to seeking fresh solutions also lies in the frank assessment of the resettlement concept itself. Indeed, the entire effort, which permanently relocated over 1.6 million refugees around the world, has been highly successful, giving a new start to these people, and they in turn have brought untold benefits to their new countries. Yet an honest appraisal must include the costs as well. The government of Laos has clearly voiced concern over the loss of one-tenth of its population, including its most highly educated and professional citizenry.[14] Vietnam and Cambodia surely have lost many potential contributions the refugees from those countries might have made toward war recovery and nation building. Although the costs incurred by the resettlement countries in terms of special programs and social services may be far outweighed by the refugees' contributions to those societies, the costs, nonetheless, must be recognized. More important, the personal costs to the refugees themselves as they try to adjust to alien cultures not always hostile but at times indifferent should be acknowledged. Many experience unemployment and underemployment and suffer from increased mental health problems from stress and loneliness. Overall, the massive resettlement of Indochina's refugees has been necessary and effective. However, an objective look at the concept by all sides could encourage their pursuit of other options, alongside, not in lieu of, the still-needed resettlement program.

14. Martin Stuart-Fox, "Refugees: A Lost Resource," *Indochina Issues*, LXX (October, 1986), 4.

Although this study focused on the UNHCR as representative of organizations protecting and assisting the refugees from Indochina, a host of other advocacy groups and assistance agencies have made and continue to make remarkable contributions, from the International Red Cross at the Thai-Cambodian border to the U.S. Committee for Refugees in Washington, D.C. As Mason and Brown concluded in their study, these groups have power, albeit limited when compared to nation-states, that should be recognized and exercised.[15] The experiences, concerns, and opinions of these organizations are an important component in the moral reasoning process for this refugee issue.

Similarly, the significant contributions of journalists to the Indochina refugee problem continue, adding information and insight and at times encouraging accountability on all sides. As was evident during the Hungarian refugee exodus, the media provide firsthand accounts, raise important questions in the debate, keep these matters before the public consciousness, and, at times, highlight signs of potential maneuverability.

The Indochina refugee issue is fraught with political and ethical dilemmas. As the nature of the problem has changed through the years, it has become clear that nations through their interests have been implicated not only in the problem but also in its solution. Presently, the refugee problem, while managed in a world far from perfect, remains unsolved in terms of its root causes. The hope for the future is that those in positions of power will possess the necessary skills and will care enough, in the words of Kenneth Thompson, "to strive to reconcile the morally desirable with the politically possible."[16]

15. Mason and Brown, *Rice, Rivalry, and Politics.*
16. Kenneth W. Thompson, "The Heritage of America" (Address, Monticello, July 4, 1986), 6.

Bibliography

Books

Aptheker, Herbert. *The Truth About Hungary.* New York, 1957.
Arendt, Hannah. *The Origins of Totalitarianism.* Cleveland, 1969.
Asia 1984 Yearbook. Far Eastern Economic Review, Hong Kong, 1984.
Bain, Leslie B. *The Reluctant Satellites: An Eyewitness Report on East Europe and the Hungarian Revolution.* New York, 1960.
Becker, Elizabeth. *When the War Was Over: The Voices of Cambodia's Revolution and Its People.* New York, 1986.
Bohlen, Charles. *Witness to History, 1929–1969.* New York, 1973.
Bursten, Marten A. *Escape from Fear.* Syracuse, 1958.
Cahn, Edmond. *The Moral Decision: Right and Wrong in the Light of American Law.* Bloomington, Ind., 1956.
Chanda, Nayan. *Brother Enemy: The War After the War.* New York, 1986.
Eisenhower, Dwight D. *Waging Peace, 1956–1961.* Garden City, N.Y., 1965.
Evans, Grant. *The Yellow Rainmakers: Are Chemical Weapons Being Used in Southeast Asia?* London, 1983.
Freund, Paul, A. *On Law and Justice.* Cambridge, Mass., 1968.
Gannon, Robert I. *The Cardinal Spellman Story.* Garden City, N.Y., 1962.
George, Terry, ed. *The On-Your-Own Guide to Asia.* Stanford, 1983.
Goold-Adams, Richard. *John Foster Dulles: A Reappraisal.* New York, 1962.
Graebner, Norman A. *Cold War Diplomacy: American Foreign Policy, 1945–1975.* New York, 1977.
Grant, Bruce. *The Boat People: An "Age" Investigation.* New York, 1979.
Haley, P. Edward. *Congress and the Fall of South Vietnam and Cambodia.* Rutherford, N.J., 1982.
Halle, Louis J. *The Cold War as History.* New York, 1967.
Hersey, John. *Here to Stay.* New York, 1963.
Holborn, Louise. *Refugees: A Problem of Our Time: The Work of the United Nations High Commissioner for Refugees.* 2 vols. Metuchen, N.J., 1975.

Hungary's Fight for Freedom: A Special Report in Pictures. Life, special issue. Chicago, 1956.

Ignotus, Paul. *Hungary.* New York, 1972.

Kiraly, Bela K., and Paul Jonas, eds. *The Hungarian Revolution of 1956 in Retrospect.* Boulder, 1978.

Kolko, Joyce, and Gabriel Kolko. *The Limits of Power: The World and U.S. Foreign Policy, 1945–1954.* New York, 1972.

Kritz, Mary M., ed. *U.S. Immigration and Refugee Policy, Global and Domestic Issues.* Lexington, 1983.

Kritz, Mary M., Charles B. Keely, and Sylvano M. Tomasi, eds. *Global Trends in Migration: Theory and Research on International Population Movements.* New York, 1981.

Lasky, Melvin J., ed. *The Hungarian Revolution.* New York, 1957.

Levenstein, Aaron. *Escape to Freedom: The Story of the International Rescue Committee.* Westport, Conn., 1983.

Lewy, Guenter. *America in Vietnam.* Oxford, Eng., 1978.

Loescher, Gil, and John A. Scanlan. *Calculated Kindness: Refugees and America's Half-Open Door, 1945 to the Present.* New York, 1986.

Loescher, Gilburt D., and John A. Scanlan, eds. *The Global Refugee Problem: U.S. and World Response. Annals,* CDLXVII, (May, 1983).

Lomax, Bill. *Hungary 1956.* London, 1976.

Lyon, Peter. *Eisenhower: Portrait of the Hero.* Boston, 1974.

Marton, Endre. *The Forbidden Sky: Inside the Hungarian Revolution.* Boston, 1971.

Mason, Linda, and Roger Brown. *Rice, Rivalry, and Politics: Managing Cambodian Relief.* Notre Dame, 1983.

Michener, James A. *The Bridge at Andau.* New York, 1957.

Murphy, Robert. *Diplomat Among Warriors.* Garden City, N.Y., 1964.

Polanyi, Michael. *Personal Knowledge.* Chicago, 1974.

Pryce-Jones, David. *The Hungarian Revolution.* London, 1969.

Public Affairs Press. *Anatomy of Revolution.* Washington, D.C., 1957.

Radvanyi, Janos. *Hungary and the Superpowers: The 1956 Revolution and Realpolitik.* Stanford, 1972.

Seagrave, Sterling. *Yellow Rain: A Journey Through the Terror of Chemical Warfare.* New York, 1981.

Shawcross, William. *The Quality of Mercy: Cambodia, Holocaust and Modern Conscience.* New York, 1984.

————. *Sideshow: Kissinger, Nixon, and the Destruction of Cambodia.* New York, 1979.

Snepp, Frank. *Decent Interval.* New York, 1977.

Stoessinger, John George. *The Refugee and the World Community.* Minneapolis, 1956.

Strand, Paul J., and Woodrow Jones, Jr. *Indochinese Refugees in America: Problems of Adaptation and Assimilation.* Durham, 1986.

Tabori, Paul. *The Anatomy of Exile: A Semantic and Historical Study.* London, 1972.

Thompson, Kenneth W. *Christian Ethics and Dilemmas in Foreign Policy.* London, 1959.

————. *Cold War Theories, Volume I: World Polarization, 1943–1953.* Baton Rouge, 1981.

————. *Ethics and National Purpose.* New York, 1957.

————. *Ethics, Functionalism, and Power in International Politics: The Crisis in Values.* Baton Rouge, 1979.

————. *Masters of International Thought.* Baton Rouge, 1980.

————. *Morality and Foreign Policy.* Baton Rouge, 1980.

————. *Political Realism and the Crisis of World Politics.* Washington, D.C. 1982.

————. ed. *The Moral Imperatives of Human Rights: A World Survey.* Washington, D.C., 1980.

Vali, Ferenc A. *Rift and Revolt in Hungary,* Cambridge, Mass., 1961.

Wain, Barry. *The Refused: The Agony of the Indochina Refugees.* New York, 1982.

Weinstock, Alexander S. *Acculturation and Occupation: A Study of the 1956 Hungarian Refugees in the United States.* The Hague, 1969.

Articles

Bailey, George. "The Fate of the Hungarian Refugees." *Reporter,* March 7, 1957, pp. 22–26.

Barber, Martin. "Trapped: Cambodians on the Border with Thailand." *Exile: Newsletter of the British Refugee Council,* III (May-June, 1983), 1–5.

Becker, Elizabeth. "Kampuchea in 1983." *Asian Survey,* XXIV (January, 1984), 37–48.

Benoit, Charles. "Vietnam's Boat People." In *The Third Indochina Conflict,* edited by David W. P. Elliott, Boulder, 1981.

Brown, Frederick Z. "Sending the Wrong Signal to Hanoi." *Asian Wall Street Journal,* April 18, 1988, p. 16.

Burrows, Rob. "Not Enough Hope To Go Around." *Refugees,* XXXIII (September, 1986), 31–33.

Chanda, Nayan. "CIA No, U.S. Aid Yes." *Far Eastern Economic Review,* August 16, 1984, pp. 16–18

————. "Vietnam 1983." *Asian Survey,* XXIV (January, 1984), 29–36.

————. "Weather Eye on Moscow." *Far Eastern Economic Review,* October 26, 1986, p. 24.

Chang, Pao-min. "The Sino-Vietnamese Dispute over the Ethnic Chinese." *China Quarterly,* XC (June, 1982), 195–230.

Cherne, Leo. "Thirty Days That Shook the World." *Saturday Review,* November 23, 1956, pp. 22–23, 31.

Colbert, Evelyn. "Stand Pat." *Foreign Policy,* LIV (Spring, 1984), 139–55.

Douglas, H. Eugene. "The Problem of Refugees in a Strategic Perspective." *Strategic Review* (Fall, 1982), 11–20.

Duiker, William J. "Applying the Lessons of Vietnam: The View from Hanoi." *Indochina Issues,* LXVIII (August, 1986), 1–7.

"The Exodus from Hungary." *United Nations Review,* III (January, 1957), 13–18.

Fraser, Stewart E. "Vietnam Struggles with Exploding Population." *Indochina Issues,* LVII (May, 1985), 1–7.

Garver, John W. "The Reagan Administration's Southeast Asian Policy." In *U.S.-Asian Relations: The National Security Paradox,* edited by James C. Hsiung. New York, 1983,
Goose, Stephen D., and R. Kyle Horst. "Amerasians in Vietnam: Still Waiting." *Indochina Issues,* LXXXIII (August, 1988), 1–7.
Hiebert, Murray. "Cambodia: Guerrilla Attacks Curb Development." *Indochina Issues,* LXIX (September, 1986), 1–7.
———. "A Change of Heart." *Far Eastern Economic Review,* May 5, 1988, pp. 39–40.
———. "Indochina Back Door." *Far Eastern Economic Review,* January 15, 1987, p. 26.
———. "The Khmer Rouge Regroups." *Far Eastern Economic Review,* December 1, 1988, pp. 34–35.
———. "A New Gerontocracy." *Far Eastern Economic Review,* January 1, 1987, pp. 10–11.
———. "Sink or Swim." *Far Eastern Economic Review,* February 23, 1989, p. 27.
"Hungary: A Nation in Flight." *U.S. News and World Report,* December 7, 1956, pp. 66–71.
Indochina Chronology, IV–VIII (1985–89).
"International Action on Behalf of Hungarian Refugees." *United Nations Review,* IV (August, 1957), 51–52.
Iyer, Pico. "Vicious Circle." *Time,* July 30, 1984, p. 84.
Kattenburg, Paul M. "Living with Hanoi." *Foreign Policy,* LIII (Winter, 1983–84), 131–49.
Kaye, Lincoln. "About Those Refugees." *Far Eastern Economic Review,* September 26, 1985, pp. 34–35.
Kunz, Egon F. "The Refugee in Flight: Kinetic Models and Forms of Displacement." *International Migration Review,* VII (Summer, 1973), 125–46.
Lake, Anthony. "Dealing with Hanoi: What Can Washington Do?" *Indochina Issues,* XLIX (August, 1984), 1–7.
———. "Normalization: Only Cautious Steps Now." *World Policy Journal,* III (Winter, 1985–86), 143–55.
Mahbubani, Khishore. "The Kampuchean Problem: A Southeast Asian Perspective." *Foreign Affairs,* LXII (Winter, 1983–84), 407–25.
Markowitz, Arthur A. "Humanitarianism Versus Restrictionism: The United States and the Hungarian Refugees." *International Migration Review,* VII (Spring, 1973), 46–59.
Nordland, Rod. "Khmer Refugees: Reaching for Oars." *Indochina Issues,* XXX (November, 1982), 1–7.
Quinn-Judge, Paul. "Hanoi's Bitter Victory." *Far Eastern Economic Review,* May 2, 1986, pp. 30–34.
———. "Knowing Thy Enemy." *Far Eastern Economic Review,* June 6, 1985, p. 6.
Paribatra, M. R. Sukhumbhand. "Can ASEAN Break the Stalemate?" *World Policy Journal,* III (Winter, 1985–86), 85–106.
Refugee Reports, VII–X, (March, 1986–May, 1989).
Refugees, 1979–88.

"Refugees: A Problem Yet To Be Solved." *Focus on Thailand*, VIII (October, 1982), 1–2.

Robinson, Court. "Southeast Asian Refugees: Critical Mass?" *Indochina Issues*, LXXVII (December, 1987), 1–7.

Roper, Elmo. "The Americans and the Hungarian Story." *Saturday Review*, XL (May 11, 1957).

Scheinman, Ronald S. "Refugees: Goodby to the Good Old Days." In *The Global Refugee Problem: U.S. and World Response*, edited by Gilburt D. Loescher and John A. Scanlan. Vol. CDLXVII of *Annals* (May, 1983), 78–88.

Stanfield, Rochelle L. "Eyeing Indochina." *National Journal*, January 14, 1989, p. 100.

Stein, Barry N. "The Refugee Experience: Defining the Parameters of a Field of Study." *International Migration Review*, XV (Spring-Summer, 1981).

Stein, Barry N., and Sylvano M. Tomasi, eds. "Refugees Today." *International Migration Review*, XV (Spring-Summer, 1981), 5–441.

Stuart-Fox, Martin. "Politics and Patronage in Laos." *Indochina Issues*, LXX (October, 1986), 1–10.

———. "Refugees: A Lost Resource." *Indochina Issues*, LXX (October, 1986).

"Suffering Continues for 200,000 Khmer Refugees." *Bulletin: International Committee for the Red Cross* (June, 1983), 1–4.

Suhrke, Astri. "Indochinese Refugees: The Law and Politics of First Asylum." In *The Global Refugee Problem: U.S. and World Response*, edited by Gilburt D. Loescher and John A. Scanlan. Vol. CDLXVII of *Annals* (May, 1983), 102–15.

Sutter, Robert G. "China's Strategy Toward Vietnam and Its Implications for the United States." In *The Third Indochina Conflict*, edited by David W. P. Elliott. Boulder, 1981.

Swank, Emory C. "The Land In Between: Cambodia Ten Years Later." *Indochina Issues*, XXXVI (April, 1983), 1–7.

Tatu, Frank. "U.S. and Vietnam: Converging Interests?," *Indochina Issues*, LXXXI (May, 1988), 1–6.

Teitelbaum, Michael S. "Political Asylum in Theory and Practice." *Public Interest*, LXXVI (Summer, 1984), 74–86.

———. "Right Versus Right: Immigration and Refugee Policy in the United States." *Foreign Affairs*, LIX (Fall, 1980), 21–59.

Thayer, Carlyle A. "Laos in 1983." *Asian Survey*, XXIV (January, 1984), 49–59.

Tinker, Jerry M. "U.S. Refugee Policy: Coping with Migration." *Indochina Issues*, LV (March, 1985), 1–7.

van der Kroef, Justus M. "Kampuchea: Diplomatic Gambits and Political Realities." *Orbis*, XXVIII (Spring, 1984), 145–62.

———. "Kampuchea: Southeast Asia's Flashpoint." *Parameters*, XIV (Spring, 1984), 60–70.

"Viet Refugees Problem Refuses to Leave." *Asian Bulletin*, VII (July, 1984), 86.

Wain, Barry. "Malaysia Fears Social Upheaval from Refugees." *Asian Wall Street Journal*, June 23, 1979, p. 5.

———. "Orderly Departure? Escape Is Still the Hope of a Million Vietnamese." *Asian Wall Street Journal*, May 6, 1985, pp. 6, 22.

Reports and Monographs

Bull, David. *The Poverty of Diplomacy: Kampuchea and the Outside World*. Oxfam. Oxford, 1983.

Catholic Office for Emergency Relief and Refugees. *Report No. 8 on Refugee Aid Work and Emergency Relief Activities*. Bangkok, October 1, 1983.

Cerquone, Joseph. *Refugees from Laos: In Harm's Way*. U.S. Committee for Refugees. Washington, D.C., July, 1986.

———. *Uncertain Harbors: The Plight of Vietnamese Boat People*. U.S. Committee for Refugees. Washington, D.C., October, 1987.

———. *Vietnamese Boat People: Pirates' Vulnerable Prey*. U.S. Committee for Refugees. Washington, D.C., February, 1984.

Chen, King C. *Southeast Asian Refugees: The Policy Experiences*. Immigration Policy Project, Center for Strategic and International Studies. No. 1. Washington, D.C., November, 1983.

Committee for the Coordination of Services to Displaced Persons in Thailand. *Perspectives: The CCSDPT Monthly Newsletter*. December, 1982, February, March, April–May, December, 1983.

———. *The CCSDPT Handbook: Refugee Services in Thailand*. Bangkok, 1983.

D'Souza, Frances. *The Refugee Dilemma: International Recognition and Acceptance*. Minority Rights Group, XLIII (London, 1985).

Forbes, Susan S. *Adaptation and Integration of Recent Refugees to the United States*. Refugee Policy Group. Washington, D.C., 1985.

Golub, Stephen. *Looking for Phantoms: Flaws in the Khmer Rouge Screening Process*. U.S. Committee for Refugees. Washington, D.C., 1986.

Hamilton, J. Patrick. *Cambodian Refugees in Thailand: The Limits of Asylum*. U.S. Committee for Refugees. Washington, D.C., August, 1982.

Hamilton, Virginia, ed. *Cambodians in Thailand: People on the Edge*. U.S. Committee for Refugees. Washington, D.C., December, 1985.

———, ed. *World Refugee Survey: 1985 in Review*. U.S. Committee for Refugees. Washington, D.C., 1986.

———, ed. *World Refugee Survey: 1986 in Review*. U.S. Committee for Refugees. Washington, D.C., 1987.

———, ed. *World Refugee Survey: 1987 in Review*, U.S. Committee for Refugees. Washington, D.C., 1988.

———, ed. *World Refugee Survey: 1988 in Review*, U.S. Committee for Refugees. Washington, D.C., 1989.

Jones, Allen K. *Living in Limbo: The Boat Refugees of Hong Kong and Macao*. U.S. Committee for Refugees. Washington, D.C., 1986.

Kane, Parsons, and Associates. "A Survey of Public Attitudes Toward Refugees and Immigrants: Report of Findings." Submitted to U.S. Committee for Refugees, American Council of Nationalities Service. April, 1984.

Kosol Vongsrisart, ed. *The Indochinese Refugees, Thailand.* Federation of Asian Bishops' Conference. Bangkok, 1980.

Lawyers Committee for Human Rights. *Seeking Shelter: A Report on Human Rights.* New York, 1987.

Lowman, Shepard C. "A Crisis in First Asylum for Indochinese Refugees: Creating Alternatives to Flight by Boat." Typescript, Refugees International, Washington, D.C., November, 1988.

National Conference of Catholic Bishops. Committee on Migration and Tourism. *Report of Journey: U.S. Bishops' Delegation to Refugee Camps in Southeast Asia,* July 5–19, 1983. Prepared by Most Rev. Anthony J. Bevilacqua, Chairman. Washington, D.C., August, 1983.

Newland, Kathleen. *Refugees: The New International Politics of Displacement.* Worldwatch. Washington, D.C., March, 1981.

Silk, James. *Despite a Generous Spirit: Denying Asylum in the United States.* U.S. Committee for Refugees. Washington, D.C., December, 1986.

Stanley Foundation. *Report of the Twenty-eighth Strategy for Peace, U.S. Foreign Policy Conference.* Warrenton, Va., October 22–24, 1987.

Tripp, Rosemary E., ed. *World Refugee Survey: 1981 in Review.* U.S. Committee for Refugees. Washington, D.C., 1982.

——, ed. *World Refugee Survey: 1982 in Review.* U.S. Committee for Refugees. Washington, D.C., 1983.

——, ed. *World Refugee Survey: 1983 in Review.* U.S. Committee for Refugees. Washington, D.C., 1984.

——, ed. *World Refugee Survey: 1984 in Review.* U.S. Committee for Refugees. Washington, D.C., 1985.

Newspapers

Christian Science Monitor, 1980–89.
New York *Times,* 1956–58, 1975–89.
Wall Street Journal, 1975–89.
Washington *Post,* 1975–89.

Papers and Dissertations

Derani, Abdul Hadi. "Refugees from Indochina, 1975–1980: Their Impact on the International Relations of Southeast Asia." Ph. D. dissertation, University of London, 1981.

Gordenker, Leon. "Organizational Expansion and Limits in International Services for Refugees." Typescript, Princeton, 1984.

Layman, Donald L. "Education and the Egalitarian Quest: The Chinese Experience." Ph. D. dissertation, University of Virginia, 1979.

Lewis, William H. "The Operations of the United Nations High Commissioner for Refugees: An Indepth Evaluation of Performance." Typescript, George Washington University, n.d.

Suhrke, Astri. "Global Refugee Movements and Strategies: An Overview." Typescript, American University, 1981.

Public Documents

Aga Khan, Sadruddin. *Study on Human Rights and Massive Exoduses.* Prepared for the United Nations, 38th Sess., E/CN.4/1503, Annex II, December 31, 1981.

California Legislature. Joint Committee on Refugee Resettlement and Immigration. *Report of the Fact-Finding Mission to Refugee Camps in Southeast Asia, October 24 to November 16, 1983.* Sacramento, 1983.

Hong Kong Government Secretariat. "Fact Sheet." No. SRD 703/5/RII. Hong Kong, May, 1988.

House Documents. 95th Cong., 1st Sess., No. Y4.J89/1:95–42; 98th Cong., 2nd Sess., No. 35-654 0; 99th Cong., 1st Sess., No. 52-922-0.

Library of Congress. "ASEAN Reaction to Indochinese Refugees, January 1–15, 1979." Typescript, September 4, 1979.

———. *Cambodian Crisis: Problems of a Settlement and Policy Dilemmas for the United States.* No. IB89020. January 9, 1989.

———. "Chronology of the Hungarian Refugee Program." Typescript, May 19, 1975.

———. *Indochinese Refugees: Issues for U.S. Policy.* No. IB79079. July 10, 1979, January 5, 1982.

———. *Radio Free Europe: A Survey and Analysis.* No. JX 1710 US B. March 22, 1972.

———. *Vietnam–U.S. Relations: Issues for U.S. Policy.* No. 86-35F. February 10, 1986.

———. *Vietnam–U.S. Relations: The Missing in Action (MIAs) and the Impasse over Cambodia.* No. IB87210. December 8, 1988.

Senate Documents. 97th Cong., 1st Sess., Nos. J-97-68, 83-102-0; 99th Cong., 2nd Sess., Nos. J-99-113, J-99-129.

Singapore.

Ministry of Culture. "Speech by S. Rajaratnam, Minister for Foreign Affairs, at the United Nations Meeting on Refugees and Displaced Persons in Southeast Asia." Geneva, July 20, 1979.

———. "Statement Delivered by the Leader of the Singapore Delegation, Mr. S. Rajaratnam, Minister for Foreign Affairs, at the Twelfth ASEAN Ministerial Meeting." Bali, June 28, 1979.

Ministry of Foreign Affairs. "Keynote Speech by the Prime Minister, Mr. Lee Kuan Yew, on the Agenda Item 'World Political Scene' at the Commonwealth Heads of Government Meeting." Lusaka, Zambia, August 1, 1979.

———. "Transcript of an Interview with Prime Minister Lee Kuan Yew by Mr. François Nivolon of *Le Figaro.*" Istana, July 20, 1979.

————. *Vietnam and the Refugees.* Singapore, 1979.

Suhrke, Astri. *Indochinese Refugees: The Impact on First Asylum Countries and Implications for American Policy.* Prepared for U.S. Congress, Joint Economic Committee. Washington, D.C., 1980.

Thailand.

    Embassy. "Refugee Problems in Thailand." Typescript, Washington, D.C., n.d.

    Joint Operations Center, Supreme Command. "Indochinese Displaced Persons." Typescript, Bangkok, June, 1983.

    Ministry of Interior, Operation for Displaced Persons. *An Instrument of Foreign Policy: Indochinese Displaced Persons.* Bangkok, September, 1981.

    "Statement by Squadron Leader Prasong Soonsiri, Secretary General of the National Security Council, at the Annual Conference on Indochinese Displaced Persons in Thailand." Bangkok, July 7, 1983.

United Nations.

    Office of the High Commissioner for Refugees. *Indochinese Displaced Persons in Singapore.* Singapore, January, 1984.

    Office of the United Nations High Commissioner for Refugees. *Convention and Protocol Relating to the Status of Refugees.* HCR/INF/Rev. 4. Geneva, 1981.

    ————. "Fact Sheet." 1982–88.

    ————. *UNHCR.* Geneva, 1982.

    Statute of the Office of the United Nations High Commissioner for Refugees. HCR/INF/Rev. 3. Geneva.

U.S. Comptroller. *A Report to the Congress: U.S. Provides Safe Haven for Indochinese Refugees.* No. ID75-71. June 16, 1975.

U.S. Congress. *Congressional Record.* 85th Cong., 1st and 2nd Sess.; 99th Cong., 2nd Sess., H11623.

U.S. Coordinator for Refugee Affairs. "An Edited Transcript of a Conference on Ethical Issues and Moral Principles in U.S. Refugee Policy, March 24 and 25, 1983." Washington, D.C.

————. *Proposed Refugee Admissions and Allocations for Fiscal Year 1984: Report to Congress.* Washington, D.C., August, 1983.

————. *Proposed Refugee Admissions and Allocations for Fiscal Year 1987: Report to Congress.* Washington, D.C., September, 1987.

U.S. Department of State. *Bulletin,* XXXV–XXXVIII, Nos. 906–69 (November 5, 1956–January 20, 1958).

————. *Country Reports on the World Refugee Situation: Report to the Congress for Fiscal Year 1984.* August, 1983.

————. *The Indochinese Refugee Situation: Report to the Secretary of State by the Special Refugee Advisory Panel.* Marshall Green, Chairman. August 12, 1981.

————. *Indochinese Refugees and Relations with Thailand.* No. 1052. February 24, 1988.

————. *Proposed Refugee Admissions for FY 1984.* No. 517. September 26, 1983.

————. *Proposed Refugee Admissions for FY 1985.* No. 610. September 11, 1984.

————. *Proposed Refugee Admissions for FY 1986*. No. 738. September 17, 1985.
————. *Proposed Refugee Admissions for FY 1987*. No. 866. September 16, 1986.
————. *Proposed Refugee Admissions for FY 1988*. No. 1004. September 23, 1987.
————. *Recent Developments in Indochina*. No. 334. October 22, 1981.
————. *Refugees: A Continuing Concern*. No. 496. June 20, 1983.
————. *World Refugee Report*. September, 1986.
U.S. House of Representatives
    Committee on Foreign Affairs. *Reports on Refugee Aid*. 97th Cong., 1st
        Sess., No. 74-150 0.
    Committee on the Judiciary. *Indochinese Refugees: An Update*. 95th Cong.,
        2nd Sess., No. 35-721 0.
    ————. *Refugee Issues in Southeast Asia and Europe*. 97th Cong., 2nd
        Sess., No. 90-514 0.
U.S. Select Committee on Immigration and Refugee Policy. *U.S. Immigration
    Policy and the National Interest: The Final Report and Recommendations of the
    Select Committee to Congress and the President of the United States*. March,
    1981.
U.S. Senate.
    Committee on Foreign Relations. *Vietnam's Future Policies and Role in South-
        east Asia*. 97th Cong., 2nd Sess., No. 90-866-0.
    Committee on the Judiciary. *Refugee Problems in Southeast Asia: 1981*. 97th
        Cong., 2nd Sess., No. 88-643-0.
    ————. *U.S. Refugee Program in Southeast Asia: 1985*. 99th Cong., 1st Sess.,
        No. 47-710-0.
    ————. *U.S. Immigration Law and Policy: 1952–1979*. 96th Cong., 1st Sess.,
        No. 44-151.
    ————. *World Refugee Crisis: The International Community's Response*. 96th
        Cong., 1st Sess., No. 48-425-0.

Interviews

Allen, Ernest, Counsellor, Canadian High Commission. Singapore, April 3,
    1984.
Applegate, William G., Joint Voluntary Agency, U.S. Embassy. Manila, April 6,
    1984.
Bayandor, Darioush, Representative, UNHCR. Kuala Lumpur, March 26,
    1984.
Berger, Arthur E., Bureau Chief, Foreign Broadcast Information Service.
    Bangkok, March 13–26, 1984.
Burrows, Rob, Public Information Officer, UNHCR. Bangkok, March 14, 1984.
Cadwallader, Ruth, Co–Field Director, American Friends Service Committee.
    Bangkok, March 20–21, 1984.
Chan Sao Sovann. Phanat Nikhom Holding and Transit Center. Thailand,
    March 23, 1984.
Coleman, Joseph, Office of U.S. Coordinator for Refugee Affairs. Washington,
    D.C., January 24, 1984.

Colin, Don, Director, Orderly Departure Program. Bangkok, March 22, 1984.

Crowley, John, U.S. Embassy. Bangkok, March 14, 1984.

Drake, John, Joint Voluntary Agency, U.S. Embassy. Singapore, March 30, 1984.

Edwards, Joan, Field Officer, UNHCR, Phanat Nikhom Holding and Transit Center. Thailand, March 23, 1984.

Feen, Richard, Office of U.S. Coordinator for Refugee Affairs. Washington, D.C., January 24, 1984.

Fortner, Jack, Officer, INS. Hong Kong, April 13, 1984.

Gomez, ———, Camp Supervisor, Sungei Besi Transit Center. Kuala Lumpur, March 28, 1984.

Grace, Dennis, Director, Joint Voluntary Agency, U.S. Embassy. Bangkok, March 14, 1984.

Gullesjo, Ann-Christine, Protection Officer, UNHCR. Singapore, March 30, 1984.

Harris, Carl, Bureau for Refugee Programs, U.S. Department of State. Washington, D.C., February 3, 1984.

Harter, Dennis, Political Section, U.S. Consulate General. Hong Kong, April 12, 1984.

Hashim, ———, Camp Commander, Sungei Besi Transit Center. Kuala Lumpur, March 28, 1984.

Hess, Richard, Joint Voluntary Agency, U.S. Embassy. Manila, April 6, 1984.

Hiebert, Linda, Indochina Project. Washington, D.C., December, 1983.

Hiebert, Murray, Indochina Project, Washington, D.C., December, 1983.

Horst, Kyle, U.S. Catholic Conference. Washington, D.C., January 24, 1984.

Hutchings, Pamela, Joint Voluntary Agency, U.S. Embassy. Kuala Lumpur, March 27, 1984.

Johnston, Frank, Australian High Commission. Kuala Lumpur, March 27, 1984.

Khun Armornphan, Camp Commander, Phanat Nikhom Holding and Transit Center. Thailand, March, 23, 1984.

Koo Yiu Fai, Deputy Manager, Hong Kong Red Cross, Kai Tak Refugee Center. Hong Kong, April 14, 1984.

Kornbluth, David A., U.S. Consulate General. Hong Kong, April 12–13, 1984.

Krug, William, Bureau for Refugee Programs, U.S. Department of State. Washington, D.C., February 8, 1984.

Lao Mong Hay, Research Fellow, Institute for Southeast Asian Studies. Singapore, April 3, 1984.

Larsen, Dan, Joint Voluntary Agency, U.S. Consulate General. Hong Kong, April 12–13, 1984.

Lasan, Dolores B., Chargé de Mission, UNHCR. Hong Kong, April 12, 1984.

Lee, Neil, Camp Administrator, Hawkins Road Refugee Center. Singapore, April 1, 1984.

Mahbubani, Khishore, Deputy Chief of Mission, Embassy of Singapore. Washington, D.C., January 17, 1984.

McHugh, Lois, Congressional Research Service, Library of Congress. Washington, D.C., October, 1982.

Meinheit, Hal, U.S. Consulate General. Hong Kong, April 12, 1984.

Nguyen Manh Hung, Professor of International Relations, George Mason University. Fairfax, Va., February, 1984.

Niehaus, Marjorie, Congressional Research Service, Library of Congress. Washington, D.C., December, 1983.

Niksch, Larry, Congressional Research Service, Library of Congress. Washington, D.C., April, 1985.

Nyfil, Denis, International Catholic Migration Commission. Bataan Refugee Processing Center, April 8–10, 1984.

Olesen, Jorgen Stoen, Intergovernmental Committee for Migration. Singapore, March 30, 1984.

Pescod, Duncan, Assistant Secretary, Security Branch, Hong Kong Government Secretariat. Hong Kong., April 13, 1984.

Peterson, Cam, Joint Voluntary Agency, U.S. Embassy. Bangkok, March 14, 15, 23, 1984.

Phillips, ———, Deputy, Malaysian Red Crescent Society. Kuala Lumpur, March 27, 1984.

Ramsey, Douglas, U.S. Embassy. Kuala Lumpur, March 27, 1984.

Robinson, Court, U.S. Committee for Refugees. Washington, D.C., September 21, 1988.

Rumpf, Roger, Indochina Resource Center. Washington, D.C., March 7, 1985.

Sakthit, ———, Minister-Counsellor, Embassy of Thailand. Washington, D.C., January 25, 1984.

Sanan Kajornklam, Colonel, Joint Operations Center, Supreme Command. Bangkok, March 14, 1984.

Schrader, Kathleen, Washington Service Center, Catholic Charities. Bataan Refugee Processing Center, April 9–11, 1984.

Schroeder, Mitzi, U.S. Catholic Conference. Washington, D.C., January 24, 1984.

Sieverts, Frank, Bureau for Refugee Programs, U.S. Department of State. Washington, D.C., February 3, 1984.

Solyom-Fekete, Vilmos, European Law Division, Library of Congress. Washington, D.C., April, 1983.

Som, Tuan Haji Mohammed, Deputy Director, National Task Force Seven. Kuala Lumpur, March 28, 1984.

Stubbs, William, Director, Refugee Section, U.S. Embassy. Bangkok, March 13, 1984.

Sullivan, Dan, Director, Refugee Section, U.S. Embassy. Singapore, March 29–30, 1984.

Sutter, Robert, Senior Specialist in Asian Affairs, Foreign Affairs and National Defense Division, Congressional Research Service, Library of Congress. Washington, D.C., 1984–88.

Thani, ———, Director, Welfare Section, Ministry of Interior. Bangkok, March 20, 1984.

Tinker, Jerry, Office of Sen. Edward M. Kennedy. Washington, D.C., January 27, 1984.

Towey, James, Office of Sen. Mark O. Hatfield. Washington, D.C., February 7, 1984.

Uris, Jeanne, Joint Voluntary Agency, U.S. Embassy. Kuala Lumpur, March 27, 1984.

van Praag, Nicholas, UNHCR. Washington, D.C., January 13, 1984.

Waggoner, Loring A., Deputy Coordinator for Refugee Programs, U.S. Embassy. Manila, April 6, 1984.

Whelan, Joseph, Senior Specialist on International Affairs, Congressional Research Service, Library of Congress. Washington, D.C., April, 1983.

Winter, Roger, Director, U.S. Committee for Refugees. Washington, D.C., February 8, 1984.

Wu, Tom, Superintendent, Argyle Street Detention Center. Hong Kong, April 13, 1984.

Yeong, Michael, Ministry of Foreign Affairs. Singapore, April 3, 1984.

Yusoff, Hamidah, Embassy of Malaysia. Washington, D.C., February 16, 1984.

Index